Let me enlist attention from THE YOUTH OF
TIMORE. For you, my young friends, these
advantages are provided. What will be you
sponse? Is there   you some bookbi
boy, like Mich   will be led b
Royal Institu   arch for whic
world will b   here some p
teacher, like   inister's son
Agassiz, bur   pursue the
of natural h   ne sophomo
college, like   n, ready to d
the questions o   ager to be train
a master econon   ot in Baltimore
nius in mathematics, like Gauss, who at three
old correcte   c, at eightee
tered the U   where he m
discovery w   meters "fro
days of Eu   at seventy-s
among the   me? If so, I
is for you, bright youths, that these doors are op
Enter the armory and equip yourselves.

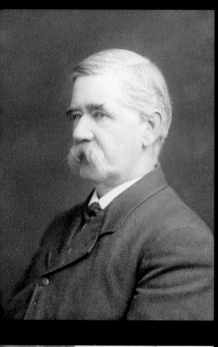

JOHNS HOPKINS
KNOWLEDGE FOR THE WORLD

1876   2001

MAME WARREN

THE JOHNS HOPKINS UNIVERSITY

Baltimore, Maryland

2000

This book has been brought to publication with the generous assistance of the W. K. Kellogg Foundation and William C. and Nancy Richardson.

Cataloging data will be found at the back of this book.

Distributed by The Johns Hopkins University Press
2715 North Charles Street
Baltimore, Maryland 21218-4319

ISBN 0-8018-6614-6

Library of Congress Catalog Card Number 00-133973

Portraits on previous pages, left to right:

ii:
HUGH KENNER, IRA REMSEN, IRENE DAVIS, ROBERT W. WOOD,
WILLIAM MCELROY, J. WHITRIDGE WILLIAMS, ISAIAH FRANK,
FABIAN FRANKLIN, G. HEBERTON EVANS

iii:
BENJAMIN CARSON, PAUL HAUPT, JOHN GRYDER, WILLIAM K. BROOKS,
LEON FLEISHER, FLORENCE R. SABIN, DEBORAH MCGUIRE,
JOHN C. FRENCH, WILLIAM FASTIE

iv:
ELLIOTT COLEMAN, MAX BRÖDEL, HORSLEY GANTT, WILLIAM G. MACCALLUM,
EILEEN SOSKIN, ROBERT POND SR., D. A. HENDERSON, ADOLF MEYER,
GERALD MASSON

v:
EDWARDS A. PARK, JOSEPH SWEETMAN AMES, FIORA CONTINO,
VERNON B. MOUNTCASTLE, DAVID NICHOLS, THOMAS R. BALL, ERNST CLOOS,
JOHN B. WHITEHEAD, EARL WASSERMAN

Endpapers:
Dedication of Gilman Hall, May 1915

Edited by Mame Warren, The Johns Hopkins University

Designed by Gerard A. Valerio, Bookmark Studio, Annapolis, Maryland

Composed by Sherri Ferritto, Typeline, Annapolis, Maryland

Separations by Martin Senn Digital Studio, Philamont
Virginia, and GGS, York, Pennsylvania

Printed by Pacifica Communications

CONTENTS

FOREWORD

When I came to Johns Hopkins as an undergraduate in the fall of 1949, the university was entering its seventy-fourth year. It had a distinguished faculty, and despite the influx of World War II veterans, it was an extremely small university and seriously constrained by annual financial deficits. Its full-time undergraduates were all male and most of them came from Baltimore, or Maryland, or a few nearby states. Part-time students in McCoy College were mostly local teachers and engineers. Students in the graduate programs at Homewood and at the Schools of Medicine and Hygiene and Public Health provided a more national and international flavor. The Peabody Institute and the School of Advanced International Studies were still independent schools, and the nursing school was managed by the hospital. The Applied Physics Laboratory was still in a former garage in Silver Spring, and if you had asked anyone what APL was, few would have known. The administration was run by a handful of people; most of them had more than one job and many of them had been at Hopkins for much of their lives. Hopkins did not begin to make its move toward the preeminence it enjoys today until the late 1950s.

Little would I have guessed then that I would be here fifty-one years later or that I would have the privilege of writing the foreword for this handsome and fascinating publication. Most of all, this is a book about Johns Hopkins people, their images captured on film and their voices recorded in more than fifty oral history interviews. Together they form an unusual mosaic of one of the world's great universities. The idea for the book originated with a faculty-student-administration committee appointed by President Bill Brody that was charged with finding ways to celebrate the university's 125th anniversary year in 2000–2001. The notion, and the challenge, was to portray the essence of 125 years of Johns Hopkins—all of Johns Hopkins—through words and pictures. The committee hoped the volume would provide an interesting and lasting memento of this historic year.

We were extremely fortunate to find a highly talented, experienced, and creative editor for the project, Mame Warren. A natural choice for this undertaking, Mame specializes in books rich with images and voices evoking the essence of time and place. The Johns Hopkins University Press published three of these, focusing on Baltimore, the state of Maryland, and the Chesapeake Bay region, and she recently produced a commemorative volume for Washington and Lee University.

At the outset we at Hopkins had one major concern. How could one possibly represent the entire university in a book like this? We feared that Johns Hopkins, known for its highly decentralized operating style, would be too complex. But Mame Warren came up with a unique idea: Organize the book around the major themes of President Daniel Coit Gilman's inaugural address, given February 22, 1876, and then weave together photographs and text from all parts of the university that relate to those themes. The result depicts a university made strong by its diversity and individualism but linked closely by a commonality of purpose, commitment, hopes, dreams, and accomplishments.

The illustrations came from dozens of sources, mostly from various archives and offices of the university but also from some alumni who were willing to share their pictures with us. Each person who was interviewed—faculty, staff, alumni, students—in his or her own way helped to shape Johns Hopkins and, in turn, was shaped by the university. Their words and their memories form the text. These candid, spontaneous comments were excerpted from the longer oral history interviews, full texts of which will become part of the university's permanent records in the Ferdinand Hamburger Jr. Archives at Homewood.

I hope you will take time to review the chronology at the back of the book. Events chronicled there reach beyond the 125-year history of The Johns Hopkins University to the founding of the Peabody Institute and our first benefactors' early planning for the institutions that evolved. Many entries are of special historical significance, but others are there solely for the human interest they portray.

No book can present all of the people, facts, character, and history of a dynamic and complex institution like The Johns Hopkins University, and there was no intention to do that. Rather, we hope that through these images and reminiscences you will gain a better understanding of America's first university dedicated to research, teaching, and public service. Examine these pages and you will see familiar feats and faces. You will also learn what Hopkins was like long before it became part of your life, what it is today, and what it may become tomorrow as it moves toward the future.

ROSS JONES, B.A. '53, Chair
for the 125th Anniversary Committee

ACKNOWLEDGMENTS

First and foremost, I want to thank Ross Jones for giving me the opportunity to assume this important challenge. It has been an honor and a pleasure to work with him, Vice Chair Paula P. Burger, and members of the 125th Anniversary Celebration Planning Committee as we prepare to commemorate this special time in Johns Hopkins' history. Together and in various subcommittees, this impressive group has pursued with enthusiasm and vigor President William R. Brody's charge to conceive memorable events and performances and to create enduring exhibits and publications.

Bob Brugger at The Johns Hopkins University Press first suggested that I might be of assistance in preparing a celebratory volume for the university's 125th anniversary. Bob encouraged me to contact Ross Jones, and Ross invited me to meet with him, Paula Burger, and Julia Morgan, assistant secretary of the university board of trustees and former university archivist. Intrigued with the idea of producing a single volume that would portray these enigmatic, highly decentralized institutions, Ross, Paula, and Julie asked me to meet with some of the icons of Johns Hopkins: Reds Wolman, Richard Macksey, Thomas B. Turner, and Jerry Schnydman, each of whom offered me fascinating insights into this venerable place. I also met Dennis O'Shea, director of communications and public affairs, whose enthusiasm for the project earned him a supervisory position once it was determined that the book would become a major element of the anniversary celebration. Dennis's encouragement, broad understanding of the university, and thoughtful editing of the manuscript have bolstered me through the last year.

Ross Jones, Julie Morgan, Nancy McCall (director of the Alan M. Chesney Medical Archives), and Dennis O'Shea are the fond trustees of this book. They have reviewed every image, read every word, answered countless questions, and made invaluable suggestions. Most important, they have shared with me their vast historical knowledge and astute political perspectives about all things Johns Hopkins. I am deeply grateful for their thoroughness, promptness, and confidence. Jack Goellner, former director of The Johns Hopkins University Press and a dear friend, administered both moral support and sage advice in liberal doses.

Prior to my arrival on campus, Dennis O'Shea asked a number of people throughout Johns Hopkins to recommend oral history interview candidates. Ilene Busch-Vishniac, Jan Corazza, Sue DePasquale, Paula Einaudi, David Fetter, Ricky Fine, Elaine Freeman, Anne Garside, Jack Goellner, James C. Hagan, Craig Hankin, Marguerite Ingalls Jones, Ross Jones, Julie Morgan, Felisa Neuringer, Edith Nichols, Judy Peregoff, Kate Pipkin, Mary Ellen Porter, Joann Rodgers, Edgar E. Roulhac, Erv Sekulow, Alfred Sommer, Gary Stephenson, Laurie Stroope, Billie Walker, Doug Warren, and Charles R. Westgate suggested many names. A tight production schedule required that the long list be narrowed. I appreciate the time these recommendations took and regret that, because of time constraints, I could not pose questions to everyone suggested.

Fifty-five people were interviewed for this book. Each was more than gracious in welcoming me into his or her life as we plumbed for Hopkins memories. Their voices fill these pages with candid and insightful commentary about the Johns Hopkins they know so well. Text drawn from the oral history interviews has been edited only for clarity. Readers should be aware that the spoken word has little in common with carefully composed prose. Instead, it reveals an immediacy of thought and a clear impression of the individual who is expressing personal experiences and convictions. I thank each narrator and refer readers to a complete list of interviewees that appears in "Who We Are." Only small segments of the interviews appear here; complete transcripts and tapes are preserved in the Ferdinand Hamburger Jr. Archives.

Many people have spent years accumulating and cataloging a vast wealth of historical records, official and private papers, and the hundreds of books and other university publications produced throughout the last 125 years (and longer, since the Peabody's history antedates the university's). While the principal sources consulted for this book are noted in the bibliographical essay, I want to give particular acknowledgment here to the people who spent untold hours making information and images available to me and my assistant, Jane McWilliams. At the Ferdinand Hamburger Jr. Archives, James Stimpert, Jennifer Rallo, Holly Callahan, Cynthia H. Requardt, Joan Grattan, Bett Miller, Amy Kimball, and others on the staff encouraged our explorations. Jim Stimpert in particular answered hundreds of questions with good humor and exacting care, often explaining distinctions that were subtle but significant. At the Alan M. Chesney Medical Archives, Nancy McCall and her able staff, Gerard Shorb, Andrew Harrison, Marjorie Winslow Kehoe, and Fran Dukissis, directed me to material that enhanced both the pages of this book and my interviews. Nancy McCall and Louise Cavagnaro (who was an administrator at The Johns Hopkins Hospital from 1953 until her retirement in 1985 and now volunteers her time at the Chesney Archives) graciously answered many inquiries and gave freely of their encyclopedic knowledge of the medical institutions. At the Peabody Institute, public information director Anne Garside and archivist Elizabeth Schaaf fielded questions and produced an invaluable time line of events at the Peabody. Ranice Crosby and Gary Lees introduced me to the riches of the Max Brödel Archives at the Department of Art as Applied to Medicine. I would also like to recognize Neil Grauer of the School of Professional Studies in Business and Education, who guided me to obscure tidbits of history and his family's personal papers and helped with fact checking.

At the Maryland State Archives, Nancy Bramucci and Jennifer Hafner found Johns Hopkins' will; at the University of Maryland at College Park, Doug McElrath and Priscilla Foley, keepers of more than a million photographs in the *News American* Photo Archive in Special Collections, opened their very accessible treasure-trove to me and permitted me to make copies of images relating to Johns Hopkins; at the Maryland Historical Society, Mary Markey provided a copy of the only known photograph of the dedication of the Peabody Institute.

Alumni Keefer Stull Jr., David Trost, Ross Jones, Bob Jones, Bruce M. Mitchell, J. E. Cooper, Jennie Stinchcomb (for Delta

Sigma Pi), Robert Torretti (for Delta Phi), and Charles E. Greene were most generous in making images from their personal collections available for consideration; their contributions reveal the student's perspective—often quite different from more formal photographs found in archives. I also thank Denise D'Oust for sending a wonderful collection of 1950s photos taken by her friend Robert C. Minnick and Nancy Norris for sharing treasures from her father's papers.

Illustrations also came from working files in the various divisions. Pat Kramer provided a multitude of images lodged at the Office of Design and Publication, and Sue DePasquale shared a marvelous hoard of pictures that have appeared through the years in *Johns Hopkins Magazine*. Edith Nichols did the same for *Hopkins Medical News* and other East Baltimore publications. Margaret Hindman in the Office of Development Communications, Mel Widomski in the Office of Facilities Management, Deborah Rager at the G.W.C. Whiting School of Engineering, Sue Dyer at the School of Professional Studies in Business and Education, Felisa Neuringer at the School of Advanced International Studies, Kate Pipkin at the School of Nursing, Ricky Fine at the School of Public Health, Anne Garside at the Peabody Institute, Jack Holmes at The Johns Hopkins University Press, Catherine Arthur and Judith Proffitt at Homewood House, Cindy Kelly at Evergreen House, and Jane Callahan in the Department of Physics and Astronomy graciously permitted me to spend hours picking through their picture files or sent images I requested. Most of these patient people also answered questions, clarified confusing information, and identified faces whenever possible. Other helpful people too numerous to name responded quickly to my urgent inquiries as I attempted to interpret precisely the activities depicted in photos.

I had the good fortune to discover the work of many gifted photographers in offices and archives throughout the university and the medical institutions. In addition, Mort Tadder was more than kind in providing an up-to-the-minute aerial view of the East Baltimore campus, and Marion E. Warren took several new pictures especially for this book. My father also made prints from negatives he had made on assignments for *Johns Hopkins Magazine* in the early 1960s and from the negatives of William H. Hamilton, the primary visual chronicler of Johns Hopkins in the 1960s. Mr. Hamilton, who worked as a technician in the psychology department, took thousands of excellent photographs of most divisions and deserves a Johns Hopkins book of his own.

Expert help from Deborah Lattimore and her staff at TechniType Transcripts assured swift and accurate conversion from voice to text. They continue to set the standard for their profession. Chip Dykes, Kent Weinhold, and Matthew Chronister of GGS in York, Pennsylvania, and Martin Senn of Philamont, Virginia, are responsible for digital separations of illustrations from the Ferdinand Hamburger Jr. Archives and the Alan M. Chesney Medical Archives. All are experts in their complex and highly technical work, and I am appreciative for their meticulous handling of fragile and unique materials.

If some physical aspects of this volume seem familiar, it is perhaps because designer Gerard A. Valerio has brought his mastery to many Johns Hopkins projects over more than thirty years, from the *Johns Hopkins Magazine* to freelance assignments for various divisions to the dozens of books he has fashioned for The Johns Hopkins University Press. This project marks the seventh volume that Gerry and I have produced together, and each experience rekindles my admiration for his artistry. I marvel at Gerry's elegant solutions to the challenge of blending words and illustrations into a vivid portrait of these diverse Hopkins institutions. Sherri Ferritto complemented Gerry's efforts by setting the type and composing the page layouts from Gerry's design.

Jane McWilliams assumed several roles here, beginning with seemingly endless hours spent pouring over scrapbooks kept by the university's first registrar, Thomas R. Ball. Jane's scholarly enthusiasm unearthed many gems and enlivened my own research. The always fascinating and often amusing results of her investigation are found throughout this book, particularly in the chronology. Once the manuscript began to take shape, Jane donned her copyeditor's hat. Her insightful questions and precise rulings on grammar and punctuation have made a harmonious whole of the many textual elements in this volume. I am also grateful to Jane for organizing the bibliographical essay and for generously providing the illustration of William K. Brooks's seaside laboratory. Most of all, I appreciate Jane's friendship, encouragement, and great good humor.

The conscientious people who keep the Office of Communications and Public Affairs running smoothly, especially Diane Carlino, Gayle Hunter, Alicia Campbell, Eileen Painter, and Tim Gillaspie, provided unfailing support, filled every request, and eased my workload. Sue DePasquale and Lois Perschetz and the staffs of the *Johns Hopkins Magazine* and the *JHU Gazette* answered questions and helped me understand the subtle nuances and the complexities of Johns Hopkins' divisions. I was particularly blessed to settle into an office at the exquisite Evergreen House; Cindy Kelly, Ben Renwick, and the wonderful people who work at Evergreen accommodated my every need. I will always remember my restorative walks through the estate's enchanting gardens and grounds.

Finally, and most fondly, for his unfaltering patience and devoted support, I thank my dear husband, Henry Harris.

MAME WARREN, Editor

JOHNS HOPKINS

"A great deal of oral history, I think, ventures into mythology.

Mythology is a certain way of conveying knowledge,

keeping traditions intact.

Sometimes it's more accurate in its way than certain kinds of history.

This is where beliefs begin to inflect the narratives."

PROFESSOR RICHARD MACKSEY, M.A.'53, PH.D.'57

I give, devise and bequeath unto "The Johns Hopkins University," a Corporation formed at my instance, under the Laws of Maryland, by Certificate duly recorded among the Records of Baltimore County, my Country Place known as "Clifton," containing about three hundred and thirty acres, and all the shares of the Capital Stock of the Baltimore and Ohio Rail Road Company, whereof I shall die possessed, (except the stock known as preferred stock of said Company, upon which a dividend of six per centum and no more is payable by said Company,) and I recommend the said "The Johns Hopkins University" not to dispose of the said Capital Stock, or of the stock, accruing thereon by way of increment, or dividend, but to keep the said stock, and said increment, or dividend stock, if any, as an investment; and I direct that the buildings, necessary for the purposes of the said "The Johns Hopkins University," shall be constructed out of the money dividends as they accrue on said stock; and that the said University and the Trustees should maintain the said University, afterwards, out of its receipts from scholars, and out of the annual revenue derived from the devise and bequest hereby made, without encroaching upon the principal fund. And I further enjoin upon the said University, and the Trustees thereof, the duty of voting and representing the said stock with diligence, zeal and perfect fidelity to the trust I have reposed in them, especially desiring that each and every Trustee thereof will abstain from all action which may tend to subordinate

BY ONE, FOR ALL

"While I leave to others the commemoration of our founder, you must let me refer to the tributes of admiration which his generosity has called out on the remotest shores of our own land, and in the most venerable shrines of European learning. The Berkeley laurel and the Oxford ivy may well be carved upon his brow when the sculptor shapes his likeness; for by wise men in the east and by rich men in the west, his gifts are praised as among the most timely, the most generous, and the most noble ever bestowed by one, for all."

DANIEL COIT GILMAN
February 22, 1876

Johns Hopkins, a prominent Baltimore merchant and investor, never married; in his will, far left, he made generous provisions to The Johns Hopkins University and The Johns Hopkins Hospital, which he had chartered in 1867. At his death in 1873, his $7-million estate was divided equally between the two institutions, the largest philanthropic bequest in U.S. history until that time.

The following year, the university's trustees selected Daniel Coit Gilman, president of the University of California, as Johns Hopkins' first president. In his acceptance letter, Gilman wrote, "The characteristics of your trust are so peculiar & so good that I cannot decline your proposal. The careful manner in which your Board has been selected, the liberal views which you hold in respect to advanced culture both in literature and science, your corporate freedom from political & ecclesiastical alliances & the munificent endowment at your control are especially favorable to the organization of a new University."

3

"The Hopkins bequest was free of the usual kinds of specific stipulations and directions that really can hogtie educational institutions when they get started. So it was essentially Gilman's creation, and he certainly did his homework. He came from an institution that called itself a university but wasn't, University of California. He had seen Yale as a student, so he had some sense of what a multi-bodied university was. But I think the idea of a graduate degree, a doctoral degree, really did evolve here. Harvard and Yale had given doctoral degrees, but they were largely honoring those people who had done work in Europe.

Gilman spent the early part of his tenure traveling around the United States, then in Europe, recruiting, but it was also an education, so he managed to see a great many people. He got some remarkable people on the earliest faculty. It had a very international edge to it, in that they were either European or European-trained."

PROFESSOR RICHARD MACKSEY, M.A.'53, PH.D.'57

When he arrived in Baltimore, Daniel Coit Gilman, above c.1876, made the selection of the faculty his priority. By the time he retired in 1901, Gilman (center of front row at left) had engaged so many scholars and medical doctors (including some who achieved world renown) that they spilled beyond the edges of the photographer's backdrop. Front row, left to right: A. Marshall Elliott, Edward H. Griffin, Paul Haupt, Basil L. Gildersleeve, President Gilman, Ira Remsen, Henry A. Rowland, William H. Welch, Harmon N. Morse. Second row: C. W. E. Miller, Maurice Bloomfield, Herbert E. Greene, Nicholas Murray, William H. Browne, James W. Bright, Henry Wood, Howard A. Kelly, William K. Brooks, William S. Halsted, John Jacob Abel, Edward B. Mathews. Third row: C. C. Marden, B. J. Vos, C. Johnston, John M. Vincent, William Sydney Thayer, Harry Fielding Reid, William H. Howell, F. P. Mall, William B. Clark, Frank Morley, J. Whitridge Williams. Fourth row: Sidney Sherwood, K. F. Smith, L. S. Hulbert, R. G. Harrison, Ethan Allen Andrews, Thomas S. Cullen, H. C. Jones, Reid Hunt, Edward Renouf.

"Without Gilman, there would have been no Hopkins. Or, since Mr. Hopkins had left the money, there would have been a Hopkins; but the idea of having what the newspapers in the 1870s called 'Heidelberg in Baltimore'—that was all Gilman. A baccalaureate program is totally outside the German university tradition. So how did Gilman do that? Well, he piled the doctoral program on top of the baccalaureate, and made the gutsy decision that the university would have undergraduates. All male, of course. That was the temper of the nineteenth century, after all.

Hopkins was condemned for godlessness because it did not have, as so many colleges that were founded earlier did, any kind of religious foundation. It was dedicated to science.

I wish I'd known Gilman. I feel enormous admiration for him, and that spirit informed me and informed The Johns Hopkins University, and I am a little sad that so few of the students and even faculty and administrators of Hopkins now bother with the history. They take it for granted." STEVEN MULLER

J. J. Sylvester almost quashed his opportunity to establish the Department of Mathematics when he demanded that his salary be paid in gold bullion. He died in 1897.

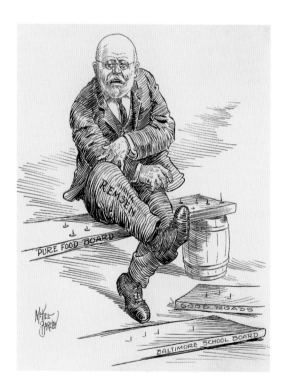

Ira Remsen, caricatured above, a member of the original faculty, became JHU's second president in 1901. Frank Goodnow succeeded Remsen in 1914. Goodnow was awarded an honorary doctor of laws degree when he was replaced by Joseph Sweetman Ames, with whom he was pictured above right in 1929.

"President Frank Goodnow looked at Hopkins and saw that the people who were most unhappy were the freshmen. He hit upon the idea of admitting students as Ph.D. candidates after a year or two of college work. Then the Depression came, and it was never really put into effect other than the possibility that you could get a Ph.D. without a bachelor's degree.

Detlev Bronk wanted no formal requirements for a bachelor's degree. Your education would be under the control of a particular faculty member or a group of faculty members. At the end of two years, you would be accepted into some department for a degree. His idea was to decrease the student body to the point that each student really could be treated as an individual.

Lowell Reed was a retired professor of biostatistics at the School of Hygiene and Public Health. When President Bronk suddenly left, they needed a president and Reed had a good reputation. He was interested in education as well as research. He did a good job of trying to get the various divisions to interact more. He looked at the whole institution instead of lots of separate little institutions.

For many years, the administration was really two people: Wilson Shaffer, dean for many years, and P. Stewart Macaulay, who was the provost. Macaulay took care of money and Shaffer took care of faculty relations, and presidents would come and go."
PROFESSOR JOHN GRYDER

In 1915, Assistant Registrar Holland, the president's secretary Miss Gwilliam, and Registrar Thomas Randolph Ball—the entire administrative staff of the university—posed in their McCoy Hall office on the old downtown campus.

"At the Bologna Center, Director Grove Haines put a French student with a German student, put an Italian student with a student from the Middle East as roommates. If you wanted to be in the diplomatic corps in Europe, you went to SAIS in Bologna, and you were credentialed. We've had fifty years of peace in Europe basically—and I submit that integral to that has been the cadre of leaders that came out of the School of Advanced International Studies of The Johns Hopkins University. You will find them in every corner of the world." WILBERT "BILL" LOCKLIN, B.S.'57

"Lincoln Gordon was an outstanding professor at Harvard whom John Kennedy had picked to be ambassador to Brazil. On paper he had the qualities that the university, the trustees, were looking for. Hopkins liked the international aspect. Milton Eisenhower was ambassador-at-large to Latin America, as Ike's personal representative. Bowman had been involved in the peace negotiations in Europe at the end of World War I and with refugees after World War II. Bronk was an internationally known scientist. So there was that tradition.

So Gordon was chosen. By then he was assistant secretary of state for inter-American affairs. He was a wonderful personality, a nice man, smart man, but he was succeeding one of the most popular and able presidents in the country at that time. It was a tough act to follow. And he walked into a very difficult time in American higher education when student unrest dominated the scene. And to make matters worse he had absolutely no experience in running a complex place like Hopkins. It was not a good time." ROSS JONES, B.A.'53

Lowell Reed (at the head of the table) became JHU's seventh president in 1953 when the Bologna Center was being planned by Provost P. Stewart Macaulay, Felice Battaglia of the University of Bologna, SAIS dean Philip Thayer, and the center's first director, Grove Haines.

In 1967 Milton Eisenhower escorted his successor, Lincoln Gordon (below left, holding hat) onto the Homewood campus. Eisenhower was an enormously popular president from 1956 to 1967; he returned as interim president in 1971 after Gordon resigned.

On February 22, 1991, Chairman of the Board of Trustees Morris Offit, right, extended his hand in gratitude to Steven Muller, president from 1972 to 1990. Between them is William C. Richardson, who had just been inaugurated as JHU's eleventh president.

"Some member of the faculty said to me that Bill Richardson was brilliant as a conversationalist in the sense that you never remembered anything *he* had said, but that you remembered what *you* had said was extraordinarily brilliant. Bill Richardson listens in such a way that he elicits from people their very best, and he leaves them feeling good. Everyone around him thrives and prospers. He was a brilliant administrator. He put conditions in place that let people do what they needed to do, and so everybody was really working effectively. It was something to behold." ELISE HANCOCK

9

President Richardson resigned in 1995 before a successor could be named, and the trustees asked Johns Hopkins' Nobel Laureate Daniel Nathans to serve as interim president. Nathans (holding a folder) joined Don Giddens, dean of the Whiting School of Engineering, in May 1996 for the rededication of the lobby of Barton Hall, where renovations were made possible by the family of Julian Smith.

"When they begged Milton Eisenhower to come back for a second term as president, he put conditions. He wanted two young trustees who were recent graduates, and he wanted a woman trustee. I've served under Eisenhower, Muller, Richardson, and now Bill Brody, but Dan Nathans, an interim president, was my favorite of them all. He was a really brilliant person, a topnotch brain in molecular biology who got a Nobel Prize, and he was the most modest, wonderful man I've ever known." MARJORIE G. LEWISOHN, M.D.'43

"Bill Brody is a wonderful president; he's a wonderful man. He's a futurist. If there's anyone who's going to be ahead of the curve and keep his institution ahead of the curve, it's Brody. And he surrounded himself with good people like Steve Knapp, his provost. This has got to be the best managed university in the country. And look at the stature of that board: people like Bloomberg, Mike Armstrong, Morris Offit. I'm beginning to understand the dedication that these people have.

Once you get involved with Hopkins, you want to be there to make it successful. The presidents before Brody, Bill Richardson and Steve Muller, are in a class by themselves. It's always, considering its size, had such distinguished, skillful people to run it.

Now, who's responsible for that? Is it the board? No, because the board keeps changing. I think it's the institution that makes people like that want to identify with it and become part of its leadership. They'll always find distinguished, talented people who want to work for Hopkins because it's Hopkins.

When I travel around in my business and I tell people I'm on the Johns Hopkins board, that's the only thing on my résumé that gets anybody's attention. Hopkins is impressive. Look at *U.S. News and World Report*, how this little institution always does so well. It'll do well in the future." ERNEST A. BATES, B.A.'58

"I've got along with all the presidents I ever worked for. They wanted to know what was the secret of staying at Hopkins so long. I told them, 'Turn right, go straight, and stay in the right lane.'" MINNIE HARGROW

When the board of trustees chose William R. Brody in 1996 as the thirteenth president of The Johns Hopkins University, he was already very familiar with the intricacies of the Hopkins institutions. Brody was radiologist-in-chief at The Johns Hopkins Hospital and a professor at the School of Medicine from 1987 to 1994. Just as important, from 1992 to 1994, he chaired the Committee for the 21st Century that examined and redefined the university's goals for the future. Here he chatted in February 2000 with his executive assistant, Jerry Schnydman, and Minnie Hargrow, who has worked for the university since 1946.

"George Peabody handled his philanthropies like he handled his business. He was constantly looking out for new ways of doing things. They tried to get him to rescue the Library Company of Baltimore, and Peabody wasn't interested in shoring up some faltering institution. He ended up founding the Peabody Institute, which was the country's first cultural center, which in one broad swipe gave the city an orchestra, a public library, the gallery of art, and the academy of music.

Peabody wanted an institution that would create a cultural revolution in Baltimore, and it did. The Peabody Library made it possible for The Johns Hopkins University to attract a respectable group of scholars to Baltimore because it had a research library, which the young university obviously wasn't in a position to create out of whole cloth. Peabody men founded the Baltimore Symphony Orchestra, Baltimore Opera, and even today they're active in Baltimore Choral Arts, Ragtime Ensemble, Baltimore Chamber Orchestra. It's staggering, the number of institutions that have grown out of this place."
ELIZABETH SCHAAF

George Peabody proposed his institute in 1857, but the building at Mount Vernon Place wasn't dedicated until 1866 when Peabody returned from his home in London. Eighteen thousand schoolchildren joined other Baltimoreans assembled for the event.

FOLLOWING PAGES:
Summer classes were offered to teachers beginning in 1909; this group enrolled two years later. The program gradually evolved into today's School of Professional Studies in Business and Education.

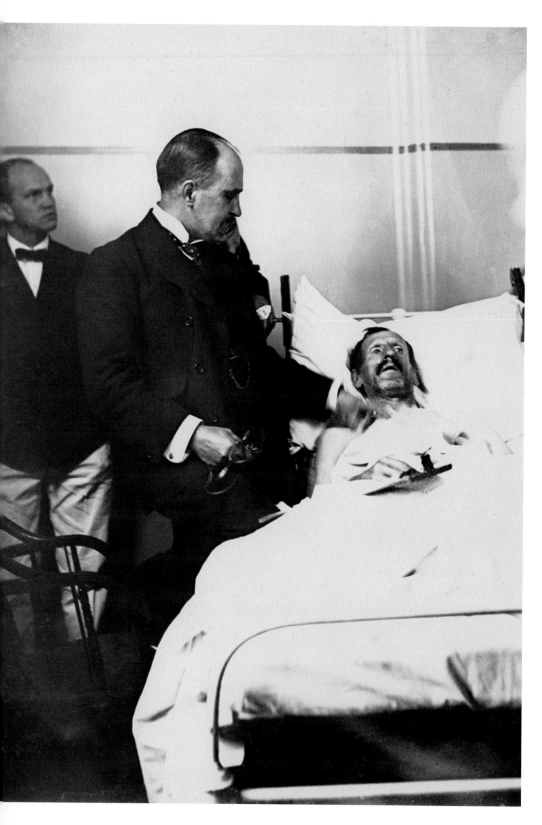

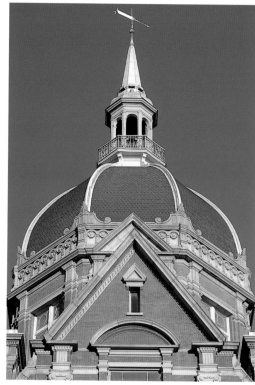

The Johns Hopkins Hospital opened in 1889 and its distinctive dome became a Baltimore landmark. Physician-in-Chief William Osler revolutionized medical education with his method of teaching students at the patient's bedside. The School of Medicine did not open until 1893, but the hospital's first bulletin, below, dated 1889, lists various courses offered. William S. Halsted wielded his favorite hammer when he presided over the first operation in the new surgical amphitheater in 1904, right. Note the use of rubber gloves, a Hopkins initiative.

"Hopkins is where discovery became a real part of academic medicine. A true academic center has three strong components: the clinical component is the ultimate, and that's what you strive for; the education component so that you have tomorrow's doctors and scientists who will make the care better; and the discovery part, the research part. That's the part that makes tomorrow's medicine better and lets you teach new things to new people.

The truly great academic centers have strength in all three, and we're one of the handful of places that really are great in all three. The whole idea of having full-time faculty paid to teach is a Hopkins innovation, and that people would do research is a Hopkins innovation." DR. CATHERINE DEANGELIS

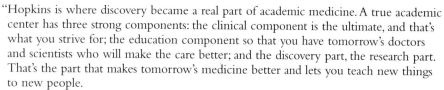

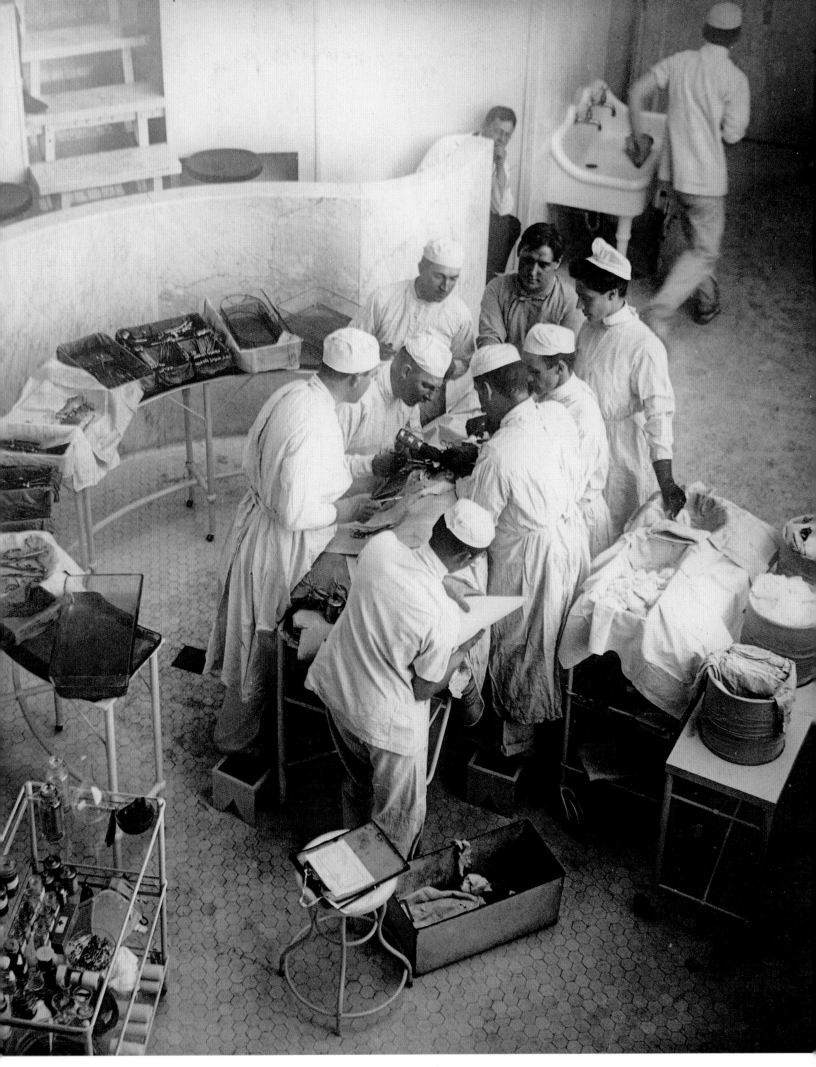

WE LAUNCH
OUR BARK UPON
THE PATAPSCO

"So, friends and colleagues, we launch our bark upon the Patapsco, and send it forth to unknown seas. May its course be guided by looking to the heavens and the voyage promote the glory of God and the good of Mankind."

Daniel Coit Gilman, 1876

"When The Johns Hopkins University was founded, the first thing the Peabody trustees did was pass a resolution that the two institutions should be affiliated at the earliest possible time. That affiliation ultimately did take place exactly one hundred years later. This is Baltimore; things move slowly. But there really was a close association between the two institutions from the very beginning. If you were looking for a Hopkins faculty member, you walked down to the Peabody Library and you found him there.

Many Hopkins people took part in a scientific lecture series at Peabody. Any of the nineteenth-century scientists who were anybody were invited to participate. When the lecture series was eliminated, all of the scientific apparatus was turned over to Johns Hopkins. Peabody Orchestra played for Hopkins' graduations and functions. So there's always been this gentlemanly give-and-take between the two institutions."
ELIZABETH SCHAAF

The university's original site was selected for its proximity to the Peabody Library, which contained sixty thousand volumes. The aerial view at left shows the Peabody in the upper right. Johns Hopkins' campus was dominated by the dome of the physics laboratory, straight down Monument Street. Above, looking east from Eutaw Street c.1910, Levering and McCoy Halls are on the left and the biological laboratory is on the right.

"Men not buildings" was the guiding doctrine of the day, according to John C. French in A History of the University Founded by Johns Hopkins, *which may explain the ill repair of the walls in the chemistry lab c.1900. Indoor sports were played in the gymnasium built in 1883. History professor John H. Latané,* far right, *must have had quite a job packing books when he moved to the Homewood campus.*

"Engineering and science have always fed off one another. Trying to understand what's happening in an electric motor or a chemical reaction is of great interest to the theoretician, and the theoretician helps the engineer understand what he or she is trying to do, so there's this symbiotic relationship. Henry Rowland and Ira Remsen and the first group of scientists here would not call themselves engineers, but they certainly were interested in practical matters.

Even before the engineering school began, the physics department was training people in what we would call electrical engineering. They were studying electric motors and questions of exactly how does the dynamo work and how you improve its performance. We had several decades of training people to be engineers but who had their degrees in physics or in chemistry." PROFESSOR STUART W. "BILL" LESLIE

"Dr. Welch I knew quite well as a young person knows an older person. He was delightful. He never married. He didn't talk trivia, but he was very outgoing in his manner. He was head of pathology at Hopkins. Then later he became head of the School of Hygiene and developed that area. When the Welch Library, named for him, was created, he was immortalized." DR. THOMAS TURNER

William H. Welch was the founding director of the School of Hygiene and Public Health. The school was housed from 1918 to 1925 in the former physics lab at 310–312 West Monument Street. This aerial photograph c. 1924 shows construction of the school's first building on Wolfe Street. At right, land is cleared c. 1877 for the hospital. John Shaw Billings's concept for the complex featured detached buildings with separate ventilation systems to prevent contagion.

"William Osler invented the idea of the residency program. Medicine had an energy at Hopkins because of Osler and Halsted and the other early greats in medicine. The whole idea of medical education as we know it is Hopkins. We are as good as we are in public health because we were first in public health. And that's Welch's doing. Hopkins was incredibly blessed with genius in the way things started." STEVEN MULLER

"You know that statue? When I was a resident, I'd come in at three in the morning and just touch the foot automatically on the way in. And we all did it! Jewish people did it, Catholics, Christians. We even had someone who was a Muslim who did it. We said, 'Help us to take care of the kids.' Almost always there's a flower or a note or something there. Some of those notes are pretty incredible." DR. CATHERINE DEANGELIS

"There were no dormitories, so all of us lived in rooming houses up and down North Broadway, North Washington, Wolfe Street. There were four Greek-letter national fraternities and one local fraternity known as the Pithotomy Club, and a certain number of students lived at these houses, but they couldn't accommodate the entire membership. Their main purpose was as dining clubs. That's where we ate. Looking back on it, it was a rather bohemian existence that we lived at that time, but we thought it was terrific." VICTOR McKUSICK, M.D.'46

"Nurses are the infantry. They're right on the front line. Wonderful, compassionate individuals, salt-of-the-earth-type individuals, and I hate to see them stressed to the point where they don't like doing what they do anymore. They play an enormous role in my success, both in the operating room and on the clinical ward, and I think physicians who recognize the value of nurses always are going to do better than ones who don't. These are people who really advocate for you and help to carry out your plan, and if you can communicate with them and they can communicate with you, your patient's going to do a whole lot better. They're colleagues, and you can't do without them."
DR. BENJAMIN CARSON

A copy of Danish sculptor Bertel Thorswaldsen's Christus Consolator, *far left above, was unveiled in 1896, the gift of William Wallace Spence of Baltimore. The medical students c. 1900 far left* and the nursing students above *were among the first of many generations to admire its majesty in the rotunda under the dome.*

Dedication of the New Buildings at Homewood
THE JOHNS HOPKINS UNIVERSITY OF BALTIMORE MAY 21st 1915.

The downtown location was never intended to be the university's permanent home. Johns Hopkins' bequest had included his three-hundred-acre country estate, Clifton, with the intention that it would be developed into a campus. For various reasons, that plan never materialized. In 1901, William Keyser and William Wyman announced that they would donate 151 acres for a new campus on Charles Street if $1 million was raised for the university's endowment. The trustees accepted the offer on February 22, 1902. The property included several structures, including Wyman Villa, left, which was razed in 1955. The move to the Homewood campus was gradual. The School of Engineering led the way in 1914; most of the Faculty of Philosophy and administrative offices followed in 1916.

In May 1915, throngs of spectators gathered for events surrounding the dedication of Gilman Hall and the inauguration of Frank Goodnow as Johns Hopkins' third president, above.

The new setting inspired students to fashion modern traditions like the Cane Club, whose members posed far left in 1930 with their coach-and-four, "the old tally-ho."

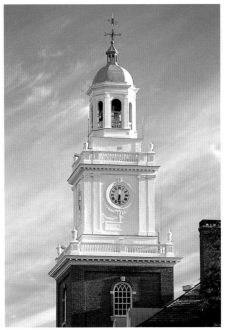

The Homewood campus developed into a nearly seamless blend of authentic historic architecture and new structures built to complement those already on the property. Homewood House, far left and below, was built in 1801–03 by Charles Carroll of Carrollton, a signer of the Declaration of Independence, as a wedding gift for his son. Gilman Hall, with its distinctive bell tower, was designed by Douglas Thomas, an 1893 Hopkins graduate. From 1935, vehicles on Charles Street had to navigate around a monument to Johns Hopkins, but the statue was moved in 1955 after being declared a traffic hazard.

"In that upper room, right up under the clock, there's nothing above us except time itself. That's wonderful, the idea of leaving the campus physically below you and ascending the last flight of stairs that even the elevator doesn't go up to, as if it's just you and the muse going up to this elevated venue.

There has been a prevailing tone in the room that pleases me. I don't know whether it comes out of the walls of Gilman Hall and the history of all the people who have taught and learned there. It's a wonderful combination of noncompetitiveness, of critical candor and reciprocal respect." JOHN BARTH, B.A.'51, M.A.'52

"I had never seen the campus when I arrived to start my freshman year. As the cab pulled into what was then a bowl (now called the beach, in front of the library), I'd never seen anything so beautiful in my life. The sun was shining, the flowers were out. It was absolutely beautiful, and I remember being so impressed with the Georgian architecture. It was everything that Norman Rockwell would have painted in a picture of an American campus." MICHAEL R. BLOOMBERG, B.S.E.'64

Meeting in the Real World

PRISCILLA MASON

Interviewed on December 1, 1999

The original home of the School of Advanced International Studies was a former school on Florida Avenue in Washington, D.C. Director Halford L. Hoskins joined students in the dining room, where conversations often were conducted in foreign languages.

The School of Advanced International Studies was started by a group of men in Washington led by Christian A. Herter, a congressman from Massachusetts, and Paul Nitze, who were cousins. Mr. Herter was a Republican and Paul Nitze was a Democrat, but they were great friends. During the summer months, when their wives took their children to New England for the summer vacation, they would talk over breakfast about affairs of the world.

One of their great concerns was that the United States was not prepared to take the leadership role which they foresaw coming at the end of World War II, that we did not have people in the business world or really even in the government who were trained in international affairs. They felt the great need for further advanced education in that area. They decided to have a survey made of the educational resources of the country, and

they found that there was absolutely no such graduate program in the whole United States, with the exception of the program at Tufts, the Fletcher School of Law and Diplomacy. So they established the School of Advanced International Studies in Washington in 1943.

This was a private, independent school. They selected as the first director Halford L. Hoskins, who had been dean of the Fletcher School. I had recently received my master's degree from the Fletcher School and Dean Hoskins asked me to be his administrative assistant in setting up the school. We bought the old Gunston Hall School on Florida Avenue.

Our first class was all girls, with the exception of two men. Faculty was made up at the last moment. John Dickey, who was later president of Dartmouth, was in the State Department. Hajo Holborn, who was a professor of history at Yale, used to commute down once a week. In

addition to teaching a few graduate students, we had a program for the military to train army officers for military government in Germany, and Professor Holborn had charge of that. And then there was Professor Linebarger, who was full time, on the Far East. Dr. Hoskins himself was a specialist in the Middle East. The curriculum was fashioned according to whom we had as faculty.

The curriculum started out as an emphasis on one area of the world backed up by a knowledge of economics. In the first couple of years this was a one-year program, but very shortly it evolved into a two-year program. This is when it began to be really, really good. Our graduates, even in the very early years, were competing with Fletcher graduates very successfully.

The original idea was that there would be an equal division between the students going into government and going into business and that gradually they would build up a corps of people in the private sector and in the public sector who would have the same training and background. They would meet each other out in the real world and make things better. They wanted to educate young Americans to go abroad and do a good job in both the public and the private sector and to have an interplay between the two to advance American foreign policy, America's position in the world.

Christian Herter was dedicated to better government, to doing the right thing for the country. He was very practical, hard working, very modest, interested in others. He spent a lot of time at SAIS. He would come to the school two or three times a week to check on administrative things, and at least once a week he would come and talk with the students.

Paul Nitze was not so involved in the early days. He oversaw the finances. When the Republicans were in, Chris Herter was in the government and Paul was out, and Paul would come and be resident at SAIS and teach. He loved the students and the students loved his teaching. Then we'd have an election and the Democrats would be in, and Chris would be out of office and he would come back to the school. So they were both extremely involved. In the early days, Chris was the one. The first four or five years, he really got the school on its feet. Chris never taught a class. He just would talk with the students informally. Paul taught defense courses, strategy, that kind of thing. He was assistant secretary of defense several

In 1950 SAIS affiliated with Johns Hopkins as a graduate division. Five years later, it opened a center in Bologna, Italy, that attracted American and European students absorbed in international studies.

president of Johns Hopkins, Detlev W. Bronk, jumped at it. He was just intrigued and right away said, "Yes, we'll do this." And he signed us up, took us over.

The Bologna Center was the brain-child of Grove Haines, a professor of European studies. He thought that Bologna was the place to set up a study center, near the oldest university in Europe. There was a great deal of cooperation with the university there. There was a lot of opposition here to setting it up, that it was going to be too expensive and it wasn't going to work; but it just took off, and now it is extremely successful.

You can't get a degree by just going to the Bologna Center. You have to spend one year in Washington. So the American students go to Bologna either their first year or their second because they want the degree. The foreign students usually spend one year in Bologna and, if they can get a fellowship, come for their second year here. But a good many just go for a year for the experience. I understand that a tremendous number of those who have been to the Bologna Center have jobs in various foreign offices in governments of Western Europe. They're expanding the curriculum to include a lot of Eastern European problems and trying to get more East European students.

Nanjing was Steve Muller's baby. No degree is connected with Nanjing. The American students are taught by Chinese professors in Chinese, and the Chinese students are taught by American professors in English. And they room together, as far as possible, one Chinese and one American student. The Nanjing Center is on the campus of Nanjing University, and so it's protected by the university. It has a library with open stacks, the only one in China.

The affiliation with Johns Hopkins was the making of the School of Advanced International Studies. The Johns Hopkins name enabled the school to recruit the best faculty and the best students.

"Bologna is a major university center in Italy and the oldest in Europe. There are a lot of students there, but the contingent from Hopkins was a little universe unto itself. In the early '60s, we had courses in international relations, contemporary German and French politics, Italian, nineteenth- and twentieth-century history, and various courses on international economics, monetary policy, and capital markets. We had students who had learned nineteenth- and twentieth-century history from various vantage points. People came with their biases—French/German issues, Jewish/German issues—which made these courses come much more alive than they ever were in an American university. Sitting there in a room with French, German, English, and American students discussing the Depression or the Cuban Missile Crisis or the Second World War, we were animated and excited. If you'd been studying economics at a European university, you hadn't revisited some of the big questions of recent diplomatic history: How do you organize the world? How do you resolve the things that have happened? Most people who went to Bologna, and I think it's true of all of SAIS, have a bit in their genetic makeup of wanting to have a better world than they entered." NANEEN HUNTER NEUBOHN, M.A.'64

times, and he was very active also in the arms negotiations with the Russians.

After the school had been going for about four years, it began running out of money. The first budgets were about fifty thousand dollars a year, and full professors were paid seven thousand dollars. It was just a whole different world. We got a little money from the government for this training of colonels and military government, but it came to the point where we felt we needed some foundation money. Paul Nitze went to John Gardner, who

was at the Carnegie Corporation. Gardner said, "We will give you sixty thousand dollars over five years. If you're going to continue to exist and get foundation grants, you've got to have a university affiliation. You're not going to be able to make it on your own."

So Chris and Paul started with Harvard. That's where they both graduated. Harvard toyed with it, but then said, "No, thank you, it's going to be too much nuisance having it down in Washington." So we went to Johns Hopkins. The then-

Priscilla Mason served as administrative assistant to three deans at SAIS before she retired in 1967 and took a seat on the school's Advisory Council.

Christian Herter, one of the founders of the School of Advanced International Studies, died in 1966, but he is honored still by a chair in American foreign policy established in his name.

In 1987 the School of Continuing Studies opened its Downtown Center to accommodate professionals who wanted to pursue advanced degrees or improve their skills.

"When you look across the array of activities that are going on in this university and the professionalism with which things are being accomplished, it's extremely impressive. It's continually amazing to find out how successful the university is on all fronts and the kinds of things it's trying to do. It's a joy, actually, to see it in progress."
NANEEN HUNTER NEUBOHN, M.A.'64

"The city has evolved to the point where world figures enjoy living here in Baltimore, which changes the character of the faculty. I think it's very important. The Peabody Library is one of the great beauties of Baltimore, really. It's a treasure.

The Baltimore Symphony has become one of the best such institutions in the country. Baltimore Museum of Art, Walters Art Gallery—it's a general quality of life. Not that we aren't beset with urban problems, and they are difficult problems, but people place value on the beauties and qualities of the city and work towards their preservation and the improvement of the problems." LEON FLEISHER

"The evening students, people who have experience out in the business world, who are in their late twenties, thirties, and forties, are a different kind of student from a youngster out of high school with only a year or two of college.

The evening students were generally highly motivated. Many of them were working with contracts and the business subjects that I was teaching. I would have to explain to youngsters in college what a mortgage was, whereas a typical mature adult understands what a mortgage is.

Day students were more adept at studying, and they were accustomed to knowing how to utilize what the book said and how to apply that material in a testing situation. The older students had to learn how to study all over again and how to prepare for examinations and tests. But in a classroom setting, with discussion and the exchange of information and knowledge, they helped each other and they appreciated each other. It was a great experience, I think, for both." JUDGE JOHN HARDWICKE

The Peabody Institute became affiliated with The Johns Hopkins University in 1977, formalizing a harmonious relationship that had existed unofficially for a century. Acquisition of the Peabody gave Hopkins yet another campus, and this one was in Mount Vernon Place, the cultural center of Baltimore. Students from other campuses were encouraged to take classes in the performing arts offered by Peabody, and Peabody students enrolled in liberal arts, science, and engineering courses at Homewood.

33

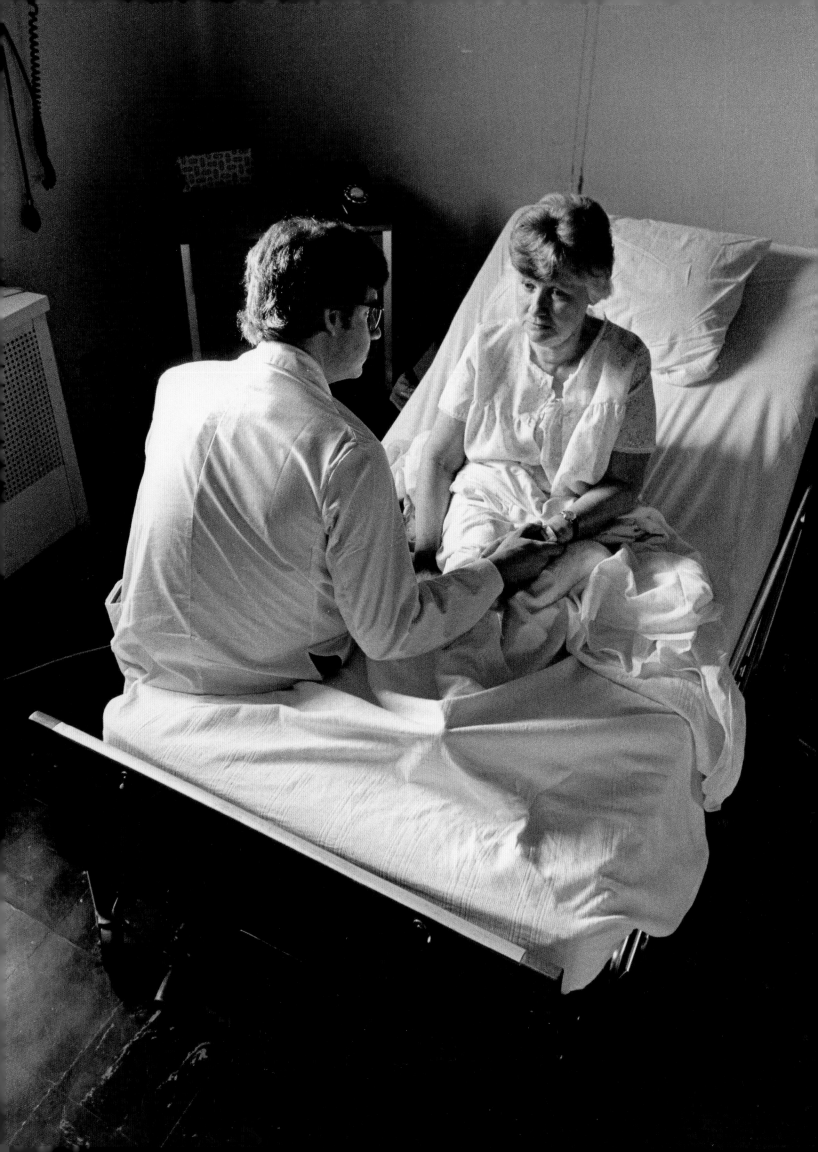

LISTEN, PONDER, AND OBSERVE

"It is well to bear in mind that the most enlightened institutions in our country, and the most enlightened countries in Europe, are those in which educational discussions are now most lively; and it behooves us, as we engage in a new undertaking, to listen, ponder, and observe; and above all to be modest in the announcement of our plans."

DANIEL COIT GILMAN, 1876

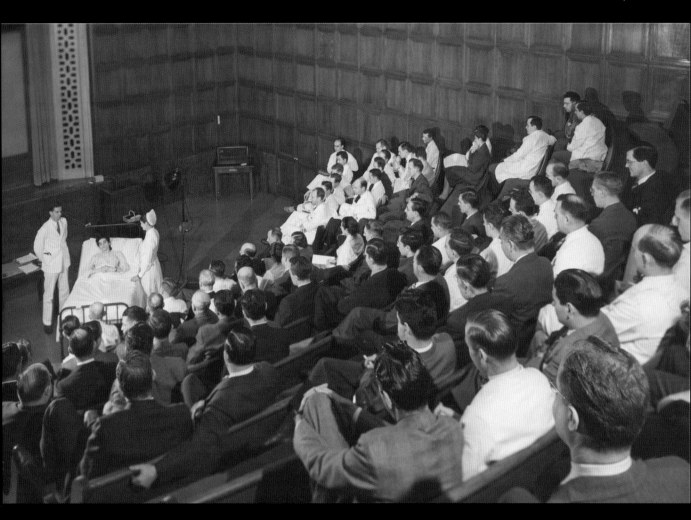

"Grand rounds, as we know them now and from my first days here, were amphitheater rounds. Patients were wheeled in on their beds or in wheelchairs. The resident would present the patient and then a member of the faculty would discuss the problem after the patient had left the room. For many years these were held in Hurd Hall and were well attended. They were moved to the Turner Auditorium in the fall of 1968.

Toward the end of Dr. Harvey's tenure, they were shifted to Saturday mornings. They had become very popular as continuing education for staff from hospitals all over the city, and for our own staff Saturday was a more satisfactory time. One could be leisurely, without having to think about when you'd have to dash off to your office or to the clinic.

But then Dr. Stobo came in as chief of medicine and there was much more attention to the women on the staff, and the realization that Saturday really should be kept sacrosanct for the staff in general. So they were moved back to Hurd Hall, in part because it's smaller and more intimate." VICTOR McKUSICK, M.D.'46

A Johns Hopkins education can take many forms, from deciphering the Dead Sea Scrolls to assisting in the launch of a satellite that will rendezvous with an asteroid. For medical students, memorable moments sometimes emerge in a quiet, candid conversation with a patient. More dramatic revelations often unfold when diseases are diagnosed during grand rounds in Hurd Hall, above.

"There was a certain amount of continuity among the faculty and administration between my grandfather, my father, and myself. Dr. Ames was president of the university when my father was there, and he'd been a professor for my grandfather.

One of my first professors at Hopkins was Frederic Chapin Lane, who was a renowned historian who taught at Hopkins for thirty-five or forty years. Almost everybody took his Occidental Civilization history course. My father had Professor Lane, and I had Professor Lane. Professor Lane always took at least one section, and I was fortunate enough to be assigned to his section, but unfortunately he held it on Saturday morning and nobody wanted to go. He held it in the basement of Gilman Hall, and he would come in on a frigid morning and throw open the window because he liked brisk air.

After the first meeting, I said to my father that I had Professor Lane, and he said, 'Oh, I had him my freshman year, too.' So I went up to Dr. Lane and said, 'My father tells me that he had you in 1932. I hope that doesn't make you feel too bad.' And Professor Lane smiled and said, 'Oh, no, Mr. Grauer. I hope it doesn't make *you* feel too bad.'"
NEIL GRAUER, B.A.'69

Herbert Baxter Adams, a founder of the American Historical Association, was a Hopkins fellow in 1876. His department included economics and politics, and the aphorism on his classroom wall makes the connection: History is past politics and politics present history.

Professors in every division made strong impressions. *Ethan Allan Andrews, right, joined the faculty under Gilman to teach zoology. Nursing students in the hospital diploma program wore starched caps in 1964, below. They were taught by both nursing and medical faculty.*

The teachers far right were enrolled in McCoy College, named to honor John W. McCoy, a Hopkins benefactor. In 1965 the part-time program was renamed the Evening College; in 1983 it became the School of Continuing Studies. The name changed again in 1999 to stress an increased emphasis on business and education.

"There was a very close relationship in those days between the students and the faculty, because the classes were so small. Dr. Ethan Allen Andrews was a professor of biology. I can remember his first lecture. He appeared at the door of the Gilman Hall lecture room, stared at the class with his thick eyeglasses, picked up a piece of chalk about the size of a bar of soap, and started drawing a line on the blackboard all around the walls of the room until he got back to the head of the room. Then he drew a ball on the end of the line and said, 'Tapeworm!' which stuck me as a hilarious way to introduce his subject.

He was a very enthusiastic lecturer. When he lectured on the chick embryo, he would draw diagrams on his vest and coat of the arteries and veins of a chicken to illustrate the circulation problems. And then he'd walk around the campus for the next two weeks without dusting the chalk off his clothes." WILLIAM BANKS, B.A.'29

"I read about this program that McCoy College was going to have because there was a shortage of teachers. We had five courses at a time, plus teaching. I took more courses than I was supposed to because every one of them was so wonderful. I really appreciated what I had at Goucher and Hopkins both; the teachers prepared us for life."
MARGARET SPARROW, M.A.T.'58

"The Evening College changed with the times. I was advising a college student on the M.L.A. program and noticed that none of the electives that I had taken were still in the program. The course work changed based on the desires of the learning population. I think the School of Continuing Studies attracted more adult learners than the Evening College. I don't remember people in their forties or fifties in any of my classes."
E. MAGRUDER "MAC" PASSANO JR., B.S.'67, M.L.A.'69

"We had to write a paper before we got a degree in English. My advisor was William Foxwell Albright, who was considered one of the giants of the faculty. He was also very approachable and very pleasant. I handed in my paper, which was thick and, I thought, impressive. I got it back about two weeks before graduation, totally marked up with no grade. I said, 'Dr. Albright, I'm going to try, but I'm not going to be able to do all this. I'm just not that good a student.'

And he said, 'Well, you don't have to do this right away. Take your time. Your expectations are much too high. This should take a year or two.'

I said, 'My parents are paying my tuition for me to graduate this year.'

'Your parents expected you to get a Ph.D. that quickly?'

'No, they want me to get a bachelor's degree.'

He said, 'A bachelor's degree? Why am I advising you?'"
SIDNEY OFFIT, B.A. '50

Hopkins undergraduates have a well-deserved reputation for overachieving; upperclassmen often enroll in graduate seminars and do well. Dress codes were easing in the 1960s, above, even as diversity increased in the student body.

Humor does creep into the classroom occasionally, though even then there's often a serious goal. Neil Grauer, known for his Blue Jay cartoons, illustrated his history notebook in the mid 1960s as Stephen Ambrose lectured about Franklin Roosevelt.

"I believe that the universal gripe that if you're taught by a teaching assistant it must be bad is nonsense. The fact is that TAs are the people who are going to be the distinguished professors in ten years. They're the ones writing the books. They're the ones enthusiastic about what they're doing."
PROFESSOR GORDON "REDS" WOLMAN, B.A.'49

Graduate students frequently lead discussions as part of their advanced education at Hopkins, bringing fresh insights into the mix.

JHU was in the forefront of introducing the concept of distance learning. At left, students in a lab in the New Engineering Building at Homewood were linked to their peers on various campuses on February 4, 1996.

"The Hut is in the back of Gilman. It is open twenty-four hours, so students will go there at two or four in the morning when the library kicks them out. The acoustics are not conducive to quiet: When someone opens the front doors to Gilman, you can hear it. You can hear everything that everyone at the other end of the hallway is whispering."
CHRISTOPHER NIEDT, B.A.'99

Virtually all aspects of the universe are open to study. Professor Douglas Poland embraced chemistry, far left. In the early 1960s, below, students were limited to scrutinizing maps; today satellite images also enhance knowledge. The Hutzler Reading Room, left in April 1984, used to be part of the main library at Homewood.

Professor Alexander Kaplan sparked the interest of electrical and computer engineering students with his own evident enthusiasm in 1997.

"If I can't be intellectually excited about what I'm doing, I don't think it's effective for the students either, and so I try to have my undergraduate courses fresh enough that I am pursuing my experience in it along with them and hope that they get some contagious reaction there. I think it works better that way; we're both exploring these dimensions together." PROFESSOR FRANKLIN KNIGHT

"When you're here for four years, there's no special treatment, there's no pampering, and it's tough academically. But if you participate in all the other things that are available, it can be a fun four years. For me and my friends, it was, in many ways, the best years of our lives. We studied together. If you didn't do well on an exam, there would be one of your classmates there to help you the next time.

In most places, pre-meds are so competitive, they never help another pre-med. It was never that way here. We always helped one another. It was almost like group learning." ERNEST A. BATES, B.A.'58

44

Well before word processors and ergonomic concerns surfaced, students hunkered in tight dorm rooms over portable typewriters, erasers at the ready. More pleasant surroundings were available by the goldfish pond in the president's garden, as the study group, below, *discovered c.1996.*

"It was an enormously serious place. In the engineering, pre-medical, and science curricula, the work was gruelingly hard. Hopkins was like an intellectual marine boot camp in that regard. But even among us writing majors and English majors and majors in liberal arts, the tone of the place seemed to be that we worked like hell late into the night five days a week, and then we binged on weekends."
JOHN BARTH, B.A.'51, M.A.'52

"Hopkins gave me every opportunity that I've had, and it made me realize that you have to think. It made me skeptical. It made me wonder. It made me ask why all the time. That's the great difference it made in me." RUSSELL BAKER, B.A.'47

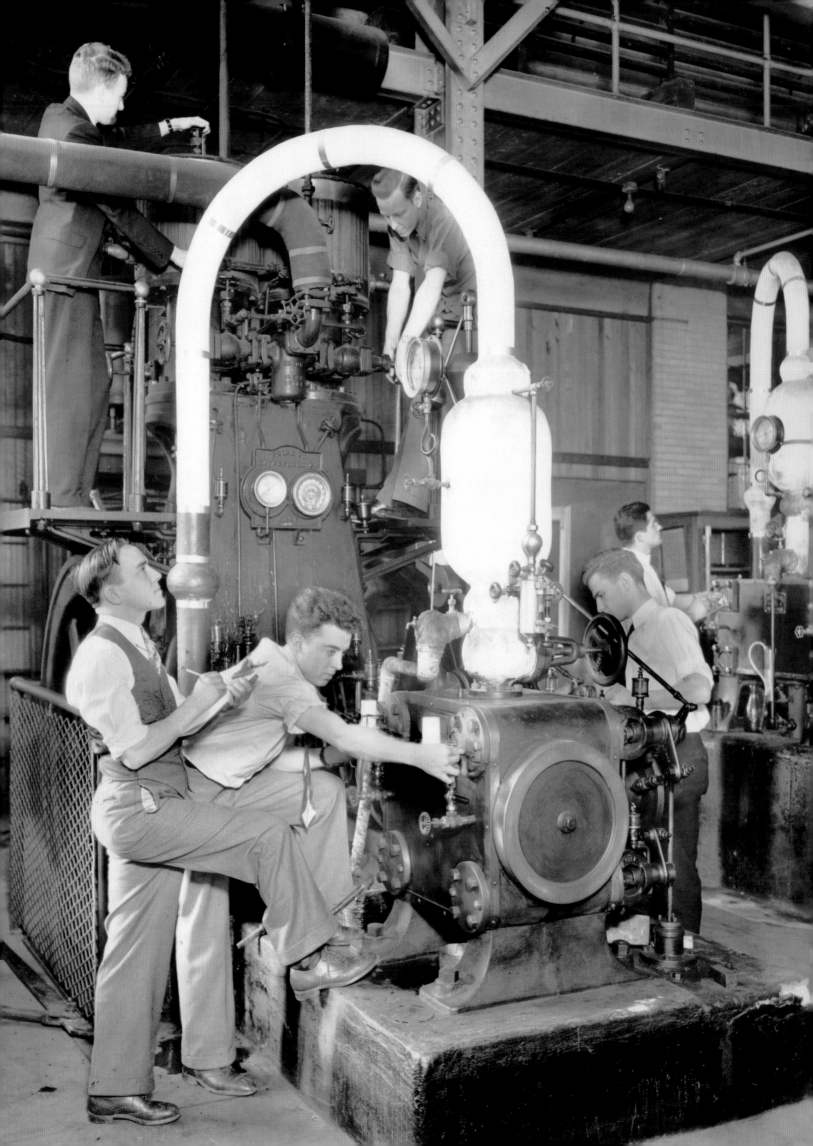

"I'd like my students to come away thinking clearly, independently, able to collect a set of data objectively, to analyze it, to come to some conclusions, realizing that this is just a technique. I like students who are willing to think about things and suggest, 'Let's try this,' because they are very bright. I learn as much from the students as they learn from me, and we have a lot of discussions one-on-one." PROFESSOR GRACE BRUSH

"Maryland Hall was in two sections. One was offices and classrooms, and attached to it were laboratories. There were metallography labs, mechanical testing labs, busting machines, impact machines, a swinging pendulum that measured energy, tensile machines. The other section was Machinery Hall and it was divided in half: the southern part was mechanical engineering and the northern part was electrical engineering. Electrical engineering did things like measuring and developing better efficiency of motors." PROFESSOR ROBERT POND SR.

By signing up for the right courses, students can easily escape the confines of the classroom. Professor George W. Fisher regularly leads field trips to look for clues to the tectonic evolution of the Appalachian Piedmont. Here, he directed attention to small-scale structures in the Cockeysville formation at the Loch Raven Reservoir.

Engineering students got hands-on experience early, since by 1914 they were responsible for the maintenance of the four boilers, reciprocal engines, steam turbines, and electrical generators in the powerhouse at Homewood.

Make It Better, Make It Cheaper

PROFESSOR ROBERT POND SR.

Interviewed on December 8, 1999

Professor Robert Pond encouraged students, like these in 1981, to explore and question every aspect of materials science. Far right above, Theodore Schneider was Professor Henry Rowland's assistant for twenty-five years; it was he who actually made the screws and working parts of Rowland's machines. In February 1954, far right below, Keefer Stull photographed his friends Tom Wild, Frank Witt, Jerry Gilbert, Mac McDonald, and Willy Gore in the radio lab. Wild later went to work at the Applied Physics Laboratory and Gore joined the faculty in computer and electrical engineering.

I went to Hopkins in 1947 to get an advanced degree in engineering. I was going to take courses, and I would be expected to do a little teaching. When I arrived, the man I was supposed to assist had quit, so I wound up with 295 students in a course that had ten laboratories. I never had time to take any courses, but I loved to teach so I really didn't mind. They let me do research. I was my own boss.

I wanted to learn about three-component equilibrium diagrams, and Hopkins didn't have a course like that. I asked my department chairman if I would be allowed to teach such a course, and he said sure, so I organized a course that I had never taken and taught it for years. It was great fun.

Rob Roy came to Hopkins as a part-time professor in McCoy College, teaching courses like Time and Motion Study. Then he became an assistant dean to Kouwenhoven; Hopkins' enrollment had increased threefold, and all of a sudden there was more work than the dean could

handle. Then when the dean retired, Rob Roy moved up. The School of Engineering had three major departments: electrical engineering, mechanical engineering, and chemical engineering, and Rob Roy developed a new department, industrial engineering. He had high hopes for the engineering school.

I was interested in innovation more than performance, so most of my papers are called U.S. patents. I learned to cast metal fibers, and I knew it should be patentable. I went to Stewart Macaulay, the provost. I said, "How do you handle an invention?"

He said, "What did you invent?"

"I invented a way to cast metal hair."

"What do you use that for?"

"It's for radar jamming. How do I go about giving it to the university?"

He swung his chair around, looked out the window for a couple of minutes, and he said, "Pond, if you think you invented something, then it's yours."

I said, "Would you put that in writing?"

He took a piece of scratch paper and

he wrote, "Anything Bob Pond invents belongs to him."

I have a lot of inventions. Now there's a man at Hopkins that's in charge of all the patents. But I came ahead of that.

If someone wanted to do research and the university didn't have the money, he would say, "Well, let me go to industry or the military and see if I can sell this idea to them, and then they will give me a contract to do the work." So everybody I knew in engineering pursued this. And you're a faculty member, so the university got some percentage of this. I used the money to hire graduate students. Everybody that I know in the engineering school did, because it's just too much work for one man to do. The more contracts you had, the more graduate students. Everybody played the game. Departments became bigger, and we got a few new departments. You can almost draw a circle around everything that's being done in the field of engineering and there's somebody at Hopkins working on some part of it, or at least it always seemed that way to me.

I've never understood why the School of Engineering went with the School of Arts of Sciences. Why did they do away with a school that was doing so well? But once we had this division of engineering in the School of Arts and Sciences, I could certainly understand why we needed to get out, because there are things that engineering students need to know, need to learn. The courses aren't the same for the guy that wants to be a chemist or a physical metallurgist or an electrical engineer. An engineer has got to know some physics and chemistry, mathematics; a physicist doesn't have to know a thing about engineering. The university realized it made a mistake, that engineering was something that was different from arts and sciences.

We have a pretty broad field, so broad that you lose your way easily. There's an excitement out there if you understand what you don't know. There's excitement about delving into it, finding out more, making it better. In engineering that's the big thing: make it better, make it cheaper.

In my field, there's a real excitement to failure. A rail breaks in two and there's a train accident, lots of people are killed. Or an airplane is flying and the canopy rips off. Or a propeller gives up the ghost. Why? There are big challenges to learn why those things happen. I've spent a whole life looking at those things.

One of the nicest things that I have in my life is I can put my finger on people who've made great advances in industry and say, "I trained that guy. That guy got his Ph.D. under me." I don't even have a Ph.D., and that guy got his Ph.D., and that's exciting.

I do something called "Fun in Metals," and I've given the talk eight-hundred-and-some times—in Japan, Canada, England, and all over this country. It's a real joy to tell somebody something new. A lot of engineers don't like to do this, but I found it an absolute joy. If you can teach somebody something that they're fascinated with, that they like, it's like giving a pearl to somebody who really appreciates beautiful things.

In the 1950s a weekend camp terminated the incoming freshmen's first week on campus. We'd play games with them, put on shows. They had a swimming pool there and we'd swim. It was mostly just a conviviality that we liked so much. Freshman Camp did a lot to break down any barrier between faculty and students. One of the reasons Hopkins is a different place is because you could find an undergraduate student doing graduate research and you could find a professor playing baseball with the freshmen. It was like a family affair. The faculty was really interested in the students.

Now it seems to me that the faculty has gotten awfully busy. It all started with con-

"Hopkins always had a place for applied work. Henry Rowland is remembered for his diffraction gratings and his ruling engine that made these very, very fine lines for use in optics and astronomy. If you wanted to buy the best diffraction grating, you went to Rowland. He had an assistant who made the grating in the basement of the physics building. Rowland was also a consultant on the Niagara power project, which was the first major alternating-current system. He was the highest paid academic consultant of anyone at the time." PROFESSOR STUART W. "BILL" LESLIE

tract work. The faculty got so busy that there wasn't time to sit down and joke with or have lunch with or know the students.

My teaching method was to communicate during the lecture with the students. I'd introduce the subject, and if two students were talking, I'd single them out and make them tell me what they thought of

the subject or what I was doing wrong. In doing that, I developed a camaraderie with the whole class.

If I were to ask a student, "Do you have any idea what Portland cement is?" it used to be, the guy would jump right in and tell me what he thought. The last year I taught, I wouldn't get an answer. My impression was the students didn't want to put themselves in a position of being wrong. There was something certainly different about it. My last year teaching was not as much fun as my first year of teaching, or any ones in between. It's a shame, isn't it?

There's something that really bothers me—it isn't just Hopkins; it's the same wherever I get my nose in—and that is this absolute penchant for success. You know, "I've got to be top of the pile." You can't take a big population and everybody's going to be at the top of the pile. That's impossible. So we ought to be doing a good job of teaching people to enjoy the fundamental things of life. That's why I find materials so exciting. Gold might be something that attracts everybody, but it shouldn't be more exciting than sand. Because from sand we get silicon. From silicon we get the chip, and the chip runs our lives, right?

Robert Pond Sr. is professor emeritus of materials science at the G.W.C. Whiting School of Engineering.

"I got to know Gordon Smith, who started a course in injury epidemiology. That same year I was alerted to a new faculty member in engineering who came from Cal Tech, Nicholas Jones. We formed a multi-disciplinary research program studying earthquake injuries and how to prevent them. This was a new collaboration between the School of Public Health, the School of Medicine, and the Whiting School of Engineering.

There's a saying 'Earthquakes don't kill people; buildings do.' That became the foundation of my next five years of academic work, pushing multi-disciplinary, multi-scientific expertise to attack the problem of reducing deaths and injuries. You cannot do it from the perspective of just medicine, public health, or engineering. That was one of the major things I took away from my Johns Hopkins experience: the importance of crossing professional boundaries.

Nick was a very inspiring teacher. He actually had me to the Whiting School to give lectures on medical consequences of building collapse. Most engineers are so focused on wind shear and relationships of the ground shaking and the mathematical physical properties that they forget that the reason why they build safe buildings is for the ultimate goal of saving lives. When I showed pictures of the search and rescue operations in Mexico City and Armenia and San Francisco after the '89 earthquake, it really hammered in that they have a public role to fulfill in designing better earthquake-resistant buildings."
ERIC NOJI, M.P.H. '87

In 1972 students established the Eisenhower Symposium to explore themes of current interest. Two years later, Mindy Farber and Chris Lee courted controversy by hosting Alger Hiss. Hiss was president of his senior class at Johns Hopkins in 1925–26, well before his troubled career at the Department of State and confrontations with Senator Joseph McCarthy.

"The Eisenhower Symposium was just beginning. It wasn't institutionalized the way it is now, where it gets great newspaper coverage and you can get the luminaries in various fields to come to Hopkins. Back then, it was just the idea of, 'Well, let's bring some people onto campus. Let's do something that's student-sponsored, but has substance.' Hopkins has such renown worldwide, we were able to entice a lot of people to come and speak. That was exciting."
HELEN BLUMBERG, B.A.'73

"A lot went on beyond the classroom. The luxury of being able, over spaghetti or a wonderful cup of espresso, to continue the discussion and probe a little more was the kind of thing that was available. Seminars at the Bologna Center often spilled out afterward because the school was small. The professor might even join them. There were about seven, possibly eight, full-time faculty and a lot of visiting faculty from elsewhere in Italy or elsewhere in Europe who would come for a day or two—quite a richness."
NANEEN HUNTER NEUBOHN, M.A. '64

Director Wilfrid Kohl got to know students at the School of Advanced International Studies' Bologna Center when he invited them to lunch in the penthouse apartment that was used for social gatherings and small receptions.

51

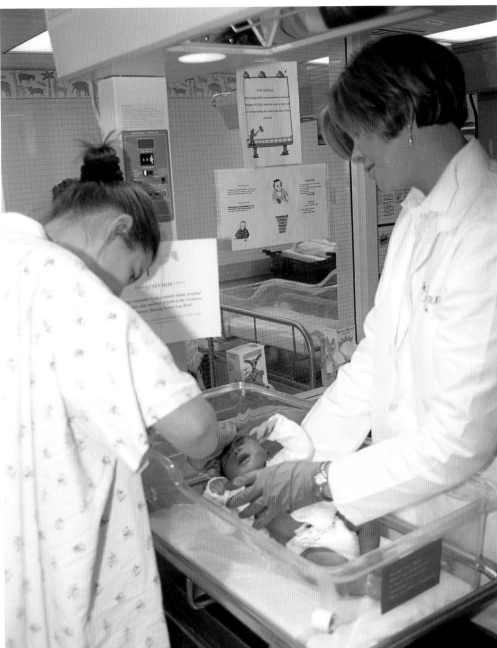

"There were many situations where nursing students knew a great deal more about how the units functioned and what was involved in the care of the patient than the medical students did. My husband rotated all the way through medical school with the same small group of people. When they were getting ready to go to surgery, I said, 'Well, I'll have a little training session. I'll teach you how to glove and gown so you don't make fools of yourselves the first day you go in the OR.' Then when they were learning how to draw blood, I explained that if they wanted to create a positive impression, they should go get a disposable towel, so that as the patient bled, they would not dirty the sheets and require the nurse to have to change the bed.

My senior year, one of the interns was a very nice fellow and he said, 'I don't know anything. Help me out.' I saw him many years later at a national conference. He had a lot of people with him, and he introduced them to me. He said, 'We used to spend the nights together alone in Osler, and Martha taught me a lot of the things I know.' I said, 'Well, we'd better explain that to these people.'"

PROFESSOR MARTHA HILL, R.N. '64, B.S.N. '66, PH.D. '87

Examinations at the School of Medicine were serious business in 1914 when the class of 1917 scratched their newly acquired knowledge on paper. Only a few women were in the group.

School of Nursing instructor Betty Jordan supervised student Emily Bahne as she examined a newborn infant in the nursery of the birthing center at The Johns Hopkins Hospital in February 2000.

Students at the School of Hygiene and Public Health organized an honor society, Delta Omega, in 1924 to promote research and scholarship. Today there are twenty local chapters around the United States. The Alpha Chapter at Hopkins sponsored an exhibit by its members in 1996.

In 1984 the Preclinical Teaching Building in East Baltimore featured a multi-media learning center, below, with the latest tools for individual and group study.

Commencement is the culmination of years of effort, and the graduates of 1989 clearly were exhilarated to join generations of distinguished alumni.

"Hopkins was a tough place, but that was part of its charm, and that's what we all shared graduation day, thinking, 'I went through four years of Hopkins. I've got to be good.' I guess students still have that feeling, but it was particularly true in our time. What a wonderful feeling it was to have graduated from Hopkins." ERNEST A. BATES, B.A.'58

THE BEST INVESTIGATORS

The best investigators are usually those who have also the responsibilities of instruction, gaining thus the incitement of colleagues, the encouragement of pupils, the observation of the public."

DANIEL COIT GILMAN, 1876

THE LABORATORY & WHARF, AT BEAUFORT.

There are two major types of research I've been involved with. One is describing the vegetation and understanding why it occurs as it does throughout the state of Maryland. The other has to do with trying to know the history. Why is the landscape the way it is today? What has been the impact of humans on this landscape? How did it change before humans were here, just related to climate?

I'm trained as a paleobotanist. I was thinking about how very closely the forest associations were related to the soil types, the water-holding availability, and how would that be different when you had a different climate regime, if you had really dry conditions, cold conditions. When the Environmental Protection Agency had some millions of dollars to spend, I began to go to some of these meetings that were related to what kinds of research were needed. Many people were saying, 'Well, we don't know what is happening to the submerged grasses. It may just be sort of a cyclical population boom-and-bust event, and they will come back eventually.' I can remember saying, 'Oh, but we can test that, because we can look at the sediment cores and we can tell you whether or not this

As early as 1878, Professor William K. Brooks opened a seaside laboratory on the Chesapeake Bay to determine the breeding patterns of oysters, the first undertaking of its kind by any university. By 1880 he had moved the lab to Beaufort, North Carolina, where its work was chronicled by Frank Leslie's Weekly. *Johns Hopkins made another major commitment to studying the environment when it launched the* Ridgely Warfield *in 1967. Two years later scientists and students were aboard, pulling core samples from the bottom of the bay that revealed an abundance of historical biological evidence.*

Expeditions in the nineteenth century ranged both near and far. In 1898–99 courses in history and geology were offered to teachers from Baltimore public and private schools. Tuition for attendance, classwork, and exams was five dollars. These classes were the first opportunity for large numbers of women to take instruction at Johns Hopkins and many enrolled, as evidenced by this photo of the geology class in the Green Spring Valley on April 22, 1899.

Geologist Harry Fielding Reid, who received his B.A. in 1880 and his Ph.D. in 1882, advanced the reputation of Hopkins science all the way to Glacier Bay, Alaska, in the summer of 1890 by naming glaciers in honor of both his alma mater and its first president. Reid (at the far right) poses with his traveling companions and naturalist John Muir (at the far left), whom they met at Glacier Bay. A member of the faculty from 1894 to 1929, Reid was also an expert on earthquakes, and beginning in 1898, he served seven years as chief of the highway division of the Maryland Geological Survey.

"Bill Fastie is big not only in size but also in his thinking. If I were to think of a single man who made the astrophysics part of the physics department as large, as reputable, as fascinating as it is, it would have to be Bill Fastie. Fastie's encouragement, Fastie's goading, Fastie's excitement about things was bursting. He did a great many good things for the physics department, for the astrophysicists, and for the university in general. A very inventive man. Fastie's foresight and his sheer delight in encouraging younger people got great things accomplished." KISHIN MOORJANI

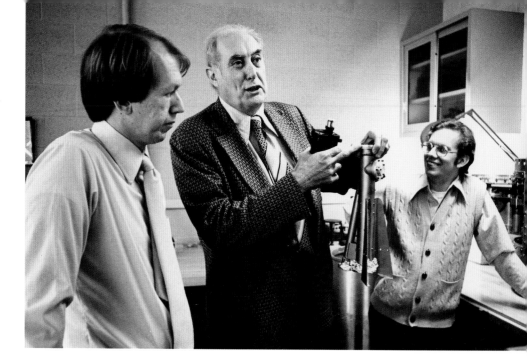

When NASA selected Johns Hopkins in 1981 as the site for the Space Telescope Science Institute, Arthur Davidsen and Bill Fastie, far left, were elated. Davidsen is a professor in the Department of Physics and Astronomy, but Fastie's credentials are more unusual. He holds no degree, having taken only a few college courses in 1936–37; the physics department then offered him a graduate scholarship, and a year later he was made an instructor. In 1952 he designed a revolutionary spectrometer that has flown on many space missions. In 1969, below left, Fastie (leaning toward the rocket) and chemistry professor John P. Doering (on the right with his arms crossed) traveled to Manitoba to launch a rocket carrying Fastie's instrument into the aurora borealis.

The Applied Physics Laboratory kept the Wolfe Motor Company sign to disguise its clandestine activities during World War II. When APL outgrew the Silver Spring location, it moved to Howard County, where its new computer building in 1960, below, featured a powerful and enormous IBM 7090.

"The Applied Physics Lab got started in World War II in an old car dealership near Washington. It was deliberately kept at arm's length from the university for reasons of secrecy and security. Its main assignment was to develop a very small radar radio tube.

A proximity fuze allows you to shoot a shell at an airplane, or it can be used against ground troops. It's preset to detonate at a set distance from the target. You hit an airplane with a shell, it goes through the wing and does a little damage, but if you explode it before it hits, it can wipe out the airplane. Same thing if you're using a mortar and you want to drop it on enemy troops, you don't want it to hit the ground; you want it to explode above them, where it causes maximum damage. It's one of the real wonder weapons of the Second World War." PROFESSOR STUART W. "BILL" LESLIE

The Applied Physics Lab conducted its first ramjet tests in April 1945 on a thirty-foot-long wooden launcher at a former coast guard station at Island Beach, New Jersey. The lab turned its expertise to developing satellites in the very earliest days of the U.S. space program. Over the years, APL often worked in cooperation with engineers and astrophysicists on the Homewood campus. In the 1980s APL built the NASA-funded Hopkins Ultraviolet Telescope, right, that was designed and managed by more than two dozen university faculty, staff, and students. The HUT flew on space shuttles in December 1990 and March 1995.

"Our first association with APL was as consultants. I made a visit with one of my colleagues to where they had a launch site for their missile test vehicles. Well, when we looked at the contraption that was about to be launched, we noticed that the missile was sagging a bit in its cradle of four booster rockets, and from our experience we said, 'That's not going to fly. It's going to dive in the water about five hundred yards from the shore.' But we were assured, no, no, the contractor had made all these calculations, and as soon as the rocket thrust went on, this would all straighten out and go up. My friend and I hid ourselves behind a sand dune. And sure enough, the missile was launched—it hit about five hundred yards from the shore. The whole thing broke up and the sustainer rocket went straight up in the air leaving a long twisting tail of black smoke. Everybody dove for cover because it was going to come down right on top of us. That experience confirmed our opinion that these people needed help."
ALEXANDER KOSSIAKOFF, PH.D.'38

The Peabody Institute and the Whiting School of Engineering initiated a double major in 1983 to train a sophisticated breed of engineer/producers for the sound recording industry. It is the only program in the country in which students have to fully satisfy the requirements of the bachelor of music degree as well as all the sound engineering requirements. Here, Alan Kefauver conducted a class in the recording studio in 1991.

"The Peabody from the very beginning has been in many ways a futuristic place. In the best of times it's been a place to try new ideas and to explore new ways of doing things.

The conservatory had the first studio for examining the scientific side of music, and that was back in the early '30s. That studio was run in conjunction with Hopkins engineering and Hopkins medical institutions.

We were the first conservatory to have an electronic music studio. This was in the 1965–1966 season. I was here when they brought the first synthesizer in the door at Peabody. My interest was early music. I had no interest in contemporary music when I came here, but I got caught up in performing contemporary music because it was so exciting. And it wasn't happening at Juilliard. It wasn't happening at Curtis. It wasn't happening at New England. It was happening here in the conservatory that was limping on from year to year, wondering whether there was enough money to pay the faculty."
ELIZABETH SCHAAF

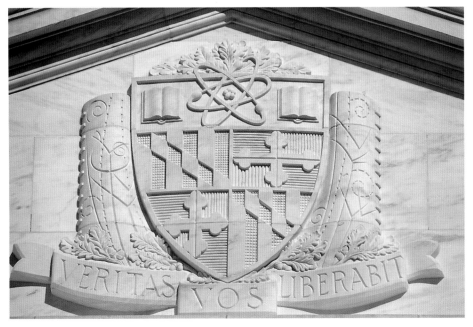

The design on the pediment on the addition that connects Krieger (formerly Rowland) and Maryland Halls is a modification of the university seal that recognizes the many achievements of Hopkins scientists and engineers, including top secret efforts during World War II relating to the development of the atomic bomb.

Students diligently working at their microscopes c. 1960 were following a long tradition of significant scientific study at Johns Hopkins.

"Reds Wolman would always come in with more unusual experiences in more unusual parts of the world than anybody else. There is no situation you can think of that Reds has not come close to experiencing, other than death, and yet he has a calmness. You say, 'Weren't you scared? Wasn't this difficult, dangerous?' And that's the time he's realizing, 'Yes, it might have been.'

Reds is living institutional history, because Reds is the son of a Hopkins professor, who also became a distinguished Hopkins professor. So he has been, from birth, related to Hopkins. He has the student's and child's view of the place, growing up, which is always a little different from an adult faculty view.

I think that's why he was so successful all along at understanding both the students, graduate and undergraduate, and faculty. And he was the best mediator that I have seen on this campus. He was more responsive, more sensitive to diverse faculty opinions and could bring people together easier than anyone else I can think of offhand, because he was the one person that every single person that I met on this campus respected, respected professionally and respected personally. Everyone would say, 'We respect Reds.'"
PROFESSOR FRANKLIN KNIGHT

"The difference between being on a Hopkins campus and being on a campus of a number of other universities is that you see here a willingness on the part of people who are professors, heads of departments, to have you walk in on them, ask for advice. They'll sit down, work with you. In so many universities, the various centers and activities are very tightly walled off and independent and there's very little communication.

It's said that Hopkins works much more like a family, and this is true. You do have a lot of rather easy interchange between people in different departments at all levels from professors to junior faculty to students. Faculty who have come here from other schools comment upon this. Hopkins has a marvelous ambiance."
PROFESSOR D. A. HENDERSON, M.P.H.'60

"The heritage of this university—the graduate education model, the German model in America, medical education, and the School of Hygiene were unique, significant contributions different from anything that existed at the time. The perpetuation of those features has to do with style, with scale, with objectives. The issues that face us, and all universities really, are to what extent this rapidly changing world of communication and information alters the way in which you try to achieve these objectives."
PROFESSOR GORDON "REDS" WOLMAN, B.A.'49

Many members of the senior faculty at the School of Advanced International Studies were present for this session of the Washington Center for Foreign Policy Research, which met for round-table discussions on Thursday afternoons in the early 1970s on the sixth floor of the Nitze Building at 1740 Massachusetts Avenue.

Invitations to William McElroy's annual oyster feast, held in the basement of Mergenthaler Hall, were greatly valued and rarely refused. Participants in the event held on February 6, 1965, seemed to have preferred Natty Boh to the Western French champagne that was also offered. Professor Gordon "Reds" Wolman, above far left, was a regular attendee.

A Healthier World

PROFESSOR D. A. HENDERSON, M.P.H. '60

Interviewed on December 21, 1999

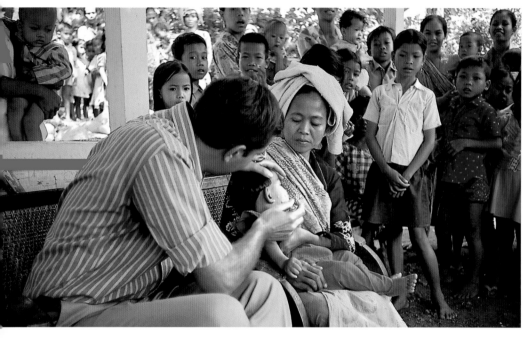

Dr. Al Sommer, a Hopkins ophthalmologist, was also a visiting professor in Indonesia when he treated this young patient in 1976. Sommer realized that giving children a two-cent dose of vitamin A could help prevent blindness and reduce mortality rates.

"In 1970 there was a catastrophic cyclone that inundated the shore of East Pakistan. Henry Mosley, junior faculty at Hopkins, and an epidemic intelligence service officer from CDC named Al Sommer were there to do diarrhea research. When the disaster happened, they shifted gears and conducted a lot of the damage assessment island by island, village by village, using epidemiological and statistical techniques which had been used in determining vaccination coverage in the smallpox eradication program. This was, to my knowledge, one of the very first instances of the use of epidemiology as a decision-making tool in disasters.

Al Sommer was trying to decide whether to become an epidemiologist or an eye surgeon. He opted for eye surgery. He got back into public health when he learned that vitamin A deficiency was a major problem of blindness in the developing world. He is now the dean of the School of Public Health, but many years ago his first idea of a career was to become an epidemiologist, and he published, with Henry Mosley, a classic paper that changed the whole field of disaster medicine." ERIC NOJI, M.P.H. '87

I came to Johns Hopkins having been an infectious disease epidemiologist in the Public Health Service. Clearly the outstanding person in the country at that time was Dr. Abraham Lilienfeld, who was chairman of the Department of Epidemiology at the Johns Hopkins School of Public Health, and he suggested I come down and spend a year with him to learn chronic disease epidemiology.

The School of Public Health in 1960 was really quite small in terms of faculty and students, so that one really got to know most of one's classmates and the faculty as well. There was a place in the

basement where everybody took their lunch, mainly just brown-bag, so you ate together very often. It was a small graduate school environment.

The opportunity to meet and talk with and work with students from a number of different countries constituted, I would say, one of the most important attributes of the school. Many of us had not traveled very much. I knew the U.S., but I really knew very little about many of the other countries. One talked about all sorts of things, not only science but culture and attitudes. You got a view of America which was different, got a view of the

world which was very different, and I would say this may have been one of the most important factors in impelling me to do more in the international health world.

Hopkins was the first school of public health, and it was created by the Rockefeller Foundation. The foundation provided scholarships to really outstanding individuals. They were young professionals who were identified as having promise and then were trained here and went back. One sees over and over again around the world these people taking leadership positions in their own countries, in international organizations, in setting up schools of public health in their own countries. Hopkins, very early on, was well recognized as the leading center in international public health.

The School of Public Health is very diverse. Our concern is the health of the public, not of individual patients. What is it that will make for a healthier America or a healthier world? What causes disease that might be preventable? This leads us into the area of vaccines that might be used on a broad scale and a very large set of activities in that area. We're very concerned about population issues and family planning, which has been, of course, very controversial over the years.

There's a whole range of things we're concerned about, occupational medical things, the environment, what is causing disease in the environment. We're concerned about mental health, concerned about substance abuse. In other words, of all the major problems that we have in the country, public health is at the center of trying to deal with these. Dr. Richard Ross, who was dean of the School of Medicine during most of the time I was dean of the School of Public Health, said to me, "You know, it occurred to me the other day that the School of Public Health is probably responsible for saving more lives in a year than we've saved in The Johns Hopkins Hospital in its entire history."

In my previous incarnation as director of the global program for smallpox eradication, we went in a little over ten years from having between ten and fifteen million cases a year to zero, and two million deaths a year to zero. During this century we estimate probably five hundred million died of smallpox. The *New York Times* estimated at one point that during this century one hundred million people have died either directly or indirectly as a result of armed conflict. Smallpox killed at least five

times that number. In other words, these are very serious problems, and with prevention, a lot of things can be done that simply cannot be done in the clinical setting.

Now, the School of Public Health is unique in another way, and that is that there are so many different disciplines represented. We really need not only physicians and nurses. We need statisticians, we need engineers, we need basic scientists, we need people involved in behavioral science who understand behavioral issues, and so forth. It's a very diverse group of people; you bring to bear talents from many different areas. This makes it a very lively place indeed.

When I first came, it was felt that the school was pretty much self-contained, and there was very little communication with the School of Medicine, even, or the School of Arts and Sciences. As time has progressed, that has changed quite significantly so that there is a lot of communication and collaborative projects with the School of Medicine and significantly with the arts and sciences. There's an intersession course for public health, which is taught from the School of Public Health, which has become immensely popular. In fact, for undergraduates now, there is a public-health major, and this has become quite popular.

You have a wonderful freedom to work in a private institution such as this that you just do not have within government—flexibility to move quickly, flexibility to do a lot of things that you cannot

do within the strictures of a federal or state establishment. Most faculty are about seventy-five percent paid through grants and contracts. They've got to be competitive to do that. There's a constant tension about getting those funds in every year, and there are some anxious moments, because once you've committed to faculty, they're paid. So this makes it a challenge, but we are able to do it.

The great experience at the School of Public Health was having people of different nationalities working together—not only different disciplines but different nationalities. And health looks different when you see it through different eyes. Eventually we built a series of activities: a population communications program, a

In 1982 Alan Ross and Allyn Kimball watched Richard Royall and Arthur Silverstein play Kriegspiel, a version of chess they considered a study in statistical probability. The School of Public Health took extraordinary precautions in sampling HIV in 1996, below.

major program in AIDS which extended internationally for obvious reasons, that whole area of population and maternal and child health. And then we managed to get started with a major program on vaccine development and testing, which began to take off. Each of these has given us a really solid base in international activities.

As a dean, you're involved in orchestrating a whole lot of different things, people, what have you, trying to provide the milieu, the ambiance within which they can realize potential. I felt this was a great adventure, and still do.

At one point I put together a symposium on refugee assistance. We had at least two or three people from every existing refugee operation going on at that time who just left the field months before. These people tell you what it's all about. You don't take it out of a book. No other school can begin to offer anything like this in terms of the quality of the students, let alone the faculty. So the experience at Hopkins is absolutely unique worldwide.

D. A. Henderson is University Distinguished Professor and former dean of the School of Hygiene and Public Health.

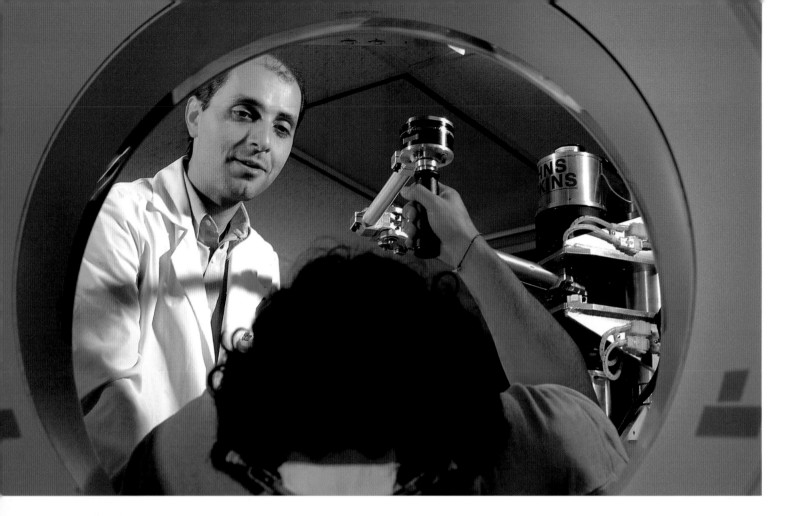

Reza Shadmehr tested imaging equipment in the Department of Biomedical Engineering in 1996.

The university awarded Vivien Thomas an honorary degree and Dr. Helen Taussig the Milton Stover Eisenhower Medal for Distinguished Service at the 1976 commencement ceremony.

Susan P. Baker, far right above, is a professor of health policy and management at the School of Hygiene and Public Health.

William Kouwenhoven checked for breath as his assistant pumped the chest in a demonstration of CPR.

"Vivien Thomas was a great guy. I passed him in the hallway one time, and I stopped to ask him who he was. He worked here in the lab, he said, and he told me to come up to his office and we would talk. That began an incredible friendship.

Both of us had been at Vanderbilt. He was a generation different from me. He always warned me about trying to change things too fast. He wanted me not to be too outspoken in the culture of this institution at the time. I didn't necessarily listen to him, but he was there as a mentor, as somebody to discuss things with, as a brother, as a colleague. I was enormously impressed with what he had done with Dr. Blalock.

Vivien wasn't able to do what he wanted to do educationally, so he got a job at Vanderbilt. Dr. Blalock was chief of surgery at Vanderbilt doing incredible work in shock, and then got interested in pulmonary hypertension. Blalock came up with a model of hooking the subclavian artery into the pulmonary artery to relieve pulmonary hypertension. Vivien Thomas started working with him to develop that model, doing the actual suturing in the lab. It was quite a technical feat to achieve back in the '40s, but they did it, Blalock and Vivien. Vivien was a technician without any definitive education. When Hopkins decided to offer the chair to Dr. Blalock, he and Vivien had a bond that made him want to bring Vivien to Baltimore.

Vivien developed the lab here. Then Dr. Helen Taussig, a great cardiologist, recognized that babies with tetralogy of Fallot—the 'blue babies'—she thought if she could develop new blood flow to the pulmonary artery, that would help them. She came to talk to Dr. Blalock about it, and Dr. Blalock said he had this model of pulmonary hypertension where he had put the subclavian artery into the pulmonary. Maybe that would work. They did the first 'blue baby' operation; the baby turned pink. Dr. Blalock, Dr. Taussig, and Vivien Thomas became famous. Hopkins became even more famous.

So here's this great event for Johns Hopkins, and one of the principal players is this man from Vanderbilt, from the South, uneducated but courageous and talented. He had developed the technique with Dr. Blalock and had performed it with Dr. Blalock on animals, and he was there to provide moral support, if not direction. When I learned all of that, I realized who this man was. He got an honorary degree from this institution. His first degree was an LL.D." DR. LEVI WATKINS

"My boss advised me to go to Johns Hopkins. He said, 'When you go to Hopkins and you get up to bat and hit the ball, they let you play. But you've got to hit the ball. Doesn't matter who you are, they'll take care of you.'" PROFESSOR DONALD COFFEY, PH.D.'64

"Johns Hopkins had a major pioneer in Professor Susan Baker, who finally got Johns Hopkins to establish a unit for injury prevention. She was a person with a master's degree, no Ph.D., no M.D., and through sheer grit rose to full professor with tenure status.

The insurance industry was very interested in reducing deaths from automobile accidents and improving the design of cars. Susan Baker published a landmark book called *The Injury Fact Book*, which revolutionized public health. Johns Hopkins, under Sue Baker's tutelage, was able to secure funding from CDC to establish a center for injury prevention and control." ERIC NOJI, M.P.H.'87

"William Kouwenhoven retired in 1954 as dean of engineering but kept working at the School of Medicine on a line of research he had entered in 1928: the effects of electric current on the heart. He and his research partners had already invented two extremely important medical devices, the electric defibrillator and the portable closed-chest defibrillator. Both were designed to restore normal rhythm to a stopped or irregularly beating heart by delivering an electric shock.

In 1956 Bill noticed that when he laid defibrillator paddles on an experimental animal's chest, blood pressure rose and blood flowed through the body. Bill and his team exploited this chance observation and developed what we now call cardiopulmonary resuscitation, or CPR." LOUISE CAVAGNARO

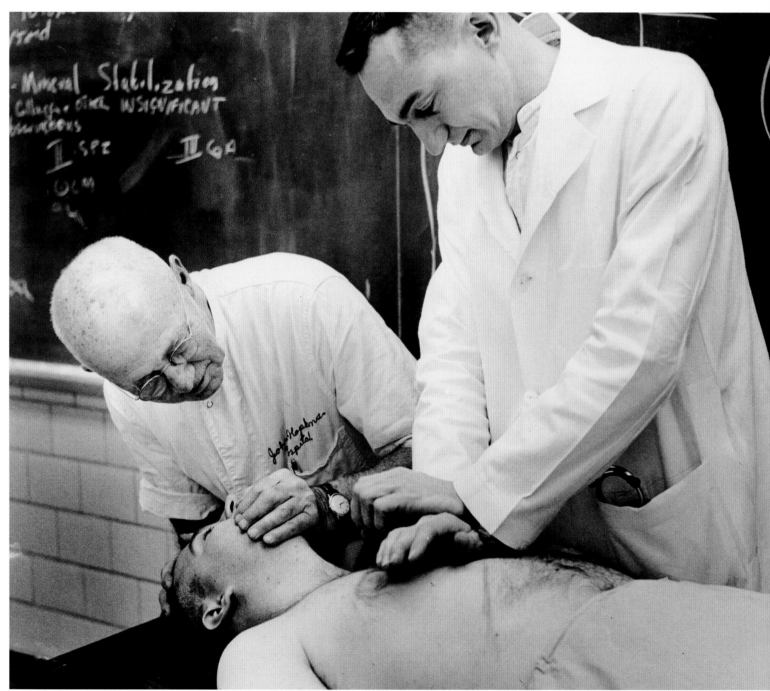

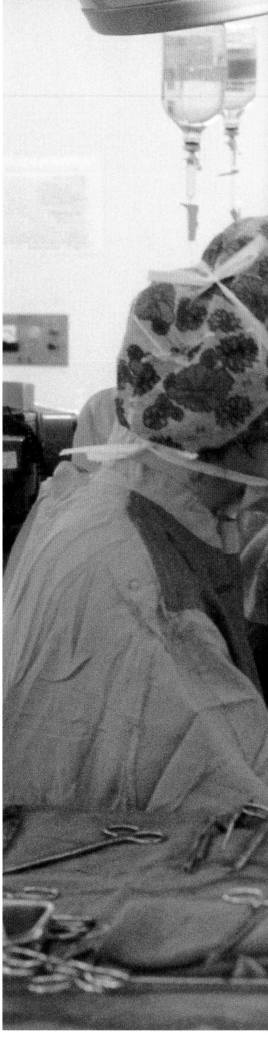

"Victor McKusick introduced me to genetics when I was in my first year of medical school in 1970. He had a little book, back then I think it was still in paperback, a primer on genetics. And I loved it immediately. As an undergrad, I was in mathematics. So it was the first thing I encountered in medical school that was mathematical in nature.

During medical school I went to Victor's clinic. Victor had a very famous clinic back then. It used to meet weekly, and patients used to come in with all sorts of rare genetic diseases. It was just fascinating. And it's incredible, virtually all those diseases we now understand, right at the molecular level. Back then no one had any idea what caused any of them.

McKusick was an unusual teacher. He didn't tell a lot of jokes. Maybe it was because of his very clear ideas, but you just got fascinated by the subject matter and the way he presented it. It was very straight, but it was spellbinding. He's taught a whole generation of medical geneticists; he's the grandfather, great-grandfather now, I guess. He's certainly my genetics mentor, the reason that I got interested in genetics."
PROFESSOR BERT VOGELSTEIN, M.D. '74

"One of the incredible things about Johns Hopkins is the breadth and depth of creativity. Dr. Michel Mirowski was from Poland. I'm a black man from Alabama. History and Hopkins and serendipity brought us together.

Mirowski was a cardiologist. He lost his best friend to sudden death. He had the idea: if we had something we could implant that would prevent sudden death, that would be a great thing. He conceived of the implantable automatic defibrillator, and he lived long enough to see it become successful. Michel is one of the very bright points, to me, about Johns Hopkins." DR. LEVI WATKINS

"The teamwork and the collegiality, the ability to work with other people of like intellect and creative ability to solve problems, that really characterizes the reason that I stayed at Hopkins all these years. I think that is the most dramatic thing about this institution."
DR. BENJAMIN CARSON

Dr. Victor McKusick, a pioneer in the field of medical genetics, has earned worldwide acclaim for his ground-breaking work. Above, he examined an EKG with genetics fellows before patient rounds in 1965.

Dr. Levi Watkins (seen here repairing a scarred heart) helped break the color barrier at Johns Hopkins Hospital when he arrived as a surgical intern in 1970. He is now a professor of cardiac surgery and associate dean at the School of Medicine.

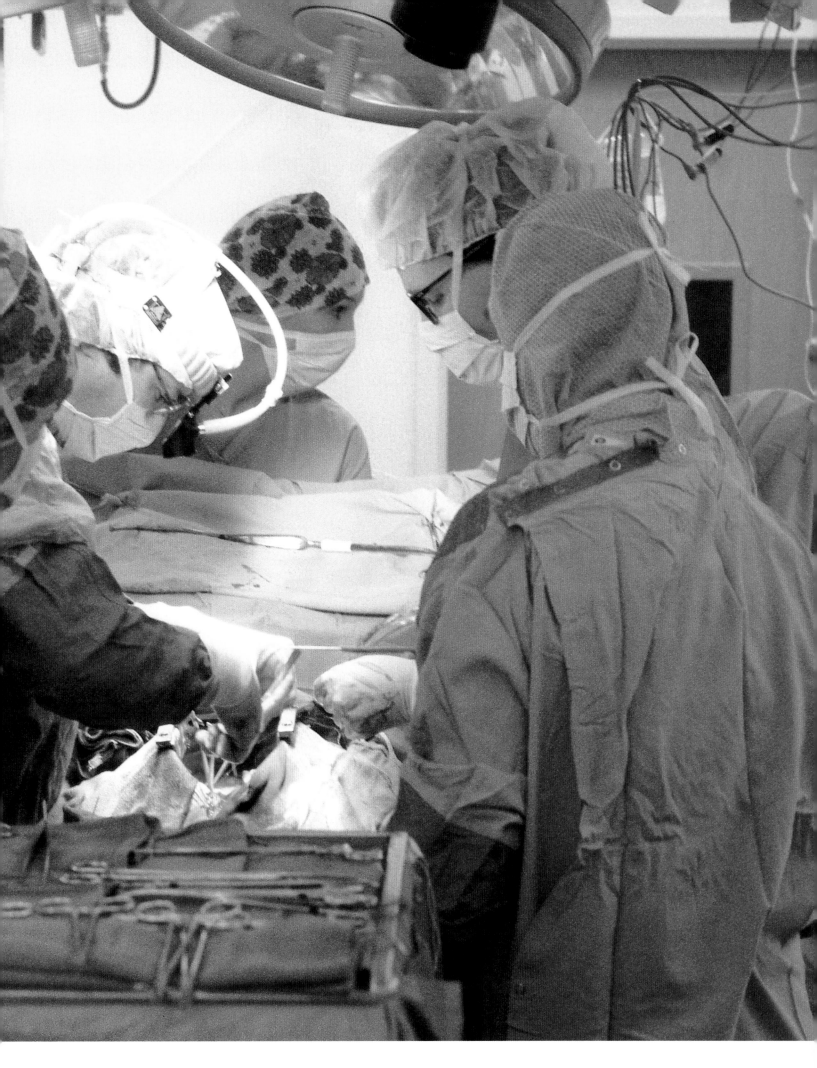

RELATIONS
TO SOCIETY

"Next to the study of Man, in his relations to Nature, comes the study of Man in his relations to Society. By this I mean his history, as exemplified in the monuments of literature and art, in language, laws and institutions, in manners, morals, and religion."

DANIEL COIT GILMAN, 1876

"The manner in which I teach I took from my teacher, Artur Schnabel. Rather than teach one-on-one, I prefer to teach in a class situation. The benefits that come from listening to somebody else have a lesson and not be under the gun oneself to produce and reproduce what is required or requested are large.

Plus, one hears three or four times the amount of repertoire. You begin to get an understanding that in music, no matter where it comes from, there are still rules or laws which most of the time are broken, but the only way to break a rule or a law is to know the law, to know the rule first, and therefore why you break it.

So I announce to all my students that they are requested to all be present for every-body's lessons. They learn that their problems are not unique. It saves an awful lot of time and energy, rather than repeating the same thing to each person individually. It's collegial, it's productive, and it brings much sooner a kind of overview to music that is very helpful." LEON FLEISHER

When Johns Hopkins affiliated with the Peabody Institute in 1977, the union brought the university its first performing arts faculty. Leon Fleisher, above in 1981, a world-renowned pianist who traces his own pedagogical lineage through five generations directly to Beethoven, has inspired students at the Peabody since 1959.

A ceremony in the great hall of the University of Bologna in 1995 marked the fortieth anniversary of SAIS's Bologna Center.

"May Garrettson Evans was a Peabody-trained musician. She was a music and theater critic for the *Sun*, and she decided to go up and interview Asger Hamerik, the director.

'Don't you think it would be a really good idea for Peabody to run a preparatory department where students could get first-rate training by Peabody-trained faculty and they wouldn't have to go through this agonizing process of relearning how to play?' And he said, 'Yes, that's a very good idea.' So she went back and wrote this big story about how Asger Hamerik was contemplating a preparatory department at Peabody. It never happened, so finally she just went ahead and did it herself, rounded up a bunch of her friends, including the wife of Harold Randolph, who had become the next director, and rented 17 East Centre Street. She figured they'd use the first floor and rent the rooms above. She ended up having to use every square inch of the building for music lessons. She had a tremendous enrollment, several hundred students, all of a sudden.

Harold Randolph thought that it would be a very interesting idea to start a program geared specifically to training teachers. The idea of having this preparatory attached was perfect because it would provide a laboratory where these young teachers could teach and be supervised, and there would also be master teachers on the faculty who would be an example, whom the younger teachers could go to for advice.

The preparatory was brought into the Conservatory of Music as a subsidiary to educate young musicians, to give them good, solid early training, and also to provide a place where young teachers could get good firsthand experience in a supervised situation. It soon became the biggest institution of its kind in the country." ELIZABETH SCHAAF

Sculptor Hans Schuler's 1941 figure of Sidney Lanier was placed on Charles Street near the Alumni Memorial Residences to commemorate the poet's association with both the Peabody Institute, where he played first flute in the orchestra, and The Johns Hopkins University, where he was a lecturer in English from 1879 to 1881.

From its earliest beginnings in 1894, the Peabody Prep has given a solid foundation in music and dance to generations of young Baltimoreans. Over the years, the curriculum expanded and more mature students also enrolled.

"Dr. Broadus Mitchell would lecture on the Bachelors' Cotillion. The title of his lecture was 'The Bachelors' Cotillion: A Conspicuous Example of Economic Waste.' He would invite several of the season's debutantes to come and model clothes while he lectured. Of course, this delighted the students. Then the night of the cotillion, you had to go down and stand on the pavement and take notes on what the dowagers were wearing, what kind of jewelry and furs, and come back and write a term paper on the subject. I doubt if they do that kind of thing now." WILLIAM BANKS, B.A. '29

When Broadus Mitchell (above) died, a *former student recalled that "he had an unquenchable thirst for equality and justice." Mitchell taught political economy from 1919 to 1939.*

"One of the most interesting conversations I ever had with anyone was about two or three hours I spent with Isaiah Bowman on a Sunday morning at his house, at his invitation, talking about the field of geography. He had written a classic textbook. I have some marvelous letters from him about why rivers meander. Several letters offer comments about why the textbooks couldn't be right and perceptions about possible future areas of research. I remember one of his phrases was, 'If the textbook says, "It is well known that . . .", you can be sure that is a very good place to begin a research inquiry.'

Bowman was very much a part of the Washington scene. He was the head of the National Research Council, the inquiry arm of the National Academy of Sciences. In addition to that, he was a personal advisor to E. R. Stettinius, secretary of state; Cordell Hull, secretary of state; and, indirectly or directly, to Franklin Roosevelt. He was pictured on the cover of *Time* magazine. He had very strong opinions and could be quite autocratic in the way in which he did things." PROFESSOR GORDON "REDS" WOLMAN, B.A. '49

"The hospital had already started desegregation before *Brown v. the Board of Education*. Both Dr. Nelson and his predecessor, Dr. Crosby, when they would have the bathrooms painted, would take the COLORED and WHITE signs off and the signs never went back.

In 1955, I talked to Dr. Nelson about desegregating so that when we had black people who wanted a private room, they would have an opportunity to have one. He agreed with me. I had a few patients complain that they didn't want black patients where they were. I always volunteered to make arrangements at the hospital of their choice and to arrange for the ambulance transfer. Nobody ever took me up on it." LOUISE CAVAGNARO

The School of Hygiene and Public Health did pioneering work in validating the significance of collecting population data. According to Dr. Thomas Turner, "statistics are vitally important to public health, and Hopkins made the world realize that."

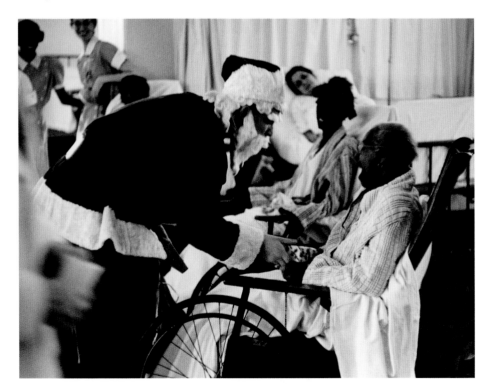

In 1918 Sir William and Lady Osler made a bequest to create the Tudor and Stuart Club as a memorial to their son, Revere, a casualty of World War I. The theme reflected the Oslers' enthusiasm for English literature. Informal gatherings of students and faculty met in the club's quarters in Gilman Hall. The meeting at far left included Isaiah Bowman, fifth president of The Johns Hopkins University.

In his 1873 letter to the trustees, Johns Hopkins stipulated that the hospital must provide for "the indigent sick of this city and its environs, without regard to sex, age, or color, who may require surgical or medical treatment." That ideal was personified in 1958 as Santa Claus greeted patients.

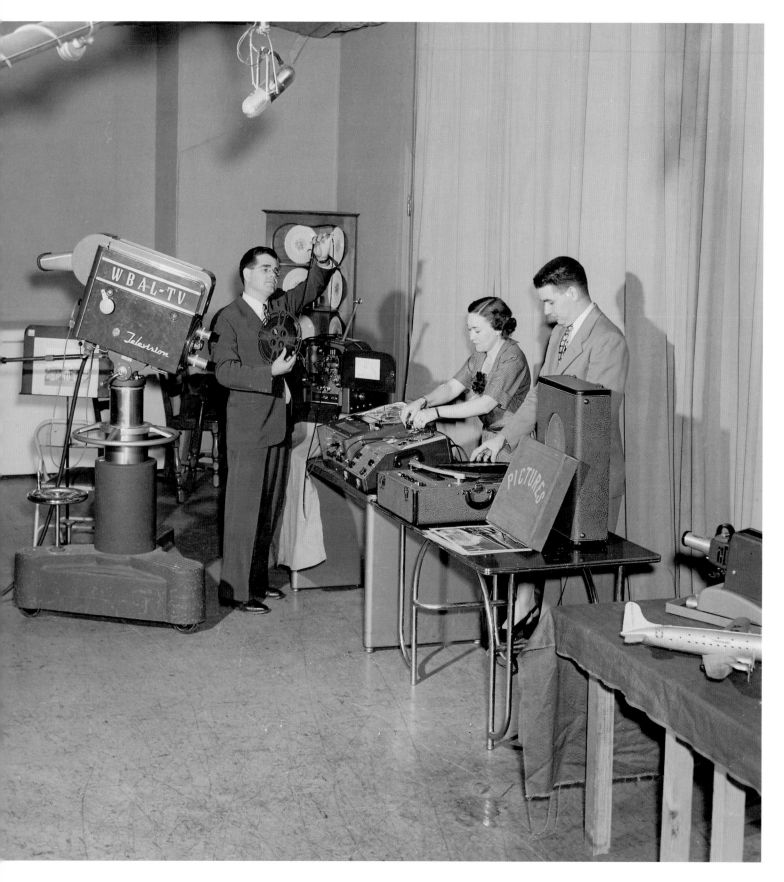

McCoy College courses covered a wide range of subjects. In July 1950, Dr. James McPherson demonstrated the use of audiovisual aids to students in a laboratory on television broadcasting.

"I've been both to business school and to SAIS. The business school probably got me the job, but SAIS was more instrumental in my getting further in my career because I had lived abroad, I had learned languages, I had tried to be on the same side of the table as the Europeans as opposed to thinking, 'Isn't it amusing that they do things differently here?' and having a good laugh and going back home. The interest in policy and public/private interface and the ability to cope in other languages stand the SAIS graduate in better stead for a long-term career in an international environment than business school training. People who have a SAIS education are the ones who become the better leaders in the long run. They've got a wider vision." NANEEN HUNTER NEUBOHN, M.A.'64

"McCoy College was just plain Baltimoreans. I don't think there were any out-of-towners. We had many returning GIs, and most of the GIs, of course, weren't kids anymore. They had seen a lot. It was kind of a sobering atmosphere. It wasn't a 'Rah, rah, rah' college crowd. We were all mature individuals because of the war. We grew up pretty fast."
ANNE E. CLARK, B.S.'49

Above, *Dr. James McLaren held an informal French language class on the upper quad.*

Participants in a summer session on contemporary Africa at SAIS posed with Dean Philip Thayer (fourth from left) in 1954.

The History of Ideas Club was founded in 1923. Its constitution defined the concept as "the historical study of the development and influence of general philosophical conceptions, ethical ideas, and aesthetic fashions, in occidental literatures, and of the relations of these to manifestations of the same ideas and tendencies in the history of philosophy, of science, and of political and social movements." In the 1930s, several noted intellectuals who had escaped Nazi Germany joined the Hopkins faculty and the club, including Ludwig Edelstein (above with pipe). Richard Macksey emphasized that "we clearly benefited from the émigré generation."

"History of Ideas was still very much a regnant Hopkins activity when I came, and we had monthly meetings which brought together not just people in history and philosophy and literary studies but in the sciences. We did a volume called *The Forerunners of Darwin* as we were getting close to the centennial of Darwin's *The Origin of Species*. The History of Ideas Club was always a place where you'd have a scientist sitting next to a humanist, next to a social scientist. Lovejoy and Chinard and Boas and people who founded the history of ideas as a discipline in the '20s established the club and then *The Journal of the History of Ideas*. They were determined that you could not do their kind of intellectual history without having input from people in the sciences as well as the humanities.

High degrees of specialization tend to take you to conferences of people who are all wearing the same underwear, and you don't get this cross-disciplinary stimulation that I think really was part of Hopkins. When I was first here, Hopkins was not as rich as it is now. It had many fewer faculty members in both arts and sciences and medicine. But it did have this very interesting and productive interaction. It was a mix of faculty from a number of disciplines, sometimes six, eight, nine, ten different departments, graduate students, a few undergraduates because the line between undergraduate study and graduate study was so permeable. They tended to be open, knockdown arguments. Papers would get read; questions would get asked. People used to complain when they would visit Hopkins to give a paper that they were worked over with a kind of rigor that they normally didn't expect as visiting lecturers. The discussions were so valuable. They weren't always brilliant, but frequently they were." PROFESSOR RICHARD MACKSEY, M.A.'53, PH.D.'57

"George Boas was a dapper fellow of enormous sophistication and polish who, however, was not snobbish at all. Boas taught this two-year course in Classics of Western Thought. He went from the pre-Socratic right up till the last semester in philosophy. The regnant discipline in the philosophy department in those days was the history of ideas, and although that's a somewhat discredited discipline now for philosophy, it's wonderful for undergraduates. We learned that ideas have history, even the idea that history is unimportant. Boas would take us through that notion: 'Let's see where in the history of Western culture the idea has surfaced that history is unimportant.'

He was a splendid lecturer, not at all histrionic, just easy, very proper—a very matter-of-fact, very witty lecturer who had a gift for illustration. He liked making the strongest possible case for ideas that he himself didn't agree with, and he was eloquent about that. He would say, 'If a lot of people have believed an idea, there must be something to it, so let us not dismiss it lightly. Let's see why that idea was so influential for so long and make the best possible case for it.'

When I came back to Hopkins, I made a pilgrimage out to his place to let Boas know that he had been the figure from whom I felt I had learned the most during my undergraduate and graduate years at Hopkins." JOHN BARTH, B.A. '51, M.A. '52

"I took course in Milton. There were only four of us in that course. It was given by Professor Don Cameron Allen, and he enjoyed it because we argued constantly about free will. This was a semester-long argument about God's perfection. If God was perfect, how could we be imperfect? If everything is preordained, then how could anybody be responsible for his own actions? This went on and on as we read through *Paradise Lost*. Is that education? I don't know, but it was a good time." RUSSELL BAKER, B.A. '47

"During the Vietnam War, we did a lot of draft counseling from my office. This was a very difficult time for a lot of people. The students' pain was very real, and they felt that nobody was listening to them. I can remember a couple who had gone to Canada to escape the draft. Then we had a number of other people that did their conscientious objection work in our office. This was a very tough time for students. In a sense, it was the loss of innocence about our country and about life in general. Some of them spent time in prison." CHESTER WICKWIRE

Chester Wickwire (wearing glasses, at right) came to Hopkins in 1953 as executive secretary of the YMCA. As university chaplain in the 1960s and '70s, he moderated many discussions about the war in Vietnam.

"The '60s came to Hopkins very late. I came here as a freshman in the fall of '65. The buildup in Vietnam was just beginning. My senior year, students took over Homewood House, which was then the administration offices. Lincoln Gordon was not on campus, which was a frequent occurrence. He had to be called back from Washington to confront the students. Compared to what was happening at Columbia or at Berkeley or any of the other major universities, I think what happened at Hopkins was pretty mild.

I remember thinking when I came to Hopkins as a freshman and was so overwhelmed with the work load that if I had entered in September of 1941 and graduated in June of 1945, I wouldn't have known there had been a war, because I was just so busy with everything that I had to do. Well, from September of 1965 to June 1969, I knew there was a war on. It certainly did make its presence known." NEIL GRAUER, B.A.'69

"Students were aware of what was going on on other campuses. Certainly the issues were in the newspaper every day—Vietnam and Cambodia, Kent State. So people were very, very upset. I think it's the only time I ever got into a real argument with Lincoln Gordon. I was in charge of, among other things in those days, the magazine. The editor did a very straightforward report on what happened on the campus. Lincoln thought that shouldn't have been reported. He began raising his voice and getting very agitated, and I was telling him I didn't agree with him, he couldn't cover things like that up. And he began yelling, and I said to him, 'Lincoln, are you yelling at me?' That took the wind out of his sails and he calmed down." ROSS JONES, B.A.'53

Protests relating to the war reached a climax in 1970 when weeks of intermittent demonstrations disrupted the Homewood campus. On April 16, students staged a sit-in on the steps of Levering Hall to denounce marine recruiters' use of the building. The next day, a larger group rallied in front of administrative offices in Homewood House. President Gordon met with demonstrators (above, holding a microphone) and offered to hold a referendum. Students held a two-day vigil and some faculty joined a strike of classes. The vote, taken April 30 with seventy percent of those eligible participating, was 1,183 against allowing recruitment on campus and 1,121 for permitting it to continue. On May 5, a memorial service was held for students killed at Kent State University.

Richard Macksey's eclectic interests have engendered many memorable classes taught under the auspices of the Humanities Center, which he helped found. Here, he met with a film class in his personal library.

"Everybody for the past forty years who has been in liberal arts at Hopkins is in awe of Dick Macksey. Milton Eisenhower used to say, 'Dick Macksey knows everything.' And that is about right. I think he does know everything.

There was a wonderful quote in a recent article in the Hopkins *Gazette*, when the professorship was endowed in Macksey's honor. It quotes some former student of his (I wish I'd said it): 'Asking Dick Macksey a question is like going to a fire hydrant for a drink of water.' And that's perfect. All I can say is, you don't mind one bit getting wet because it's just so refreshing and invigorating to get that splash." NEIL GRAUER, B.A.'69

"I'm innovating a course with Sara Castro-Klarén, which is going to be, if it succeeds, a general introduction to Latin America. It requires a certain intellectual compatibility as well as a certain common approach toward work. She is from Peru and I am from Jamaica, so we have a non-mainstream approach to the hemisphere.

Sara Castro-Klarén is more interdisciplinary than most. She does the reading in history and I do the reading in literature, and we bring up general ideas which we involve the students in discussing. We hope to bring in participants from outside the university in different fields—painters, musicians, people in literature—to talk about their work."
PROFESSOR FRANKLIN KNIGHT

William Foxwell Albright taught archaeology for almost thirty years. His eminence in the field brought many challenges; in 1948 he helped verify the authenticity of the Dead Sea Scrolls. Sara Castro-Klarén, director of the Program in Latin American Studies, joined the faculty in 1984.

"Right from the start the press fit into Gilman's vision for the university. He saw publishing as a way to advance knowledge by disseminating it, in his words, far and wide. So we began publishing just two years after the university opened its doors, and that makes us the oldest university press in this country. In 1978, when we reached our hundreth year, there was a dandy fuss made—proclamations by the mayor, the governor, President Jimmy Carter, even a joint resolution by the Congress—because it wasn't just a birthday in Baltimore, you see, but the centennial of university publishing in America. I like to think Gilman would be happy about the thousands of books and journals his press has published since that beginning." JACK G. GOELLNER

Proudly displaying some of their books and journals (along with other essentials), the staff of The Johns Hopkins University Press assembled in 2000, above, by the renovated church at 2715 North Charles Street that has been their headquarters since 1992.

"Crisis simulation started as a fairly spontaneous activity among a small number of students back in 1984. Four students suggested that we make this into a small seminar that would have academic content in terms of crisis management. It's never had more than eight, at most nine, in the control group designing scenarios, giving the world as it would be in whatever date the crisis is envisaged. For a month we essentially play history, and then we have a two-and-a-half-day fairly intensive crisis. It's not war games, though there is usually some military aspect to it. It's a schoolwide activity and isn't based in any one field of study, which is one of its virtues. (I think it's probably the school activity that has led to the largest number of marriages.)

It's very much a role-playing activity. The first week after we've selected the players, they have to write their CVs as players, which are totally separate from their real life. All of us then have to live with this new character for the following month. Quite often we have people who completely have to change their political beliefs.

We try to insert domestic political pressures, a very agile and usually quite imaginative press corps, and most of the time a Congress as well as an international component. We had the kidnapping of former President Carter in Latin America. We had a computer breakdown of the stock exchanges. We've had several crises dealing with the Gulf and Iran in the early days—Russian involvement in Iran.

Students have to get out of their normal groove, have to deal with the unexpected and work against a timetable; they feel a sense of pressure. You can't exactly parallel what crisis management is in government, but some people have felt that it's done even that."
PROFESSOR FREDERICK HOLBORN

Routines are modified at SAIS when Fred Holborn's classes go into crisis simulation mode. "Pope Thelonius I" (Ted Osius) made a dramatic entrance bearing an umbrella in 1992, perhaps to protect him from fallout resulting from a bomb that supposedly had been dropped on North Korea.

Crises rarely occur at the Villa Spelman in Florence, Italy, far left, where graduate students mingle with great minds in the humanities. The Johns Hopkins Center for Italian Studies was established in 1972; it was renamed in 1985 to honor Charles S. Singleton. Seminars there are usually oriented toward art, literature, and language, but scientific workshops are held at the villa occasionally.

A Pressure Cooker

FORREST TOBEY, M.M.'97, D.M.A.'97

Interviewed on March 21, 2000

Lind and Murdock of Baltimore designed the Peabody Institute, and a Baltimore County quarry supplied the marble. The cornerstone was laid in 1859, but the building's completion and dedication were delayed by the Civil War.

I lived in India from 1987 to 1990 and taught music at an international school in the foothills of the Himalayas. The year I got there, the conductor of the Delhi Symphony passed away, and I was able to walk right into the conducting position. Being music director for three years gave me a lot of podium time.

Before I left for India, I'd come across Fred Prausnitz's book *Score and Podium*. I thought it was the most brilliant treatise on conducting I'd ever seen. There are a lot of books out there on conducting, but this one was so detailed and professional and erudite, it spoke to me in a really clear way. I realized I wanted to study conducting seriously; I wanted to study with Fred Prausnitz. He is on the faculty at Peabody, and *Score and Podium* came out of his experiences as a teacher.

Typically in conducting at the graduate level, if you were lucky, you would do a couple of rehearsals with the orchestra and you'd mark conductors' scores and

maybe you'd get to do one concert. Fred Prausnitz created a situation where the best players at the Peabody were paid a decent wage to be an orchestra so that twice a week the conductors would have an orchestra to practice on. Everything was videotaped, and Fred would deconstruct you and try to get you to become better at the art of conducting. If you're a pianist, you get a piano and you practice it. If you're a violinist, you get a good violin and you can practice all you want to. If you're a conductor, how do you practice? I thought Fred's was a fantastic program.

So in 1989 I flew from Delhi to Baltimore to audition. Audition week at Peabody is a frightening, overwhelming situation because you've spent your whole life trying to be a musician and you're putting it right out there in front of all these professionals. Are you really good enough? The whole faculty gets involved in audition week. It's at all levels from a pianist who's a senior in high school to

the people coming in as conductors, which is purely a graduate-level situation.

I knew there were probably thirty or forty people auditioning, and I knew they were going to choose four. I was looking forward to being able to observe other people before I went on. Well, I was first one up. It was Debussy's *La Mer* and some Mozart. I didn't realize that the orchestra had never played the Debussy piece before, and I didn't feel it went all that well. But then I got into the Mozart, and there was a point where I actually jumped up off the podium. On one level you don't do that professionally, but Fred said that was a sign of real involvement in the music.

I went back to India and got a telegram some weeks later that I had been not only accepted but also given a piano-teaching assistantship. For three years I was the assistant in the piano pedagogy department. At the undergraduate level you have to graduate with piano proficiency; it doesn't matter what instrument you play. It's a basic tool for any musician because you understand chord structure and chord progressions in a way you can't on any other instrument. So I had two classes in piano pedagogy, and then I would meet with pairs of students once a week for private lessons. The singers I would tend to push a little more because they work with pianists a lot. They rely on pianists to accompany them. If they're going to be in opera, they're going to be in coaching situations. It's a very important skill to have.

The average Peabody student is obsessed. The pressure is very intense, especially at the level of a Peabody Conservatory, or a Juilliard or Oberlin or Eastman, because you want to be a professional. You want to make a living playing, conducting, composing music, and it's not easy. It's a difficult choice to make.

Most people don't make the choice; it just makes you. You reach a point where you realize there's nothing else you want to do, as impractical as it may be. I think it's pretty typical of students at Peabody.

The Peabody is a pressure cooker. It's right there in downtown Baltimore and it's just that little block. Everything's compressed. I can't imagine it before the new building was built with more practice space and the library, which was a great resource. It's exciting because everyone is spurring everyone else on to be better. I became far more serious and focused and professional than when I came.

The sense of history at Peabody is nice. The neighborhood of Mount Vernon is a

Forrest Tobey conducted a "virtual orchestra" in Times Square. Below, Peabody students gathered for conversation in Mount Vernon Place.

great space with the Walters and Center Stage right there. And downtown had experienced a renaissance, so it was a good place to be.

My very first semester, even as I was studying conducting and taking some of the history classes that one needed for the degree, as an elective I took the introduction to computer music and I was hooked. Geoff Wright had established a program that was of great benefit to a motivated student. His philosophy is, "We're going to create the studio, give you time in there. Just to go in and make music. Try not to break the computer. Learn the technology."

Geoff Wright goes back to the days when he would write a composition for computer music in code and then take it up to Hopkins, and they would process it in some way and send it off to Stanford. When Stanford would get around to it, they would run the program on some computer at two in the morning, and eventually Geoff would get a reel-to-reel tape back and actually hear what the piece sounded like. The 1990s, when I started, were a seminal time. Macintoshes were getting faster, more affordable, and there was this whole way of communicating with computer software with synthesizers. Things were just beginning to happen in real time.

I became fascinated by the possibility of using gesture in computer music—there's an expressiveness to human gesture. The conductor's art is partially a way of communicating to musicians, but it's also a way of showing the music. You're gestur-

ing with your arms and your facial expression, communicating that to the players and, to a certain extent, to the audience, and communing on a certain level with the mind of the composer. I decided if I was going to do this, I needed to learn computer programming. For my final project, I wrote a little thing called "Mouse Music," where you move the mouse and it would scoot along certain little graphic things that I put on the screen and music would happen. I don't know where it came from, but getting the computer to understand my gestures and respond musically was something I focused in on early.

A year later, I was reading in a journal about an instrument that had been invented by Don Buchla called the Lightning. It was amazing. You could hold these wands in your hands, and you could communicate to the computer just through gesture in space, without any physical connection. It was so similar to what a conductor does in communicating with an orchestra that it seemed like a natural thing. I asked Geoff Wright if he'd be willing to drop fifteen hundred bucks to buy this instrument so we could explore it. And he said, "It sounds great. Let's get it."

I researched everything that others had done, took all the advanced-level classes in computer music that Peabody had to offer, and I got good enough at programming to write my own program that allowed me to conduct a computer. I taught it how I conduct, so that it understood my particular gestures, and started performing with it, and people began to notice what I was doing. Geoff Wright thought it was a cool project and was really helpful. I ended up evolving this composition called *Five Elements Embracing*, which was influenced by my time in India. I wanted it to be accessible to a listener, to have a dynamic that would be expressive in a simple way, that would communicate to an audience and not be threatening and not be distancing. And I guess it worked, because it always gets a good response.

One performance I did was at the Maryland Science Center. Dr. Brody was in the audience and asked if we could collaborate when he gave a lecture to the heads of all the high-tech companies in the Virginia-Delaware-Maryland area. Rather than just give a talk, we did this whole Lightning shtick. He had Lightning in his hands and I had a pair in mine, and we did this interactive performance. It was a fun collaboration and an honor that he

singled out the work as being a really important thing that was going on at Johns Hopkins.

Last year, I got this call from Geoff Wright saying, "These people who are putting together the Times Square 2000 Millennium celebration found out about what you're doing with the Lightning and they want to see it." It was a huge, huge deal. The entire show had to be timed to the second. I ended up writing music that didn't work for them because I didn't realize they were looking for very commercial music. We brought in Charles Byungkyu Kim, a composer and electronic musician at Peabody, who was experienced in doing film score writing. Charles very quickly wrote a couple of really nice pieces. That was what they were looking for. It was an interesting collaboration. On

New Year's Eve, we got up there and performed three times in the middle of Times Square. Don Buchla had to reinvent the Lightning to be able to cut through the signal interference. We pulled it off, and it was very gratifying.

The press from all over the world were there. I've got videotape of ABC News carrying this live from Times Square and really good comments from Peter Jennings that no one else has on a résumé. Peabody's willingness to allow me to explore these unique ideas that I had was very significant. They were very, very supportive.

Forrest Tobey is director of the 21st Century Ensemble in Alexandria, Virginia.

"Science seems to get to the essence by focusing on smaller and smaller and smaller. Art does just the opposite, finding its answers by becoming larger and larger and larger, more all-inclusive. So they're mirrors, opposite sides of the same coin." LEON FLEISHER

"How do you define a grand and wonderful event? It's so taken for granted here at Peabody. You can walk into Griswold or Leakin Hall on almost any day of the week in the springtime and hear a performance so impressive that it's just mind-boggling. We've all gotten very complacent about it. We've had wonderful, wonderful people here over the years, and fabulous faculty and visiting artists. It's hard to think of a time when something incredible *wasn't* going on." ELIZABETH SCHAAF

"I think the affiliation of the Peabody Conservatory of Music with Hopkins was a big step forward in broadening the cultural curriculum. Homewood was getting to be a super vocational training school for all kinds of experts on narrow subjects. There's a lot more to treasure in life than just your job—things like music and the visual arts. Hopkins is building a center at Homewood now to provide a place for students to pursue the arts and broaden their lives." WILLIAM BANKS, B.A.'29

The student-run drama club, the Barnstormers, took its name from its former headquarters in the Barn at Homewood. Productions, like this one in 1983, feature student casts who are usually directed by fellow undergraduates. The Barn is now the home of Theatre Hopkins, a community-based, semi-professional organization with nearly a thousand subscribers to its annual four-play season.

Several times each year, the Departments of Voice and Opera stage performances in the Peabody's Friedberg Hall. The audience's enjoyment of The Marriage of Figaro in 1997 was enhanced by surtitles.

GENIUS, TALENT, LEARNING AND PROMISE

"Young men of genius, talent, learning and promise, you can draw.
They should be your strength."

DANIEL COIT GILMAN, 1876

"I enjoyed the diversity among the student body. Hopkins is not just a bunch of preppies who all dress the same and drive the same cars and come from the same background. At Hopkins there's always been much more representation of populations in general.

When you look at Hopkins publications, it's not all just white guys in the picture. There are many women, minorities. They still have a long way to go in terms of representation on the faculties. I was lucky, I had a couple of women professors when I was an undergraduate." HELEN BLUMBERG, B.A.'73

"What impressed me most about Bill Richardson is that this very gentle man had everything benign about him, but yet I felt there was a very tough tensile strength there. He could make the very tough decision and, more importantly, he knew how to embrace people, to get them to feel good about that decision." MORRIS W. OFFIT, B.A.'57

President Gilman's definition of Johns Hopkins' strength would be more expansive today. It would certainly include Katrina Bell McDonald (wearing red), who joined the Department of Sociology in 1994. McDonald encourages students to explore the dynamics of race, class, and gender.

Bill Richardson's presidency was marked by a sense of personal engagement throughout the Hopkins family, far left.

"I came to Johns Hopkins to study for a graduate degree in political science in 1953. Part of the arrangement was that I would teach some of the sections of Dr. Malcolm Moos's class. There were five of us junior instructors and I was the only woman. The students, most of whom were Korean War veterans, were older and bigger and smarter than I, and they knew it and I knew it. It was a very interesting first year.

Going to my first section meeting I was full of great excitement and enthusiasm. I can remember writing on the board my name and the room number in Gilman Hall where I could be reached. I had a seating chart passed around. I remember saying, 'Thank you very much. Now, if you'll be kind enough to stay in these seats for the first two weeks, I will get to know your names. Are there any questions?'

This rather large person in the back row raised his hand and said, 'What did you say your telephone number was?' Well, of course, the whole class erupted. It really went from bad to worse.

After class, I fled back to the office and three of my buddies were there. They said, 'What happened?'

At that moment, here was this great creature who had asked me what my telephone number was, standing in the doorway. He said, 'Is Barbara here?'

My wonderful friend said, 'Miss Johnson is here. What do you have to say to her?' And, of course, it put a whole new cast on things and the person went away.

After two or three weeks, things began to settle down, but it was a baptism by fire."
BARBARA JOHNSON BONNELL, M.A.'54

In May 1960 the approach of any female was enough to draw the attention of admiring undergraduates. Most women on campus then were graduate students or support staff. Only one woman, Registrar Irene Davis, held a position of authority.

"Our Ph.D. program in biomedical engineering really is first class, well supported by the National Institutes of Health, and able to attract outstanding students. We allow these very good students to do research with anybody in the university, so they work in various laboratories both in East Baltimore and on the Homewood campus.

It's interesting that biomedical engineering developed at a time when the School of Engineering had merged with the Faculty of Philosophy to become the School of Arts and Sciences. After the Whiting School started, a number of faculty had biomedical interests, so an undergraduate major evolved and David VandeLinde, who was dean of the Whiting School, asked us if we would be willing to operate this undergraduate program. These students were among the best and the brightest of the Homewood undergraduates; the quality of these students convinced us to assume responsibility for the program. Our faculty has done a superb job of advising and mentoring these students, and the program has grown to the point that it is today the biggest undergraduate major in the university.

Murray Sachs succeeded me as the director of biomedical engineering. He developed the concept of a Biomedical Engineering Institute—a joint venture between the School of Medicine and the Whiting School of Engineering—that would include people from the Department of Biomedical Engineering and people from all of the engineering disciplines who had an interest. He did it by getting Dean Ilene Busch-Vishniac enthusiastic and developing a strong faculty consensus. Then he got the Whitaker Foundation to fund part of it and Jim Clark to fund the building." RICHARD JAMES JOHNS, M.D.'48

By 1996 some of the most qualified applicants to the Whiting School of Engineering's graduate programs were women. Once they arrived at Homewood, they were also spirited competitors in games of Ultimate Frisbee played on the lower quad.

97

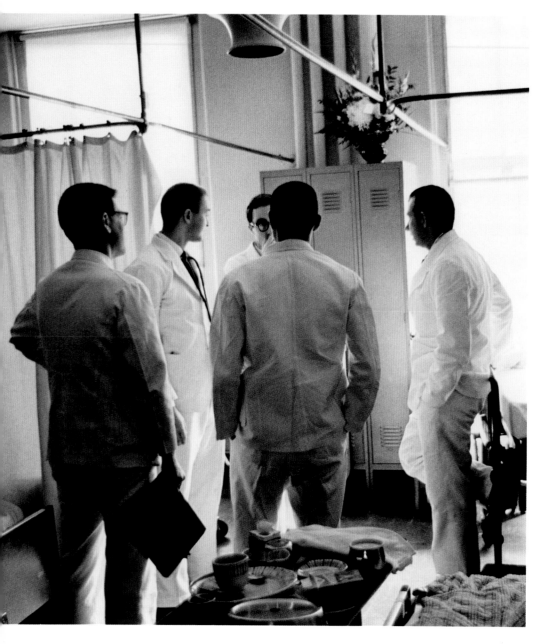

"There is a very special Hopkins ethos. One wonders where it comes from, and I think that it is attributable, as much as anything, to William Osler. Osler was a superb teacher. The teaching in the clinical years was spectacular. It wasn't lecture teaching; it was at the bedside and patient-oriented. Part of the Hopkins ethos is that if you're at Hopkins, you must be good. It's very encouraging and enlightening if people think that you're going to achieve something.

The Oslerian tradition is that you are first a physician and then a specialist. If you are an internist worth your salt, you should be able to handle most problems that came along. I hope that principle still continues. Clinical medicine is very important. Research is on a pedestal, too, but I think good clinical medicine is respected at Hopkins. You don't get rated as a number-one hospital for nine years running unless you have very good clinical medicine being practiced." VICTOR MCKUSICK, M.D.'46

The rounds in progress above c. 1960 contin- ued William Osler's practice of teaching at the patient's bedside, a method of medical training that is now employed throughout the world.

In the earliest days of the School of Medicine, faculty members appeared to be almost as young as their students. Harvey Cushing, Howard Kelly, William Osler, and William S. Thayer (who was Osler's resident from 1891 to 1898) posed with a class that included a cluster of four women.

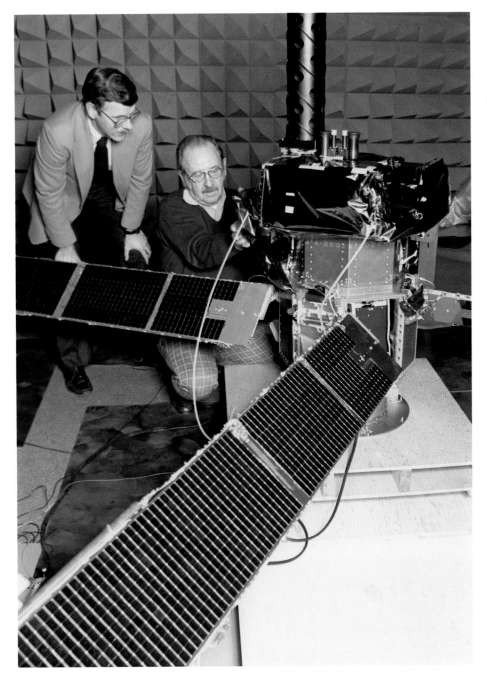

"APL built instruments to ride on satellites built by the Jet Propulsion Lab that went to Jupiter and Saturn. We were measuring the composition of particles in space with little mass spectrometers that bent particles to see their mass, so you could identify whether we were dealing with an atom of carbon or nitrogen or iron or whatever by seeing how the magnetic field bent them as they came into the instruments."
ALEXANDER KOSSIAKOFF, PH.D.'38

"I've always respected Hopkins, deeply. And it's funny—I started into university work because I was a '60s person and I did not want to be part of what I then thought of as the war machine, so I came to Hopkins. Go figure.

Johns Hopkins receives the most federal research funds of any university, and I don't mean just for medicine. APL was basically a branch of the navy for many, many, many years, doing all sorts of amazing stuff like mapping the bottom of the sea. They made the early weather satellites, which were intended for navy use. Satellites that were designed and built at APL went up successfully, stayed up, and most of them served long beyond their intended time. They were damn good engineers; if you're going to put up satellites, they might as well stay up." ELISE HANCOCK

"Johns Hopkins School of Public Health has consistently been rated the number one school of public health in the United States and draws students from all over the world because of the excellent reputation of its faculty for research and commitment to teaching. All my courses were taught by tenure-track faculty, in most cases by full professors.

These students then go on and achieve stellar careers in government or academia. The alumni phone book is a great resource for people who are now ministers of health, or vice presidents of countries, deans or presidents of medical schools or schools of public health. They inspire students to come to Johns Hopkins for schooling."
ERIC NOJI, M.P.H.'87

When Charles L. White showed Kenneth A. Potocki details on the Applied Physics Laboratory's 250-pound high latitude ionospheric research satellite in June 1983, APL had been in the satellite business for a quarter century. Above, that same month Lee Dubois searched a data file on tracking satellites while Matt Ganz and Greg Bailey looked on.

In 1985, the School of Public Health was concentrating on issues just as complex, but more down-to-earth.

"Peabody is a place where the traditions of music are respected and honored and perpetuated, but it's also a place that's oriented toward tomorrow. That's why you train young musicians. It's always been a place where you could try out new ideas and look at new ways of doing things and hear new voices. That's been its strength over the years."
ELIZABETH SCHAAF

The Peabody community honored Awadagin Pratt with its Alumni Young Maestro Award in 1995, above left. Pratt excelled by completing majors in conducting, violin, and piano. In 1992 he won the prestigious Naumburg International Piano Competition and has made his career at the keyboard.

Ray Sprenkle, left, spun not only vinyl but also countless anecdotes about music history at both the Peabody and the School of Continuing Studies.

"There's one classroom, Gilman 500, that's right underneath the bell tower. It has windows that are almost floor to ceiling. You get great views. You can say what you want about the positives or negatives of the academic experience, but you have arrived in the ivory tower when you are in Gilman 500 looking down on the rest of the campus and talking about theoretical poetic aesthetics."
CHRISTOPHER NIEDT, B.A.'99

"My last year, I learned that there was a writing course being given in the teachers' college at night. They had it hidden away in Maryland Hall, a place where you buried engineers.

There was a group of people who, like me, all hoped to sell stories to the *Saturday Evening Post* and become rich. The guy presiding was Elliott Coleman. Elliott made no attempt to teach. You would write, and then you would read your story, then people would tear it up. Writers all detest each other, like cats and dogs. I learned a lot from having my stuff torn apart.

Elliott would try to guide us into what we ought to be reading. We were all reading Fitzgerald and Wolfe and Hemingway. I got to the point where I could write a Hemingway story better than Ernest Hemingway. Elliott was very tolerant of all this for a while. Finally, one evening he lost his patience and said, 'Hemingway is swell, but he's out.' And he started arranging lectures: Joyce, and Proust. It was very primitive when I was there. The following year Elliott got it moved into Gilman Hall. It became the Department of Writing, Speech, and Drama, and the university accepted it, probably over the steaming bones of the English department. And then it turned into the Writing Seminars. Quite an institution, I understand." RUSSELL BAKER, B.A.'47

Alice McDermott, winner of the 1998 National Book Award for fiction, continued the round-table tradition of the Writing Seminars, listening intently as a student discussed his story in February 2000. McDermott had recently been named the first Richard A. Macksey Writer-in-Residence. Macksey himself admitted that he so admired McDermott as a teacher that he sometimes sat in the lounge below her Gilman tower classroom "just to eavesdrop."

Some students dispensed with ties in an economics seminar on May 15, 1963. Even Professor Carl Christ shed his jacket, but the one nun still wore a full, and no doubt warm, habit.

In 1950 Owen Lattimore, director of the Walter Hines Page School of International Relations, declared, "I owe allegiance to no one except my country and my conscience." He was responding to charges by Senator Joseph McCarthy that he was "the top Soviet agent in this country." The trustees granted Lattimore leave with pay so that he could defend himself. Charges were eventually dropped and he returned to teach in the Department of History until 1963. Far right above, Lattimore met with students at City College on March 7, 1951.

"I joined the faculty in 1973. It was an intimate community. People were very serious about the work they did. The intellectual pursuit was up front, mainstream, and focused.

You could have a seminar, which is what the graduate institution is based mainly on, which dealt, for example, with Latin America, but the audience would be people from the medical school because they had an interest in demography or public health, or from the Department of Economics or from political science. People never identified themselves by department; sometimes it was difficult to know what department they came from. It was non-competitive. I remember having very strong differences of opinion and afterwards we would go to the faculty club and continue the discussions in a very tranquil way. It remained a professional difference of opinion that never affected personal relations.

It's a changed university now. It's a little larger, there are certainly a lot more undergraduates. I think Hopkins knew what it was about in the '70s and the '80s. I think it is less certain that there exists a consensus what Hopkins is about today, and that's a big difference over twenty-five years." PROFESSOR FRANKLIN KNIGHT

"Owen Lattimore was a kind of ghost who roamed the fourth floor. He was not permitted to teach, but he was permitted to come to the oral examinations of Ph.D. candidates. A student from India who had a topic that not very many people understood or knew anything about went to defend his thesis. The candidate said Lattimore asked the most penetrating questions. They were just extraordinary. 'We went on for two hours, and at the end,' he said, 'I felt so good, because I'd really had a very interesting and challenging conversation with someone whose mind I respected.'"
BARBARA JOHNSON BONNELL, M.A.'54

"Owen Lattimore was a fine teacher. He didn't have a Ph.D. I remember the night Lattimore came back from Asia when Senator McCarthy had tarred him with the Communist brush on radio and television. He was welcomed in Levering Hall; the faculty came to stand by him. I was out in the hall, standing on my tiptoes to try to see what was going on. I sensed the coming together of the faculty to support freedom of speech and freedom to teach."
ROSS JONES, B.A.'53

Overhead projectors became standard equipment in many classrooms by the late twentieth century. They were used regularly during weekly seminars in the Department of Mathematical Sciences where professors, postdoctoral fellows, and distinguished visitors presented highlights of their work.

105

"Bob Scott is one of the great men of Johns Hopkins. He was a successful lacrosse coach, a successful athletic director, but his greatness goes beyond the athletic center. He is a guy of great integrity, and he taught values to his players. When you played for Bob Scott, you learned how to play lacrosse, you learned how to win, but you also learned how to be a decent person. He would tell us, 'It all comes out in the wash.' That was a favorite expression of his. If you tell the truth, you don't have to worry about the truth coming out later.

You had to dress properly. If you went on an away trip, you wore a coat and tie. Period. When you were playing, you had to have your shirt tucked in. Scotty was a straight arrow, and you knew that.

We had almost nine hundred people for his retirement party and it was fabulous."
JEROME SCHNYDMAN, B.A.'67

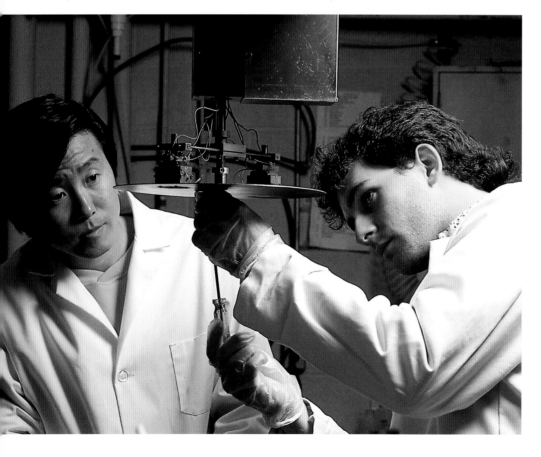

Henry Ciccarone and Bob Scott, above left, defined Hopkins lacrosse for years. Scott, on right, became head coach in 1953, a year after he graduated. Ciccarone, an All-American midfielder under Scott in 1962, succeeded him as coach in 1974.

Gang Xiao and Jeffrey Childress worked on a multi-source deposition system—and their Ph.D.s—in the condensed matter physics lab in the Bloomberg Center in 1988.

106

"Mentoring is having someone who takes you by the arm and leads you through the politics, the science. I go to a meeting, and I take one of my mentees with me. When I meet my friends, my mentee is there. Time comes for a job, I pick up a phone and say, 'Joe, I've got a wonderful person here.' A mentor can get a mentee through the door, maybe not keep them in the room, but you've got to get through the door. If you don't have someone who's there pulling for you, you're going to have a heck of a time.

Your mentor will tell you which grant to go for and whom to call, or he or she will call for you. A mentor will tell you, 'Look. Why are you doing that study? Where do you think that's going to get you?' or, 'Where do you want to be in five years, and how do you think you're going to get there?' If you do this, let me tell you what's going to happen. If you do that, this is probably what's going to happen. All the forks in the road, all the door-openings, that's what a mentor does." DR. CATHERINE DEANGELIS

Catherine DeAngelis decided on her career at the age of four. "People kept giving me nurse's kits, but I knew I wanted to be a doctor." She came to Johns Hopkins to join the pediatrics program in the old Harriet Lane Home and eventually rose to the level of vice dean in the School of Medicine. In 2000 she took a leave of absence to become editor of the Journal of the American Medical Association.

What Makes Scientists Tick

PROFESSOR BERT VOGELSTEIN, M.D.'74

Interviewed on December 22, 1999

"I was at a dinner party with Dan Nathans once, and there was a picture of a nice family of Midwestern farmboys. They were this perfect little line, one a year. And Dan said, 'Yes, but there's a blip in the data,' and he pointed out that one of the kids had his knees scrunched out because he didn't fit. It just amused the hell out of me that Dan would be the one to notice the blip in the data. Because that's what he does." ELISE HANCOCK

When I was a teenager, I read a book put out by Hopkins called *The Making of a Physician*, which impressed me, and I thought I wanted to go to medical school here, which I did. I did my internship and residency here, and then I went away for a postdoctoral fellowship for a couple of years at the National Institutes of Health. Then I came back in 1978, and I've been on the faculty ever since.

By the time I got to medical school I knew I wanted to do research. Research is complex, just as medical practice is complex. You go to medical school and you learn a lot about physiology and anatomy and biochemistry, but that doesn't mean that you know how to treat patients. In order to treat patients, you have to see patients, examine them, learn how to interact with them. That's the art in medicine.

Science is the same way. You take courses, you learn somewhat different things than a physician does—maybe biophysics, more detailed biochemistry, molecular genetics—but you don't really know how to do research until you try it. You learn that in the laboratory. You learn how to work the tools, how to formulate questions, how to answer questions.

Just as physicians have to do an internship and residency after they're trained and get their M.D. degree, scientists also do internships and residencies. They're not called that; they're called postdoctoral fellowships. But it's the same thing. It's an apprenticeship. It lasts for the same period of time: three to five years. And only after that are they thought qualified enough to actually practice science and be hired, say, by a university to do research and to teach.

People in our lab work eighty hours a week. They're here all the time. They have a goal, each of them, and sometimes they appear to make an important step toward that goal, but the emotion that is elicited by the experiment that's successful is not "Eureka!" It's, "Hey, this is really interesting. I wonder what's wrong," because you're conditioned by months and months and years and years of failure. Every time something looks good, it's virtually always followed by a realization that it's not as good as it looks and something is terribly wrong. And then it usually takes quite a long time, weeks to months, to reproduce the experiment and to rule out all the potential artifacts that could have caused the false excitement. So experimental science certainly has its moments when one is very excited, but it is so difficult that that moment is fleeting, and it's rapidly overtaken by back-to-reality and a lot of additional experiments to verify it or refute it.

So research is not an instantaneous process. It's a long, drawn-out thing. It's still very satisfying. People who really enjoy science enjoy it because of the day-to-day, the little things that go right, and the underlying idea that you're working on something that can one day be important. That's what really makes scientists tick, the little things that work. The Eurekas come all too infrequently to really make a scientist satisfied, and sometimes they never come during your whole life.

Back in the mid '80s we were looking for evidence of a cancer gene which we expected to be on chromosome 17. Susie Baker, a graduate student, had a goal to find that gene. Now, back then no cancer gene like this had ever been found, so it was almost a humorous thesis project. We really didn't expect her to find the gene; we just expected her to make some progress toward mapping where the gene might lie on the chromosome. But during the course of those studies, she evaluated a gene called P-53, which we didn't believe at the time was likely to be the culprit. So she designed a strategy to see if that gene was involved.

It was a Friday afternoon in December in 1988, about three o'clock, and she was looking through her sequence and she said, "Bert, look. It looks like there's a mutation here." So I looked at it and the mutation was not a very impressive one. It was the kind that you wouldn't think would make any difference, but it was a mutation. We looked at it and we knew that it would be exciting if it were true, but we were both skeptical.

The next step was to make sure that the change really was a mutation that was

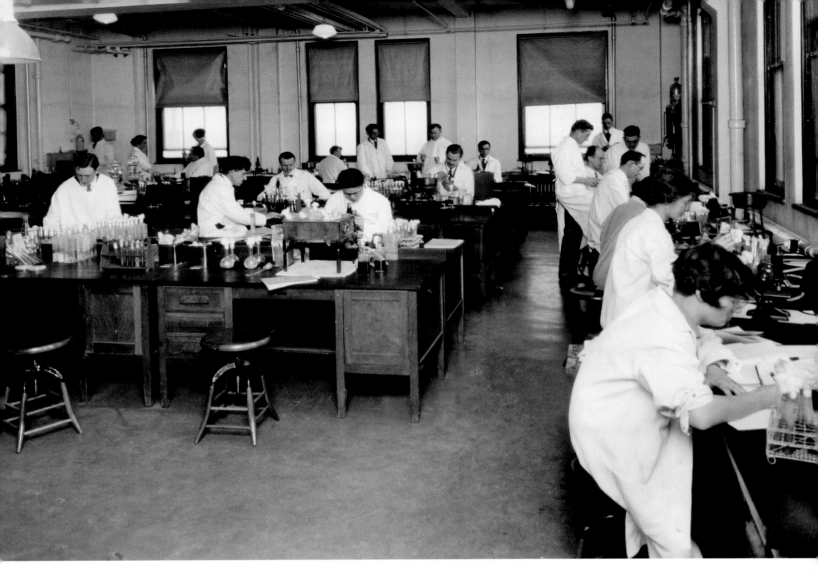

"I had a meeting with Dr. David Blake, the associate dean of the School of Medicine for research, who was pretty blunt. He said that the criteria for promotion and longevity for faculty at Johns Hopkins was not the number of publications. You could publish a thousand publications, but if they did not advance the field, they would not be worth as much as one paper that changes one's field. There were cases of specialists at Johns Hopkins Hospital in cardiology, neurology, orthopedic surgery, who changed their fields by the invention of a new surgical technique, discovery of a new drug to cure disease, publication of a paper that fundamentally altered the practice of cardiology or neurology—and the faculty member who published that paper would be promoted." ERIC NOJI, M.P.H. '87

not found in the patient's normal cells, which Susie did. It took her about three weeks to verify that. Now it would take about half a day, but with the technology back then, it took quite a bit longer. And then we looked at other cancers, and every single cancer she looked at, she found a similar mutation.

It took us about two months to realize

Daniel Nathans and Hamilton Smith, winners of the 1978 Nobel Prize for Medicine far left, and public-health students studying bacteriology above are among the legions of researchers who have labored in Hopkins labs over the years. At right, Professor Kam Leong analyzed biomedical polymers in 1988 while Mark Richards, a B.S./M.S. candidate, and Nai-hong Li, a postdoctoral fellow, watched.

that we had discovered a cancer gene that was likely involved in most cancers in the world, that was going to start a revolution in cancer research, which it did. P-53 was named Molecule of the Year a few years later. It's now the most active area of cancer research. It's been that way ever since Susie discovered it. So that was about as close to a Eureka as we get, but it wasn't "Eureka!" It was, "Hmm. This must be an artifact."

Hopkins develops a great crop of young people who are, when they're ripe, picked by other institutions. It's a shame, but that's the way the world works. I consider this place home. I like the atmosphere. I think it's a unique place, wonderful students, very supportive administration, and they let you do your thing. They try not to interfere. It's the same thing we do with our students and postdocs. We provide guidance and we provide resources, but we let them blossom themselves.

Bert Vogelstein is professor of pathology and of oncology and cancer biology at the School of Medicine and an oncology investigator at the Howard Hughes Medical Institute.

Susan Barger, a specialist in the conservation of paper and the preservation of early photographic artifacts, conversed with technician Gary Bowdon and a student in her materials science laboratory in 1988.

"Postdocs are people who already have a doctoral degree, M.D. or Ph.D. They're here doing further training and research under specific mentors. They're making incredible discoveries. For example, Bert Vogelstein has ten or twelve postdocs in his laboratory doing the research in molecular biology. These are incredibly rich, productive researchers and trainees.

There are twelve hundred postdocs at this university. They had no organization, no representation, no uniform stipends, no uniform benefits, no specific length of training. They were assigned to one professor or the other. If the professor happened to have money, they would get money. If the professor didn't, they would work for nothing practically. They came to me in my role as associate dean. My title was to handle the interns and residents, but we have more postdocs than we have interns and residents. They were very clever in their choice of words. They told me they felt like they were on the back of the bus. I knew what they were talking about. So over the next few years I tried to articulate their issues before the Advisory Board. We were trying to bring them into our academic family and I think we have. *Science* magazine heard about it. They singled out Johns Hopkins as providing leadership in the way postdoctoral education should be done."
DR. LEVI WATKINS

Eva Wong, a graduate student in materials science engineering in 1996, experimented with the luminescent properties of phosophors and hoped that her work might lead to a new generation of flat displays.

"The result of research cannot really be foreseen. The people who contributed to lasers were not looking for something that would be very effective in doing operations on the eye. Even in 1960, it was a joke to say that the laser was a solution in search of a problem. Now lasers are being used from scanning devices and pointers to surgical instruments and weapons."
KISHIN MOORJANI

Charles Roger Westgate holds joint appointments in the Whiting School of Engineering and at the Applied Physics Laboratory. Many alumni recall the time and energy he invested in their education with appreciation and fondness.

111

STRONG, BRIGHT, USEFUL AND TRUE.

"We are trying to do this with no controversy as to the relative importance of letters
and science, the conflicts of religion and science, or the relation of abstractions and utilities;
our simple aim is to make scholars, strong, bright, useful and true."

DANIEL COIT GILMAN, 1876

"It seems like a lot of people have a plan for their lives and Hopkins is the first step to get there. Everyone seems to be going to med school or grad school or law school. Everyone's really absorbed in academics.

I was talking to a friend about whether or not there is a Hopkins type. I guess the only thing they have in common is they're very driven, they're usually good at science. I always got the impression that they were a little bit nicer, that there were fewer real jerks at Hopkins than at other schools." CHRISTOPHER NIEDT, B.A.'99

The stress of moving-in day in 1986 was made more enjoyable for freshmen and their families when Josh Liberman appeared with refreshments, far left. The orientation committee in 1995 took its logo, above, from the interstate on which many new arrivals had just traveled.

"Bill Brody is a wonderful person, warm and easy to deal with, and the students love him. He and his wife, Wendy, roller-skate to meet the freshmen. I think he's an excellent administrator and really human and caring, which is what Hopkins is so good at." MARJORIE G. LEWISOHN, M.D. '43

Since 1995 President Bill Brody and his wife, Wendy, have surprised and delighted arriving freshmen by greeting them in full Rollerblade regalia. It's unlikely that President Daniel Coit Gilman gave a similar reception to the class of 1893, but they seemed hale and hardy and virtually all had hats when they posed in the entrance of McCoy Hall on the old downtown campus.

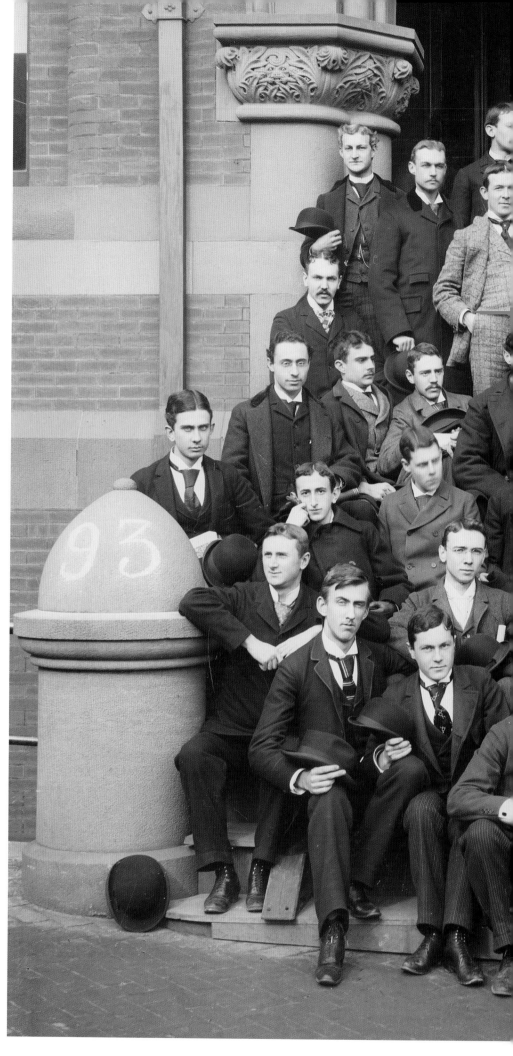

115

The student body acquired an early international accent when Japanese students joined its ranks. Members of the class of 1901 apparently used themselves as subjects for their chemistry experiments, *far right*.

Although the university never made its home at Clifton, Johns Hopkins' country estate was used for outdoor athletic events, *below far right in 1888*. Scrimmages between the freshman and sophomore classes, *below*, often drew blood.

To Dr. H.B. Adams,
With the best Regards
of his Pupil,
Inazo Ota
J.H.U. 1885.

"In those days hazing consisted of requiring freshmen to stand at attention and do this, that, or the other, and the sophomores carried paddles. If the freshmen didn't perform up to the standards of the sophomores, they'd whack them with a paddle.

There were several battles during the class banquets. Our sophomore year an expedition from our class went down to Annapolis and disrupted the banquet that the freshmen were having in the armory and this turned into a fight. Several of the participants landed in the Annapolis jail for the night." WILLIAM BANKS, B.A.'29

Charles Carroll, the original owner of
Homewood House, built the Barn in the
early nineteenth century to shelter his cattle.
When the university moved to its new campus,
the building became a student center housing a
barbershop, three lunchrooms, and work areas
for various activities. In 1983 it was christened
the Merrick Barn to honor Robert Merrick,
who had underwritten its restoration. Merrick
also funded the transformation of Homewood
House (where he had lived as a graduate
student c.1920) into a museum.

Cotillion Board members relaxed on the steps
of Levering Hall c.1946, the year a one-story
addition enlarged its cafeteria facilities.

118

"We didn't have any place to hang out except at the Barn, which was cozy but full of noise and confusion and bad food at the lunch counter. The upstairs was cut up for offices for the different activities, the *News-Letter*, the *Black and Blue Jay*. The old Barnstormers Club used the loft to build the scenery for the annual shows they gave down at the Lyric Theater." WILLIAM BANKS, B.A.'29

"Dr. G. Wilson Shaffer was a great, great person. He was very supportive of athletics. He was upset when they developed the NCAA tournament in lacrosse, because he felt it was going to move it closer to the professionalism that you see in college basketball and football. He said, 'It should be there for the students to come and watch.' When exams were over, everything should end.

When the football team beat a lot of the great teams one year, they were invited to the Tangerine Bowl. Dr. Shaffer wouldn't let them go. He said, 'There's no reason to go. We had a wonderful season. Now it's basketball season. Let's move on.'

Dr. Shaffer was my mentor. He was more than just somebody who helped me pick my courses. He would congratulate me for doing well in the classroom. He would tell me how proud he was of me. He would tell me how happy he was that I was succeeding on the lacrosse team. He was somebody who would give me insight into how to act in the classroom, on the field, in life. There are hundreds and hundreds of people who would say the same thing, so I'm not unique." JEROME SCHNYDMAN, B.A.'67

All eyes were on G. Wilson Shaffer when Johnny Milligan presented him with an honorary H-Club key c.1948. Shaffer was named dean of the College of Arts and Sciences in 1942 and dean of the Homewood Schools in 1948. He held a lifelong interest in sports and was appointed associate professor of physical education in 1939; in 1948 he transferred to the psychology department, a position he maintained along with the deanship until he retired in 1967. Shaffer made a lasting impression, particularly on those who took his class in abnormal psychology. Shaffer Hall was dedicated in his honor in 1968.

"Nursing students lived in Hampton House. All they had do was walk across the street and they were at work. Hopkins was their life for the three years that they were in nursing school. There are many happy memories that revolve around their work in the hospital, but also the social life. That brought them in very close contact with students from the School of Medicine." PROFESSOR STELLA SHIBER

"Hopkins had wonderful dances. All the big-name bands came—Woody Herman, Jimmy Dorsey, and I can't remember how many others—so I danced to all of them. Glenn Miller was the best. They would have the dances at the Alcazar, and the place would be full every time. Sometimes when we went to dances we wore our evening dresses on the streetcar. Everybody did it. Once in a while the boy would borrow his father's car; hardly any students had their own.

We would dance to the music on the radio—these big bands were all on the radio, so we could dance all night long. We were annoyed when Roosevelt would make a speech because we couldn't dance then." MARGARET SPARROW, M.A.T.'58

Johns Hopkins had no ballroom of its own; when big names played, dances were held downtown. World War II veterans made up much of the student body when Duke Ellington, above, entertained at the Alcazar on June 7, 1947.

Jubilant—if temporary—guardians crowded around the four-hundred-pound terrapin they had just released from captivity in College Park. The Hopkins undergraduates filched the University of Maryland's mascot on May 23, 1947, and posed with their prize at 3 A.M. Adding insult to injury, the Blue Jays walloped the Terps 15–6 on the lacrosse field later that day.

120

"Hopkins or Maryland was national lacrosse champion year in and year out, so there was an intense rivalry. On the eve of the Hopkins-Maryland game, a group of guys in the dorm got into a parade of cars and drove over to College Park after midnight. The symbol of the University of Maryland at College Park is this terrapin that has to be four feet in diameter—and it's bolted. Our guys had some engineers in the group and they had cased it very carefully.

Meanwhile, back at Homewood, outside the Alumni Memorial dormitory, other students were building this barricade covered with barbed wire. I said, 'What the hell are you doing?'

They said, 'We're bringing in the terrapin.' The four-hundred-pound terrapin had been seized and was en route back to Baltimore with a stream of University of Maryland cars behind it in hot pursuit.

I said, 'Don't bring it in here.'

So they went in the woods behind the faculty club and hid it. This was now four o'clock in the morning. I called the police. Hopkins kids were behind the barricade with fire hoses pulled out of the dorms. Maryland guys were storming across the campus. Police were everywhere. The Maryland guys did not recover the terrapin, and the police finally broke it up. That afternoon, the Hopkins boys presented the terrapin to the Maryland team at halftime." WILBERT "BILL" LOCKLIN, B.S.'57

When students at the hospital's nursing school gave a dance, above, *they often invited medical students as their escorts. Some preferred dates who were closer to their own age and turned to undergraduates from Homewood or other nearby schools.*

Levering Hall was built by the YMCA in 1928–29 on land provided by the university. Its lounges, meeting rooms, and cafeteria became the primary social center at Homewood, especially for students who commuted.

"When you came out of Gilman, you went down to Levering Hall. There was a piano that Corbin Gwaltney would play occasionally. The *News-Letter* office was underneath, and the Student Council met down there. The cafeteria was a great social center. That's where everybody went to kill an hour or to shoot the breeze, to argue. Get a cup of coffee and cigarettes. Everybody smoked." RUSSELL BAKER, B.A.'47

"We would serve breakfast, lunch, and dinner in Levering Hall. At dinnertime we had lines to the door. We served good-quality food, and the Evening College would come in and eat dinner. People taking class at night depended on eating their dinner before they'd go to school; they'd leave work and go right on there and eat dinner. So that's why we had such a mob. We had just about as many for dinner as we did for lunch. We were open five days a week and half a day on Saturdays." MINNIE HARGROW

"I was told that I was going to be the first African American in the arts and sciences school. Well, I had not applied intending to be a pioneer, but I wanted to go to Hopkins. I was a bit surprised when I got there that I didn't have a roommate. I called up the admissions director and he said, 'Well, Ernie, we thought that was a bit much, to ask a student to room with you. We're trying to minimize the problems, so if you don't mind, you will not have a roommate.' Well, I was a little upset, but the second day, twenty people offered to be my roommate. I was just overwhelmed by that.

But as it turns out, I did not accept any of them, and the reason is I met the African-American students who lived in Baltimore, the townies. Baltimore at that time was segregated. The restaurants were still segregated, the movies. The school systems were just beginning to desegregate. Hopkins was ahead of its time in letting these students come. So this was much more traumatic for them than for me because I had been in integrated school systems before.

My room became the meeting place for them. It was where they left their books, their sandwiches, their coats. That room became one of the most popular rooms in the dorm. It was very good for the African-American students because they got to see dorm life.

The entire time I was at Hopkins, there was not one incident of discrimination. At no point was I ever treated less than any other student. It wasn't true off campus, but on campus you would have never known that I was the first in arts and sciences. My cohorts who lived in town—they were in engineering—they, too, did not have any problems."
ERNEST A. BATES, B.A.'58

When Kelly Miller entered the graduate program in 1887, he was Johns Hopkins' first African-American student. However, Miller transferred to Howard University to complete his degree. It was not until the 1950s that Hopkins again welcomed black students, including Ernest A. Bates, right c. 1955.

Ross Jones snapped his brother Bob and buddies David Jennings, Craig Haight, and Jack Sutherland when they stacked themselves on the wall in front of the Alumni Memorial Residences in 1953, above. Bruce Mitchell captured '50s life in the dorms on film, including Dave Mellits and Dan Desantis playing chess. Their contemporary Ernie Bates recalled, "we'd stay up until three and four in the morning playing."

Members of the Student Council met on November 20, 1961, above far right, to discuss issues of concern to Homewood undergraduates. Television and cold beer afforded a break from scholarly activities in a fraternity house c. 1960, far right. Local students particularly benefited from such camaraderie. Jerry Schnydman said, "It allowed me to meet and socialize with a bunch of people that I wouldn't have because I was a commuter. I made some great friendships in my fraternity and in other fraternities."

"When I was an undergraduate I had no idea of the breadth of Hopkins. I don't remember being the scholar that had this great academic thirst for knowledge. I was a nice young middle-class kid who was maturing. I think the mistake a lot of parents make—and a lot of kids who are very serious make—is they think that the main reason to go to college is to get a set of facts. The main reason to go to college is to learn how to deal in this world with others, learn that others have feelings and need help. Those skills are so much more important. And those are the ones that really do take four years to learn. The handful of facts you learn, if you did a cram course, you could learn those pretty quickly. You don't need to spend four years of your life doing it." MICHAEL R. BLOOMBERG, B.S.E.'64

The counterculture arrived at Johns Hopkins in the mid 1960s and took much the same form as it did on virtually every college campus in the United States. Dorm rooms became galleries for posters proclaiming allegiances to political organizations and popular performers, above. Hopkins hosted a wide range of musical groups when Odetta, Flatt and Scruggs, Nina Simone, Charles Mingus, Thelonious Monk, Ravi Shankar, Simon and Garfunkel, Frank Zappa and the Mothers of Invention, and the Mamas and the Papas came to Baltimore. Chester Wickwire, who coordinated many of the events, remembered that "we held lots of concerts in high schools all over the city when we couldn't get Shriver."

Heightened political awareness also stimulated efforts to increase minority enrollment. By the time this proud graduate and her family celebrated in the Hutzler Reading Room at right, students from around the country and around the globe were registering on all levels in all divisions.

"Milton Eisenhower said when he first came to the campus, everybody walked around the campus with their head down; they never looked at anybody and never said hello. He tried to personally change that. He lived on campus, and he had a little light next to his study door. Whenever that light was on, students knew that they could come over and talk to him, and they did. They were very rewarding times for him." ROSS JONES, B.A.'53

"It was a tumultuous time. There was a lot of emotion out there, and yet there was also a shadow cast by what was going on in Cambodia and Vietnam. Nixon was so easy to hate. There were all these elements coming into play: coeducation, the rise of feminism, the Black Power movement.

It was an extraordinary time. But when you're going through it, you don't stop to reflect; at least you don't when you're eighteen-, nineteen-, twenty-year-olds. You're too busy being of-the-moment. It was an exciting time to be a college student, if you were lucky enough that you could be in college." HELEN BLUMBERG, B.A.'73

Milton Eisenhower took enormous pleasure in entertaining students at Nichols House, the president's residence on the Homewood campus. Neil Grauer recalled that in the 1960s, "a lot of students took warmly to him, and rightly so, because he was genuinely interested in them. He was the undergraduates' best friend at Hopkins."

Hopkins Boys

JEROME SCHNYDMAN, B.A.'67

Interviewed on June 17, 1999

I grew up in Baltimore County, but everybody in my family had gone to City College high school, so I passed by Johns Hopkins on my twenty-five-minute drive to school every day. I began playing lacrosse when I was in the eighth grade, and every day I thought, "Wouldn't it be incredible if I could play on Home-wood Field?"

I was accepted at Hopkins and I enrolled. I lived at home, and my father dropped me off every day to go to school at Johns Hopkins. In those days, an awful lot of Baltimoreans commuted to Hopkins. I didn't have my own car, but my mother would let me use her car if I needed to stay late to study. I always participated in intramural activities. I was in a fraternity. By the time I was a senior, I was very involved in all aspects of the campus.

So, for me, the only thing I missed out on, really, was living in the dorm freshman year, because after the freshman year everybody moved into apartments. There were students who lived in the dorms after freshman year, but it was a pretty small number.

My advisor was Earl Wasserman. This guy, to this day, is one of the most brilliant people I've ever known. Wouldn't have known a baseball from a football, but he was a wonderful, wonderful guy. Even though I knew my chances were not good for a good grade, I decided to take his one-semester course on Keats and Shelley just because I thought, "Here is a world-famous professor whose books are being used all over the world, particularly at Oxford and Cambridge." I learned an awful lot. I got a C-minus; I was probably lucky to get that because it was very, very difficult for me. Dr. Wasserman said, "Schnydman, my colleagues in the English department tell me that you are a fabulous lacrosse player, that if they gave out grades in lacrosse, you'd get an A. So if we average the A in lacrosse and the C-minus I gave you, you probably would be close to a B." I thought that was so kind of him because I knew that he probably didn't even know where the lacrosse field was. That was a great moment for me, that he would say that to try to make me feel better.

I was president of the Interfraternity Council, so every time there was a problem, the dean of students would call me into his office. Kelso Morrill felt no student at Hopkins should do anything wrong because it might dishonor Johns Hopkins. And I respected that. I've tried to live that way myself as a student, as an employee. Hopkins is far greater and more important than anybody who works here. I learned that from Dr. Morrill.

We had an Interfraternity Council boat ride, and people really got drunk. The water police escorted the boat back early. Everybody had to leave. On Monday

morning, there was a note in my box to go see Dr. Morrill. He was incredulous. He kept saying over and over, "These are Hopkins boys. How could they act like this? They're Hopkins boys." He couldn't understand anybody who would do anything that could bring dishonor to Hopkins. After maybe fifteen or twenty minutes of telling me how boys need to act and how things should be done, he said, "Okay, that's over." And then he talked to me for ten minutes about lacrosse.

Hopkins is the kind of place where nobody tells you what to do. You're treated as an adult. You have to take responsibility here as a student. It's a smorgasbord, and you can take whatever you want. If you want to take an upper-level course and you don't have the requirement but you think you're ready to take the course, then you talk your way into the class. You can do research as an undergraduate. You're encouraged to do that. And, to me, that's what makes Hopkins great.

And it's the same working here. This is a very decentralized place. The dean of arts and sciences may as well be called president of arts and sciences. President Brody says that being president at Hopkins is like being the caretaker at a cemetery: there are a lot of people under you, but nobody's listening.

The people here care about Hopkins.

They care about doing a good job. Students care about doing well in the classroom. There's a feeling here of excellence, that we're going to do it as well as we can and we're going to do it better than anybody else. I think all that helps to make Hopkins a great place. The overriding greatness of Hopkins is its creativity, and you can only have creativity if you have freedom.

Dean Kelso Morrill seemed more absorbed with cards than students in 1962, above. *The raucous freshman-sophomore rivalries of earlier generations were nearly forgotten by the time the class* far above *gathered for its dignified banquet. Rowdy behavior still prevailed at the Shipwreck Party at Delta Upsilon in 1953,* far left.

Jerome Schnydman is executive assistant to the president and secretary of the Board of Trustees of The Johns Hopkins University.

Baltimore's occasional snowstorms offer the perfect excuse to escape from studies, as these fellows discovered c. 1973. By that time only faculty members regularly wore jackets and ties to class. Indeed, some students in 1974 joined the streaking fad and stormed Gilman Hall one night almost in the altogether—hats and shoes added a curious aspect to the new look.

"When Stewart Macaulay hired me after the war, he said I was to be assistant director of admissions and social and athletic director of the dormitory. At three o'clock every Sunday we had dinner in the dining room. We had waitresses in the dining room. We had a guy play the piano, and we would sing the alma mater.

I observed that dress was getting to be a little more casual than I was satisfied with. The guys were coming in from the athletic fields sweaty; they didn't have a tie or jacket. I said, 'You know, it's a disgrace to have you here in this condition. Next Sunday I'm going to be at the front door. No one is going to get past me who's not wearing a jacket and tie.'

The next week, I was there at the front door at five minutes till three and they all started streaming out of the dorm. Every single one of them had on a jacket. Every single one had on a tie—not a stitch of other clothing, not a shoe, not a sock, not trousers, not a shirt—just jackets and ties. I just died. We had these nice ladies who were serving us, and they roared. They thought it was hilarious. We stood there and sang the alma mater, and they sat down and ate. The next Sunday everybody came fully dressed, and I didn't have any more trouble." WILBERT "BILL" LOCKLIN, B.S.'57

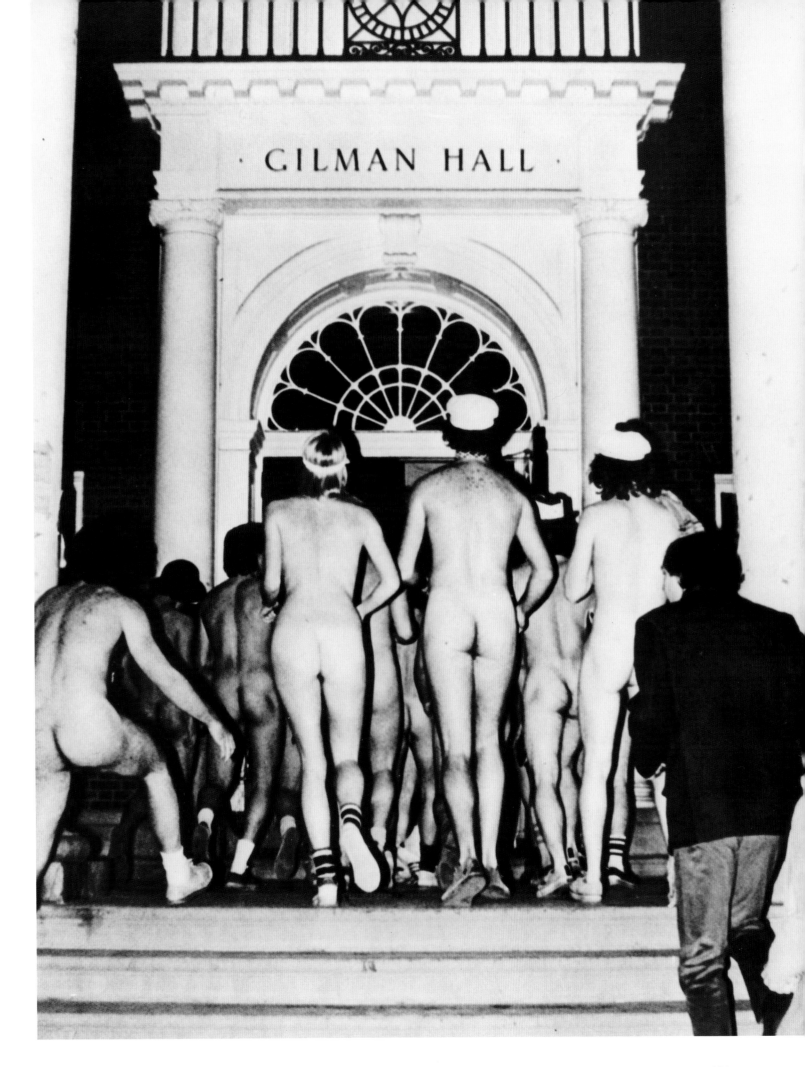

In the former dress code of nursing, students wore distinctive attire. The students sitting in a hospital nursing station in September 1967 at right wore white scrub dresses, indicating that they were assigned to a specialty area. Blue uniforms were the standard for students.

Professor Frederick Holborn acknowledged that in recent years the majority of his students at the School of Advanced International Studies rarely see the Homewood campus, though some do take advantage of the Eisenhower Library. Since 1963 most academic and social activities at SAIS have centered on the Nitze Building at 1740 Massachusetts Avenue, far right.

Members of the Black Student Union gathered in 1983 for a group portrait, below. Formed in 1968, the organization sponsors social events, lectures, and community services such as tutoring disadvantaged children.

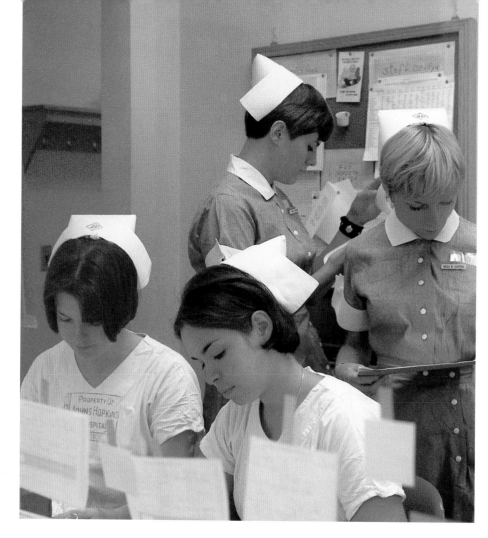

"Dr. Rich, who taught pathology, had a recitation session every Monday morning. He always started at the end of the alphabet, so Fred Zeigler could be assured of being the first to be asked a question. One of the first questions was, 'What is death?' None of the answers were acceptable; he would produce counterarguments showing that each was a stupid answer. He got to Carl Schultz, and Carl said, 'It's when you stop eating.'

Dr. Rich said, 'That can't be true. There are people with anorexia nervosa who don't eat for prolonged periods of time.'

And Carl Schultz said, 'Well, Dr. Rich, have you ever seen a dead person eat?' Dr. Rich was outraged and ended the session for the day."
RICHARD JAMES JOHNS, M.D.'48

Each year a fresh class of medical students begins anew the rigorous but rewarding process of learning the body's intricacies.

In November 1964 the Johns Hopkins swimming team worked out in the uncompleted pool of the Newton White Jr. Athletic Center, above. Coach Bill Klarner and his squad were optimistic that the pool would be finished in a few months. Another generation of swimmers conjured up its third consecutive NCAA Division III championship with a little sorcery in 1979 when Co-captains Dean Buchenauer and Mike DiCio tossed the names of all the competing teams into a giant hat and mumbled an incantation. David Trost's camera caught the magical flash just before a large sheet of paper emblazoned with a rabbit and JHU was pulled out of the hat.

"We went coed in the 1970–71 school year. Joyce Hogan was our first female coach. Squash and tennis were our first two women's sports. We then moved with basketball, and it was natural that we would move to lacrosse. Swimming was a natural; the coach who handled men's swimming handled women's swimming. Steve Muller said, 'Whatever the women want and will support as participants, we'll provide for them.'

We have had marvelous success with our women's teams because we've had some wonderful coaches. We've had championships in women's soccer, field hockey, basketball, swimming, and lacrosse. Janine Tucker's done a superb job as lacrosse coach. Her first four years we won three conference championships, and now we have moved to the Division I level in women's lacrosse and are more than holding our own." ROBERT SCOTT, B.A.'52

The same year that undergraduate women arrived on campus, the university abolished its requirement that freshmen take a physical education course. Developing women's sports took time, but by the turn of the twenty-first century, Hopkins fielded nine women's intercollegiate teams.

135

Brendan Schneck flew past Washington College's defense as he moved the ball downfield on March 25, 1981.

Fans clambered to every possible perch to see Hopkins clobber Maryland 19–13 in April 1978, left.

"Kelso Morrill stressed fundamentals. That was a hallmark of lacrosse under Father Bill Schmeisser, who played in 1906–07 and then helped coach all the way up through 1941. Kelso was a part of the Schmeisser tradition of emphasis on the little things. Hopkins always tried to play the smart game. Sometimes we didn't have the better athletes compared to some of our opponents, but we did try to pay attention to detail—positioning, helping your teammates, moving the ball properly, passing the ball where it can best be caught and handled. The emphasis on the little things really was important and a big part of our style of play. If you can get the team to prepare, to respect their opponent and be a little scared of whom they're playing, then they're working hard and concentrating.

When I was head coach, we had Sunday meetings that lasted about five hours. Wilson Fewster would give the coaches the scouting report and we'd decide how we were going to approach the game, who was going to play, different plays that we were going to use. Monday afternoon we'd have a light workout, then Wilson would present his report, challenging our guys and building up the opponent. He'd give all the straight facts, but he'd say, 'You're going to get killed. Those guys are so much faster.' He would heat up our players to where they just couldn't wait. Tuesday, Wednesday, Thursday, we had three hard-work days, made all of our preparations, scrimmaged hard. One of our second teams would set up the opponent's tendencies and plays so we'd get a chance to practice against some of the specifics. Friday we'd have a very light workout, finishing touches, go easy. And then Saturday we'd go hard." ROBERT SCOTT, B.A.'52

"Lacrosse was something that everybody seemed to be involved in, whether you'd never been to a lacrosse game till you got to Hopkins or you'd grown up with a lacrosse stick in your hand. Even people buried in their labs surfaced enough to know what the score was the next day."
HELEN BLUMBERG, B.A.'73

Coach Fred Smith gave a pep talk in the locker room in June 1951 at right. Smith had played on a string of championship lacrosse teams from 1947 to 1950 just before he was named head coach. The Blue Jays enjoyed another championship season in 1979 under Coach Henry Ciccarone. That year the game against the Terps was close, but the Jays won 13–12, below.

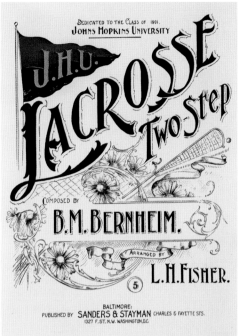

"Conrad Gebelein was the band leader. The band was always there during lacrosse games. When the team huddles up just inside the fence, they know that when they break for the sidelines, the band's going to start playing 'Dear Old Johnny Hopkins.' And they know after every goal the band's going to play 'To Win, to Win.'"
JEROME SCHNYDMAN, B.A.'67

Over the years Hopkins lacrosse has inspired several musical compositions. The Blue Jay mascot greeted young fans in 1983, above, while dedicated band members watched the game above left.

"I remember being so moved watching the Peabody students with the Soviet students. When the concert was over, the students all jumped up, waving pieces of their instruments, the violinists waving their bows and the drummers waving their sticks. They wanted to meet the students who played the same instrument.

The Soviet students had nothing—violinists without resin, horn players with only one mouthpiece. Yet because everyone made music at home, you could still buy virtually anything in sheet music, and it was cheap. When the Soviet students discovered that their American friends had been unable to get sheet music, they started taking them to a music store, and, oh, they were so excited. And there was much drinking of vodka. The connection that the kids made, to me, was really the high point." ELISE HANCOCK

The Peabody Symphony Orchestra journeyed to Moscow in 1987 and established new ties. Above, violinist Ann Palen spoke the language of music with a Soviet counterpart.

Far left, Laura Middleton observed the view from her dorm as Jennifer Ruzietti gazed at her new friend.

Scholars suddenly took up residence on the beach when dogwood blossoms and warm weather inspired a mass exodus from the Eisenhower Library.

"Johns Hopkins is probably a little more humane than back in my student days. Social life was never a big deal. Your social life was over in those row houses off the campus. If anything, it was the opposite of a party school. Bloody serious, but high intellectual adventure, rigorous standards, which I still admire enormously."
JOHN BARTH, B.A.'51, M.A.'52

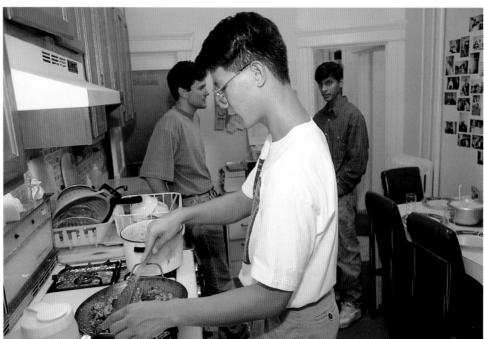

142

"Robert Hieronimus wanted to do a mural. We didn't have any money, but I said, 'All right. You can do something here.' Well, he started and he wouldn't stop. He did all of the upstairs area; he came on down the steps. He was very much into what they call symbology." CHESTER WICKWIRE

"The undergraduate lifestyle is better now that there's housing for more students. A lot of the social life at Homewood revolved around Charles Village. P.J.'s Pub and Charles Village Pub were the two places that people would hang out. They would broadcast sporting events. We would go over and watch college basketball games. On Monday nights they had all-you-can-eat chicken wings for four bucks.

There was a grocery store in Charles Village, Eddie's. A diner opened my last year of college, and that was big news. We used to make the trek over every once in a while and get chocolate malts, especially during exam time." KELLY GEBO, B.A.'91, M.D.'95

Gabrielle Bonne found a quiet place to study on the second floor of Levering Hall in 1991. Surrounding her was Robert Hieronimus's mural The Apocalypse, *which he painted in 1968.*

Upperclassmen usually settle into group apartments in the Charles Village neighborhood, far left. Local businesses provide groceries and other necessities and even an occasional summer concert on St. Paul Street, left.

143

Since 1909, summer sessions have attracted
part-time students pursuing both bachelor's
and master's degrees. Some of those who social-
ized in front of Shaffer Hall in 1974, above,
probably also enrolled in the Evening College
during the regular academic year.

Students at the School of Hygiene and Public
Health come from all over the world. These
1992 graduates and their families brought
an international ambience to the East
Baltimore campus.

"Our class at Hopkins was very local in character. Approximately half came either from Baltimore City College or Baltimore Polytechnic Institute, so that as freshmen we tended to know each other, which enabled us to have a great deal of cohesion right from the beginning. That certainly couldn't be true now that a typical class coming into Hopkins is from all over the world." WILLIAM BANKS, B.A.'29

"We expect you to be great. And we will work as hard as we can to make you great. I know of no place else where people work as hard to help each other. People who've never been here and don't know us think that this is a cutthroat place. They don't understand it's just the opposite. We have the opportunity to take from among the best, and we have among the best teachers to work with them. Great begets great begets great. You're expected to be great and you are. Everybody has every faith in you."
DR. CATHERINE DEANGELIS

Some of the most inventive students at Johns Hopkins are participants in the Center for Talented Youth. Professor Julian Stanley became fascinated by youngsters with exceptional talent in mathematics and established the center in 1979. Since then its programs have expanded to other campuses around the United States. The young scientists above conducted their experiments in 1983.

THE MORNING HAS DAWNED

Then, turning to the other side of the picture, when we see what admirable teachers have given instruction among us in medicine and surgery; what noble hospitals have been create what marvelous discoveries in surgeries have been made by our countrymen; what ingenio instruments they have contrived; what humane and skillful appliances they have provided on the battlefield; what admirable measures are in progress for the advancement of hygiene and the promotion of public health; when we see what success has attended recent efforts t reform the system of medical instruction; when we observe all this, we need not fear that t day is distant—we may rather rejoice that the morning has dawned which will see endowments for medical science as munificent as those now provided for any branch of learning, and schools as good as those which are now provided in any other land."

DANIEL COIT GILMAN, 1876

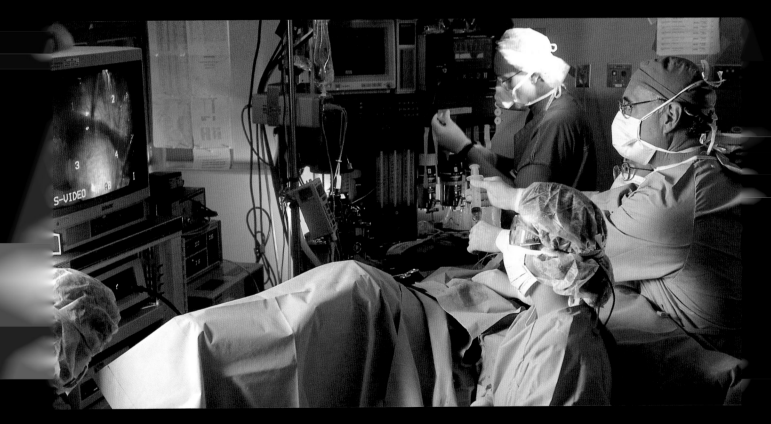

came for an interview. It's quite an imposing place. The buildings had the names of people with whom I was familiar—the Blalock Building, the Halsted Building. I saw all these pictures of incredible surgeons. I was quite impressed in terms of history, but also I was very favorably impressed with the substance. After spending a day and seeing the excellence of the training and the quality and the cordiality of the people, the only question in my mind was would they take me out of all these applications they get from around the

Shortly after the 1965 meal at far left, the faculty luncheon club in the Welch Library disbanded. Later conservation studies showed that emanations from the club's steam table had damaged Sargent's The Four Doctors, *especially the face of William Halsted*

The Harriet Lane Home for Invalid Children, far right above, opened in 1912. It featured large windows to provide natural light and ventilation. In 1940 the American Legion Auxiliary donated an Inclinator elevator for moving wheelchairs up a stairway, above. When the Harriet Lane Home was demolished in 1974, faculty and staff kept bricks as mementos.

"Harriet Lane is the name every pediatrician knows; it is still one of, if not *the* best pediatric training programs in the country. If you were a 'Harriet Laner,' you're always a Laner. Harriet Lane, a weathy widow, left a bequest to build a home for poor children. The whole idea was you'd find the best care and you'd give it to them, and it didn't matter if they could pay for it or not.

So Harriet Lane's name is sacred to every pediatrician who's ever stepped foot in here. By the time I was here, only the outpatient services were there. It was not air-conditioned; it was blistering in the summer. You were just sweating like crazy. I don't know how anybody learned anything. But it was wonderful. And when they tore it down, people were really upset.

The Harriet Lane name will never die. When I came back and started the primary care clinic, that clinic's known as the Harriet Lane Primary Care Clinic."
DR. CATHERINE DEANGELIS

"The model of the university where people come and sit and learn is going to be complemented by the professor who goes to the students. The student will sit at his desk at home and listen to the lecture that is given by a professor from his office. This is not the far-off future. It already happens." KISHIN MOORJANI

Closed-circuit television links such as the one below at the Kennedy Institute in April 1968 were a harbinger of today's distance learning. Now named the Kennedy Krieger Institute, the center began in 1937 as the Children's Rehabilitation Institute. It provides interdisciplinary services to children and adolescents with disorders of the brain.

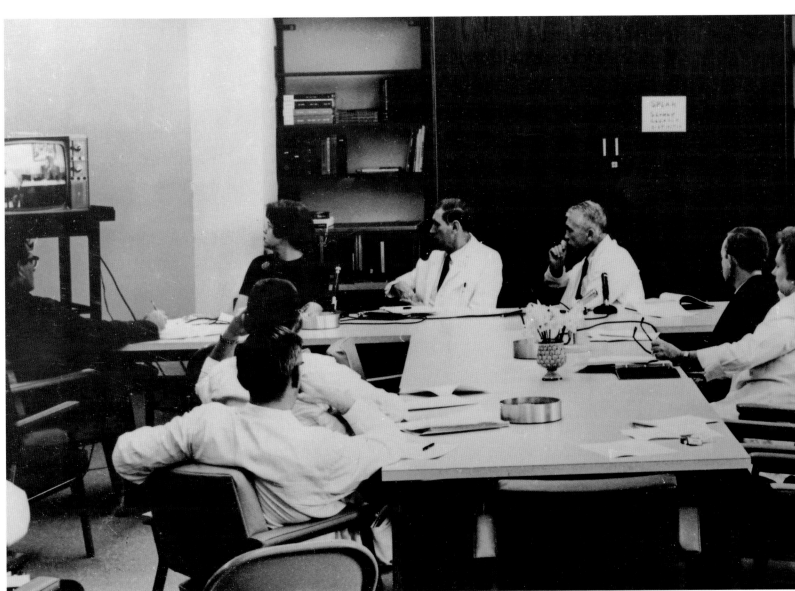

Dr. Victor McKusick and his colleagues at the Moore Clinic discovered and described many genetic anomalies, including those of people with congenital short stature. His Heritable Disorders of Connective Tissues, *first published in 1956, established medical genetics as a clinical specialty. A 1946 graduate of the School of Medicine, McKusick has received widespread recognition highlighted by the 1997 Lasker Award for special achievement in medical science.*

"Dr. J. Earle Moore ran a venereal disease clinic closely linked to the School of Hygiene and Public Health. About 1951 or '52, penicillin had come in and been a great success in the treatment of syphilis, and Dr. Moore realized that this wasn't as exciting an area as it had been. At the same time he realized that in his files he had a tremendous collection of patients with all sorts of chronic diseases, so he converted his clinic into a multifaceted chronic disease clinic.

In 1957, Dr. Harvey asked me to take over. We renamed it the Moore Clinic. The deal I made with Dr. Harvey was that I'd be permitted to develop a division of medical genetics within the Department of Medicine on the same footing as all the other divisions, having a triple role of teaching, research, and patient care. I argued that genetic disease is the ultimate in chronic disease since you have it all your life. You're born with it.

Medical genetics was institutionalized at Johns Hopkins July 1, 1957, and rather quickly the Moore Clinic became synonymous worldwide with medical genetics in general and medical genetics at Hopkins specifically. A very exciting group of fellows who trained in the Moore Clinic went on to populate programs elsewhere. In 1991 medical genetics became one of the certified boards." VICTOR MCKUSICK, M.D.'46

"Helen Taussig was a very driven person. The patient was everything. She had no sense of time when she was dealing with a patient. She'd just stick with it until it was done. She had a great knowledge of congenital heart disease and trained a lot of people around the world. She was a great internationalist, great social activist." DR. RICHARD ROSS

"I was very impressed every time I saw Helen Taussig. As an intern and a resident, it was exciting for me to come to Hopkins and see people that were legends, and to see them in the flesh. Harry Klinefelter was on the faculty. We all knew about Klinefelter syndrome, and there he was walking in the hallway right next to me. Incredible!"
DR. BENJAMIN CARSON

"People who come to Hopkins are an unusual group. They're very bright, very motivated, very hardworking. They're real accomplishers. People go away, but more often than not they end up coming back because it's an organization that is unique.

The School of Nursing hired a faculty member from the School of Public Health to teach our nutrition course. Someone asked about her husband; he was in his late seventies. She said he'd retired. 'Oh, I didn't realize that.'

She said, 'Well, it's not a great big difference. Now instead of coming in seven days a week, he only comes in six days a week.'

And I thought, 'Only at Hopkins.'" PROFESSOR STELLA SHIBER

In the early 1940s, Dr. Helen Taussig (above left with a patient and far above with younger colleague Dr. Catherine Neill) proposed a surgical procedure to correct a type of congenital heart malformation. After Dr. Alfred Blalock performed the first "blue baby" operation, their names were linked to this pioneering procedure, the Blalock-Taussig shunt.

Dr. Thomas Turner, above, was dean of the School of Medicine from 1957 to 1968. He then became archivist for the medical institutions and wrote Heritage of Excellence, a history covering the years 1914–1947.

151

On May 6, 1961, members and guests assembled for the annual Pithotomy Club show. Why the sign proclaimed 100TH PITHOTOMY is not clear since the club began in 1897 and the tradition of hosting a program to lampoon the faculty dated from 1914.

"The Pithotomy Club is unique to Hopkins. It was the top students. I don't necessarily mean academic-wise, but the most attractive group were in the Pithotomy Club. I was not a member, but I've been to many, many parties there. We drank a hell of a lot and ate a little. We worked very hard and didn't drink during the week, but weekends we frequently did." DR. THOMAS TURNER

"I was a very regular attendee and found the annual Pithotomy Club show very amusing, both as a faculty member and as a student. Many were very raunchy; the most clever weren't excessive. It was a marvelous satire on the members of the faculty. All the little idiosyncrasies of the professors would be imitated. Sometimes the professors would get very put out about it. Some refused to attend." VICTOR MCKUSICK, M.D.'46

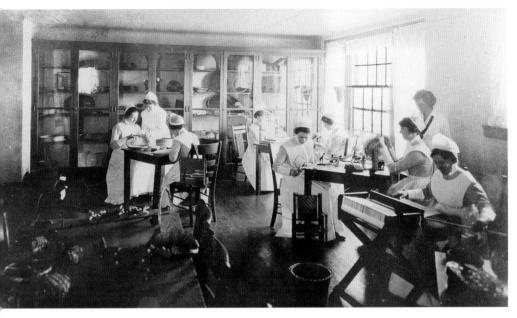

In a letter written in 1873, Johns Hopkins instructed his trustees "to establish, in connection with the hospital, a training school for female nurses. This provision will secure the services of women competent to care for the sick in the hospital wards, and will enable you to benefit the whole community by supplying it with a class of trained and experienced nurses." The School of Nursing opened with the hospital in 1889. These nurses were busy in the work area of the Phipps Psychiatric Clinic, which was completed in 1913.

In 1936 Dr. Edward Kelly explained the origins of an East Baltimore tradition: "During the spring of 1931 there was an epidemic of sweepstakes and lotteries among the house officers and nurses at the Hopkins, and fertile minds, which should have been occupied with abstruse medical problems, were pondering over ways and means of transferring loose cash from one pocket to another. The turtle derby, a sudden inspiration, came as a climax to the gambling season." In 1961, above and left, doctors and turtles performed to raise funds for charity.

153

"As soon as I finished the hospital diploma school, I went full time to college. I originally planned to go to Georgetown University. I wanted to take ancient history and English literature and classical music, and they wanted me to take advanced surgical nursing and community health nursing. I said, 'Oh, no, I've had those already. I went to Johns Hopkins. I worked at night alone in charge of Osler. I had a census tract in East Baltimore in the Eastern Health District.' When I think back on it, I laugh, because I thought I knew all I needed or wanted to know."
PROFESSOR MARTHA HILL, R.N.'64, B.S.N.'66, PH.D.'87

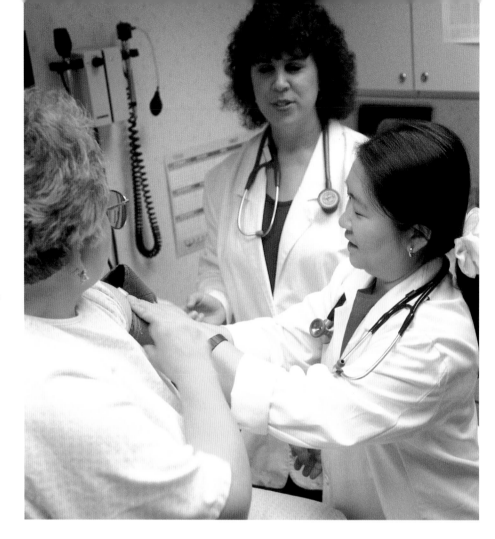

When The Johns Hopkins University School of Nursing opened as a new academic division in 1984, it welcomed students who considered learning to be a lifelong pursuit. Below, undergraduate Christiani Guerrero examines a newborn under the watchful eye of graduate student Sharon Rumber in the hospital nursery in February 2000.

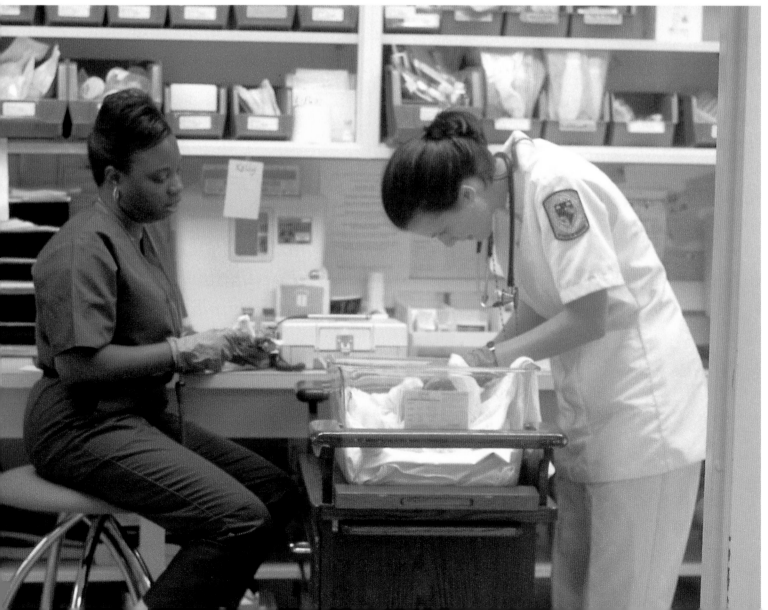

"As a medical student, there are two ways to approach nurses. Some feel, 'I'm the doctor and you're the nurse, and you need to listen to what I say.' Some medical students realize that nurses have far more experience than they'll ever have and listen to what they have to say.

I remember taking care of a patient with diabetes and being a little unsure of myself and the nurse saying to me, 'Kelly, you probably want to increase the insulin.' I thought to myself, 'She's been doing this for a lot longer than I have,' and I listened to her. She kept saying to me, 'You probably want to check their blood now.' 'You probably want to give them this now.' She knew exactly what I should be doing. By the next morning the patient was fine. I remember thinking to myself, 'She got me through that.'

We wouldn't be able to function without nurses. They take care of patients minute by minute, and we come by two times a day or night. Nurses are definitely your eyes and ears." KELLY GEBO, B.A.'91, M.D.'95

Far left, *nurse practioner and faculty member Janet Selway supervised a student as she examined a patient in 1998. The School of Nursing tied for fifth place in the 2000 ranking of graduate schools by* U.S. News and World Report, *and Dean Sue Donaldson affirmed, "Our goal is always to remain on the cutting edge of advances in the field of nursing and to set the standard in quality health care delivery."*

"The East Baltimore campus was originally fourteen acres. Buildings have been torn down and replaced by new buildings in existing space, but additional space has been acquired. The neighborhood was quite concerned that Hopkins was pushing them out; there was some bitterness. It was a white neighborhood around the hospital when I came, and that changed.

Broadway was once the boundary on the west side, but buildings came up on that side. The first one was Hampton House, a nurses' home built in 1932 and then expanded. Then, where a church had been, are the big outpatient center and the big new oncology research center. Back in the '60s there was a grocery store, and different shops, and some parking. Those structures have become different components of the Johns Hopkins institutions, some used by the university, some by the hospital. They built housing for house staff and now that's gone. There's a parking garage for the outpatient center back there, then the Cooley Center—a big gymnasium and swimming pool—named for Denton Cooley. On the Wolfe Street side, the School of Public Health was one building in the middle. They've added one, two, three wings onto it, and a fourth wing is going to be under construction soon." LOUISE CAVAGNARO

The horizon of the East Baltimore campus continues to evolve as some older buildings are razed to make way for newer, more modern facilities. The original building with its dramatic dome seems destined to survive since it was added to the National Register of Historic Buildings in 1976. At that time it was officially named to honor John Shaw Billings. Above, left to right, the Robert M. Heyssel Outpatient Center, Reed Hall, and Hampton House stand across Broadway.

Big People and Little People

KELLY GEBO, B.A. '91, M.D. '95

Interviewed on August 31, 1999

In the 1990s, students at the School of Medicine came from a variety of backgrounds. As always, they demonstrated an intense interest in becoming the best doctors possible.

First day of medical school, somebody asked a question about calcium channels. I had no idea what the question meant; I had no idea what the professor's answer was, and I realized everybody in that room was way smarter than me and I was just not going to get through. That was it. I called my parents and I said, "I'm going to try to get your tuition check back because we've made a huge mistake." They kept saying, "No, no, no, you can do it. You can do it."

Our first year courses were biochemistry, anatomy, physiology, and cell biology, and we used to go to class from nine until five. We got Wednesday afternoons off. I had never been in class for eight hours a day and then had to go home and study at night. It was just way beyond what I had ever anticipated.

Second year you get a lot more exposure to patients and you learn how diseases work and how they affect the body. That was just awesome. It was fun to see how heart attacks happen and cancer works and how you stop it, because you take pharmacology and learn how drugs work. You begin to interview patients. You put on your little white coat and you go into the hospital.

Then third and fourth year you learn about how to interact with people, how to put together their symptoms with diseases, and how to decide what you're going to do. You take eight weeks of each rotation—surgery, pediatrics, internal medicine, obstetrics—then you take four weeks each of psychiatry and neurology.

You have to decide what you're going to grow up to be. One of my professors said to me, "You know, Kelly, you have to decide between big people and little people and between medicine and surgery, and then everything else sort of falls into place." Trying to make those decisions was very difficult because everything was really exciting.

I really thought I was going to do pediatrics. I liked taking care of kids, but I became very emotionally involved with them. There was one kid in particular that I really got to like and the child died, and that was a very difficult experience for me. It was hard to distinguish where Kelly-the-doctor stopped and Kelly-the-friend started. Shortly thereafter, I took

care of a child who was abused. She was three months old. That was what crystallized for me that I couldn't do pediatrics. If adults were going to abuse their bodies, that was one thing, but for an adult to abuse a child, I just couldn't stomach that. And that single experience made me choose internal medicine.

At the end of second year, you were assigned a faculty member, and you worked with that person in their clinic one day a week. You got to know their patients pretty well because you saw them over the course of three years. As you got increasingly better at medicine, they gave you more and more responsibility.

My mentor was just magnificent with patients and magnificent at teaching and very interested in helping people improve their lives with medicines and lifestyle changes, but also he was awesome in helping me to understand how you communicate with people and how there's a lot of different treatments. Really what it comes down to is talking with people and helping them to understand what their disease is and how to treat it. And then the diseases you can't treat, you help patients come to terms with living with it and eventually dying with it.

My mentor and I e-mail each other almost every day. He has been very involved in my career ever since then, and I can call and say, "Hey, what do you think about this?" or "What would you do in this situation?" He helped me decide that internal medicine is what I wanted to do. A lot of my peers who were assigned to either a pediatrician or an internist ended up choosing the field of the person that they were assigned to because you get to know them so well and you really enjoy what they do.

Match Day changes the rest of your life. You pick a specialty and you apply to programs. You send in an application much like your medical school application with your transcript and essays and recommendations. The programs review them and then ask the best candidates to come for interviews. You probably have between three and eight interviews, depending on the program and the specialty. Then at the end of the interview season, there's a day where you go into the computer and enter the programs that you are interested in. The programs rank their candidates, and a computer mushes all this information together from all over the country.

Then on Match Day, you get together

ple, so there are definitely strong bonds. In college, everybody's taking different courses. In medical school, you all take the same thing. Every day you're together all day long. You know everybody's business about everything.

Hopkins has this trifold motto of research, teaching, and patient care. A lot of places are good at two of the three; we were expected to be professionals in all three. Patient care makes your research seem much more realistic, and it helps reinforce why you're looking at these questions. Research helps you learn more about people and diseases and why things happen and helps you to want to teach medical students, interns, and residents how to take care of patients. They all come together.

The people at Hopkins are the smartest people I've ever met. They are people who can be presented a case and tell you exactly what the patient has, even after that patient has been examined by a hundred people. It's based on their fund of knowledge. That's one thing I've really thrived on, learning so much from my colleagues and from the other people that I work with. My parents keep saying, "You've got to move away from Hopkins." And I can't ever imagine leaving because

The class of 1897 (right with some of their professors but without their one female peer, Mary S. Packard) was the first to graduate from the School of Medicine. Above, a pediatrician greeted a young patient in the old Harriet Lane Clinic.

for breakfast. The tension is so high you could cut it with a spoon. At twelve o'clock everybody goes into the lecture hall and gets an envelope. Some people open their envelope while they're standing in front of the dean; some people take it outside; some people let their spouse open it. There are a lot of tears shed and there's a lot of champagne flowing. There are a lot of people who are very happy with where they get, and there are a few people who aren't very happy. But ultimately it all works out.

The day before graduation, there's a skit about all the things that happened during medical school. We had somebody raise their hand and ask that question about calcium channels. Everybody realized that they had felt they were the dumbest person in the room and hadn't wanted to admit that to anybody else. Everybody I knew in medical school at

some point felt, "I'm never going to get through this. I'm never going to be able to do it." And we all did. There were three people who dropped out of my class in the first few weeks for various reasons, but everybody else graduated. Some people took a year off or some people did different things, but ultimately we all graduated.

You become very close to those peo-

it's so interesting and there are so many people who are so smart that you're constantly learning. Every day that's exciting for me—to learn new things.

Kelly Gebo is a fellow in the Department of Medicine at the School of Medicine and a recent M.P.H. graduate of the School of Public Health.

Helen Abbey (far above in 1995 with colleague Harvey Fischman), a highly esteemed professor of epidemiology, was honored with the first Golden Apple, the School of Public Health's annual teaching award. Drs. Phillip Sartwell and Paul Harper chatted with Professor Rowland Rider in 1969 (far above right). The school's library is named for chronic disease epidemiologist Abraham Lilienfeld.

"The School of Hygiene and Public Health has grown enormously. We bought up all the houses down Monument Street and we used those. When the hospital opened up a new building, they found that they really didn't need Hampton House, so I struck a deal for the School of Public Health to take that over. Every year was a struggle to find more space. We built laboratories, and by the time we finished them there were new research grants in and they were fully occupied the minute we moved in."
D. A. HENDERSON, M.P.H.'60

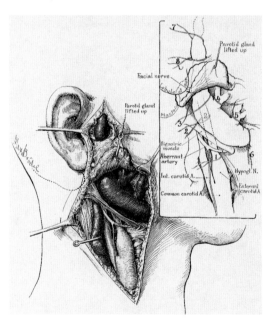

Johns Hopkins gained a gifted artist when Max Brödel (far above left in his lab and right in his studio in 1917) arrived in 1894. In 1911 Brödel became the first director of the Department of Art as Applied to Medicine, which has trained generations of medical illustrators. Graduate Timothy Hengst, left, returned to join the faculty from 1977 to 1986. Above is a drawing from the Brödel Archives.

159

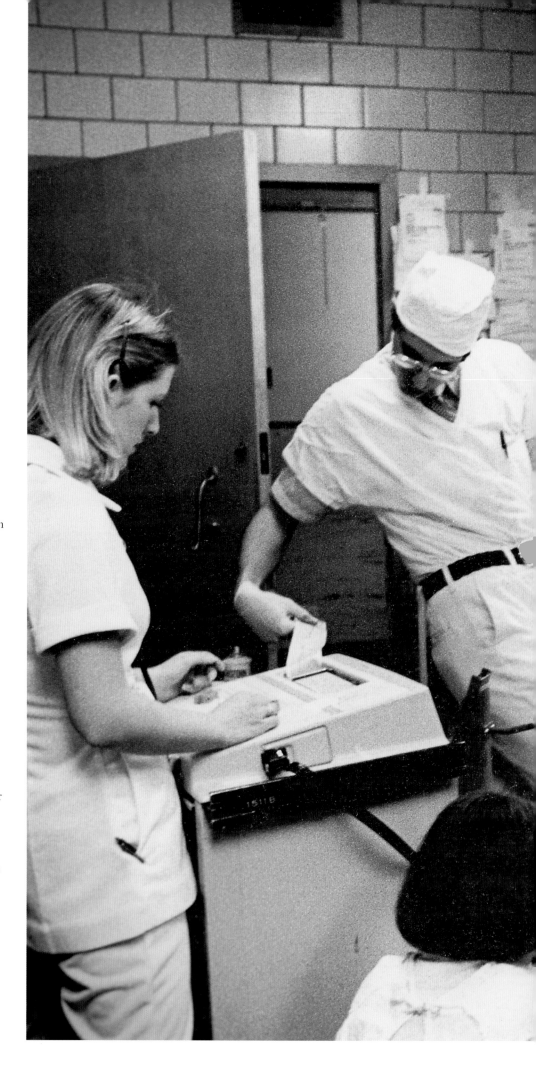

"Emergency medicine, almost by definition, is a very broad field. You have to be
able to handle the child with asthma, the
patient coming in with diabetic ketoaci-
dosis, the patient with the foreign object
in their ear, the patient with a heart
attack, the patient with an eye infection,
a patient with cocaine poisoning or heroin
overdose. You see everything, little kids,
gynecological problems with women—
you have to be able to deliver babies—
gunshot wounds, internal medicine
problems, or a patient choking because
of an asthmatic crisis due to allergic
exposure." ERIC NOJI, M.P.H.'87

"The accident room was a fabulous
experience. You'd see fifty patients over
a twenty-four-hour period, but you'd
see four or five really unusual, serious
problems that required your attention
to unravel them and to bring about treatment. I think disease has changed a lot.
You used to see people with typhoid fever
in the summer come up from the Eastern
Shore of Maryland. A current-day intern
wouldn't know what you were talking
about. Tuberculosis was very common.
Infectious diseases were big because it was
very early in the antibiotic era; penicillin
was not even a decade old when I was an
intern, and it was in very short supply."
DR. RICHARD ROSS

Donald Coffey, Drew Pardoll, and Bert Vogelstein, right, *reviewed notes on their theory that the cell's system of making DNA might be different from what had been visualized previously. Coffey recruited both Pardoll and Vogelstein to work with him on cancer research. Richard Johns,* below, *directed Hopkins bio-medical engineering from its inception.*

"Don Coffey is the mentor's mentor at Johns Hopkins. He spends a huge amount of time with young people, just trying to make sure they're on the right track. His door is always open to virtually anyone at Hopkins but certainly to people that he's helped recruit or participated in training. He's full of wisdom and always good to talk to. A lot of people, including me, have taken him up on his generosity frequently over the years."
BERT VOGELSTEIN, M.D.'74

"Bert Vogelstein is really big-time good. This kid can walk on water. I can walk on water, but it has to be frozen. This kid is a water walker. He's one of the the best scientists in the world. I did nothing except get him here and get out of his way. That's my contribution."
PROFESSOR DONALD COFFEY, PH.D.'64

"The provost put out a report looking at salaries of women across the university, and the report made the School of Medicine look like an abomination. The dean was beside himself. Dean Ross asked me, 'What do you think?'

I said, 'I think the bottom line is probably pretty accurate. I'm sure that women are not paid the same as men. I'm sure they're not being promoted at the same rate. I'm sure there's not the same mentoring. But this isn't the way to show it.'

So I did a study and it blew everybody's mind. Allowing for rank and years and eliminating all the department chairs, women weren't being paid the same, weren't being promoted at the same rate, weren't being mentored. All I did was present data. Well, the department chairs went bonkers, because nobody wanted to be seen as unfair. These are truly great people and they didn't like it.

I said to the dean before I started, 'Look, if we find out that there are inequities in salaries, it's going to cost you money because the departments aren't going to be able to foot the bill.'

He said, 'Okay, I'm ready for it.' And God love him, he kept his word.

It took us two years. For the last seven years, there's been salary equity. Women are being promoted. In the 106-year history, two-thirds of all the women professors have been promoted in the ten years since we started this initiative."

DR. CATHERINE DEANGELIS

Former medical dean Richard Ross (for whom the Ross Medical Research Building, far above, was named) and retired hospital president Russell Nelson conversed in 1977.

163

"The hospital trustees felt that they were the businessmen and that the School of Medicine faculty were academics who didn't understand anything about business. I went head to head with these trustees and said 'Hogwash.' Johns Hopkins medicine has nothing to do with the bricks and mortar of the hospital, it has to do with the quality of the faculty. That faculty is research, teaching, and clinical. The chairmen of those departments were the chiefs over on the hospital side.

The trustees started to understand. They knew that the marketplace no longer allowed for the luxury of divided governance. Finally we came up with a configuration where the dean of the School of Medicine became the CEO of Johns Hopkins Medicine. Now the head of the hospital reports to that CEO. So for the first time in Hopkins' history, we clarified the role of the School of Medicine and the hospital.

It's working like a charm, and that's why Hopkins medicine is absolutely thriving. The right people are making decisions, and the CEO of Johns Hopkins Medicine reports to the president of the university. We're the first health system in the country to really pull this all together. This is one of our crowning achievements." MORRIS W. OFFIT, B.A. '57

"Virtually everyone who spends time here develops an uncommon affection for the place. Perhaps this is due to our connection with Hopkins' illustrious history. My hypothesis is that it's due to a peculiar virus, call it JHV, that gets into the chromosomes and there expresses its genes for the rest of one's life. In some cases, myself included, it mysteriously gets into the germ line and affects future generations. Unlike other viruses of its type, the sting of JHV is no more painful than that of a tiny arrow. However, it may loosen purse strings, and on appropriate occasions, it may cause those afflicted to hear the voice of Osler or Halsted or Welch or Kelly or Brödel or McKusick whispering in a friendly voice, 'Now don't you screw up, hon!'" DR. DANIEL NATHANS

As expansion continues in East Baltimore, the Billings Building and its dramatic dome remain the predominant icons for the Johns Hopkins Medical Institutions.

Research abounds at Johns Hopkins, but rarely do colleagues have the pleasure of celebrating a Nobel Prize. In 1978 Dan Nathans (at left above) shared his joy with Paul McHugh.

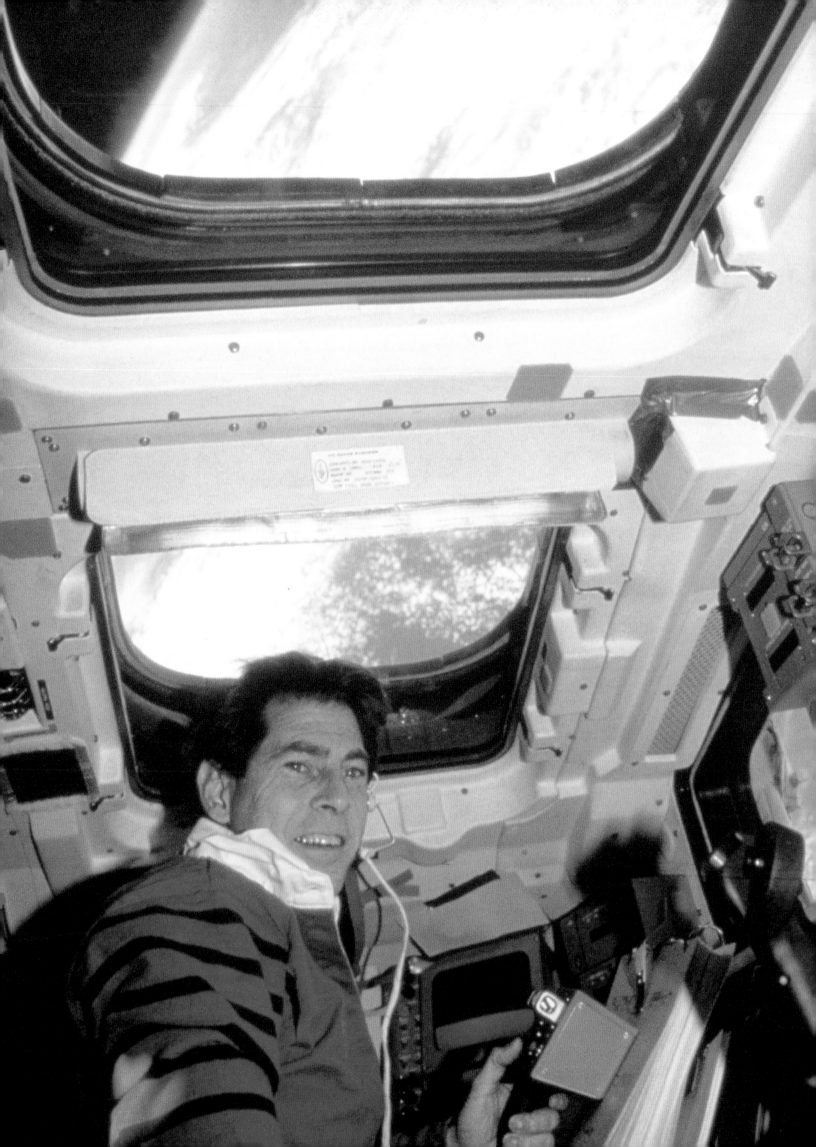

A GOOD SERVICE

At present the heads of all the governmental surveys acknowledge the difficulty of finding men enough, qualified enough, to carry forward efficiently such work in all its manifold departments, astronomical, geodetical, topographical, meteorological, geological, zoological, botanical, economical. If our University can provide instructions in these departments of physical research, looking forward to the future developments, not only of Maryland and the Atlantic seaboard, but also of the entire land, it will do a good service."

DANIEL COIT GILMAN, 1876

We started tutoring in the Maryland penitentiary. Once we got going, we tried to involve students in as many kinds of meaningful experiences in the city as we could, so we were not only tutoring, we were also working in hospitals; we were working in mental hospitals. We were working with people on parole, on probation, with juvenile delinquents.

Tutoring was not as sophisticated or as well-developed as it became. It was a shotgun kind of thing at first. On a Saturday we might have as many as four hundred tutors going down into the city.

At a later time, we had students trained to go into churches in the suburbs and talk about problems in the city. We had such a tremendous group of students who wanted to do something. Students had to do a lot of things that you normally might have staff do, and it helped them to grow up. A lot of them now are with the Office of Public Defender. Some of them are judges. Some head up the Center for Poverty Solutions and Baltimore Neighborhoods, Inc." CHESTER WICKWIRE

Johns Hopkins' first astronaut, astrophysicist Sam Durrance, operated the Hopkins Ultraviolet Telescope during missions in 1990, far left, and 1995. Monitored by a team of Hopkins scientists and engineers at NASA's Space Flight Center, the HUT made observations that significantly advanced scientific knowledge of distant astronomical objects. Above, a Hopkins student tutored a youth with soaring aspirations.

167

"Three or four hundred students volunteer on various committees for Spring Fair. It's a not-for-profit activity. Soliciting craftspeople to participate, selling ads in the book, contacting the set-up people—the kids do all that. The campus turns into a fairground. It's an opportunity for students to let loose, to relax. And it's an opportunity for the community to see a different face of Hopkins—and great community relations, inviting all these people on campus. High school students come on campus and think about coming here, seeing what a neat place it is. Spring Fair serves many purposes."
JEROME SCHNYDMAN, B.A.'67

"I remember being a freshman, not really knowing what to expect. Thursday before Spring Fair, trucks just started pulling up. Overnight there was this circus-like atmosphere with games and rides and food. It was a fun thing that definitely broke up the monotony of course work. It was something to look forward to, which made me want to participate.

It's a tradition now: my roommates come back not for Homecoming but for Spring Fair. It's something that we did as roommates, so we look forward to it every year."
KELLY GEBO, B.A.'91, M.D.'95

In 1972 a group of students hoped that inviting the neighbors in would be a terrific way to improve Hopkins' rapport with the wider community. They held a festival called 3400 on Stage (poster far above) and more than five thousand visitors came to browse exhibits, hear lectures and music, and watch movies. By 1974, above, hundreds of children came with school groups. Amusement rides, far above, provided thrills. The event caught on as an annual tradition known as Spring Fair with themes like 1987's Safari, far left.

Undergraduate athletic teams have joined Johns Hopkins' international efforts numerous times. In 1928 in Amsterdam (right) and again in 1932 in Los Angeles, Hopkins lacrosse players represented the United States in demonstration games at the Olympics when the sport was being considered for inclusion in future games. Subsequent lacrosse teams competed in England and Japan.

Twenty-eight members of the 1986 baseball team became sports ambassadors when Professor Wayne Smith of the School of Advanced International Studies arranged a week-long excursion to Cuba. Two years later the Blue Jays welcomed a team of Russian players to Homewood Field, below.

"Hopkins has this ethos that commands loyalty and reverence. You don't just see it in the faculty; you see it everywhere. In any successful organization there has to be loyalty to the institution. Working at the Hopkins Medical Institutions has never just been a job to most people, and that is what makes it successful." DR. RICHARD ROSS

Since its inception in 1927, the Women's Board of The Johns Hopkins Hospital has enhanced the quality of life for patients and staff through its volunteer service and donations from money-making enterprises such as shops, eating places, and special projects. Above, Women's Board volunteers served lunch at the Corridor Café in 1954.

Pediatric nurses gathered their patients (many of them clutching toys) for a group portrait on Christmas Day 1900, above. When the Harriet Lane Home opened in 1912, it welcomed children of all races.

In 1894 a new facility "exclusively for colored people" opened with amenities similar to those in the white public wards. True integration at the hospital began in the 1950s and came gradually to various departments.

"I took over the Marburg Building in the 1950s. Twenty-six dollars a day was the most expensive room I had, and it wasn't paying our cost. They had increased from ten dollars a day not too long before I came. We had a lot of patients who paid nothing. Dr. Nelson got the State of Maryland to pay some money to Johns Hopkins Hospital. We were taking care of more indigent patients than the University of Maryland, which was state supported, more than the Baltimore City Hospitals, which were city supported. Endowment funds didn't begin to support all the free care that we were giving." LOUISE CAVAGNARO

"When I came to Johns Hopkins in 1927, I spent half a day in the clinics and the other half doing research in the laboratories. Full-time faculty, a relatively small group, were paid a salary; their income was not at all from patients. Then we had another large group of part-time faculty who received little or no salary but were an integral part.

In the summer many of the faculty took off for Maine. In those periods I would go on the wards as a house officer. There would be twenty to thirty patients lined up on each side of the ward, the sickest being closer to the nurses' desk in the middle. As they recovered a bit, they were moved farther down. These patients were looked after by the residents." DR. THOMAS TURNER

"Lottie Cole, a black woman who's a personal friend, said to me, 'My dad used to tell me that he couldn't enter the front door of the hospital. I told him that was not true, but what people perceive and what's true can be quite different.' In the old days, free care was provided in the dispensary building, the Carnegie Building, on Monument Street. So if black patients came in there because they weren't feeling well and then the doctor decided they had to be admitted, they were admitted from there." LOUISE CAVAGNARO

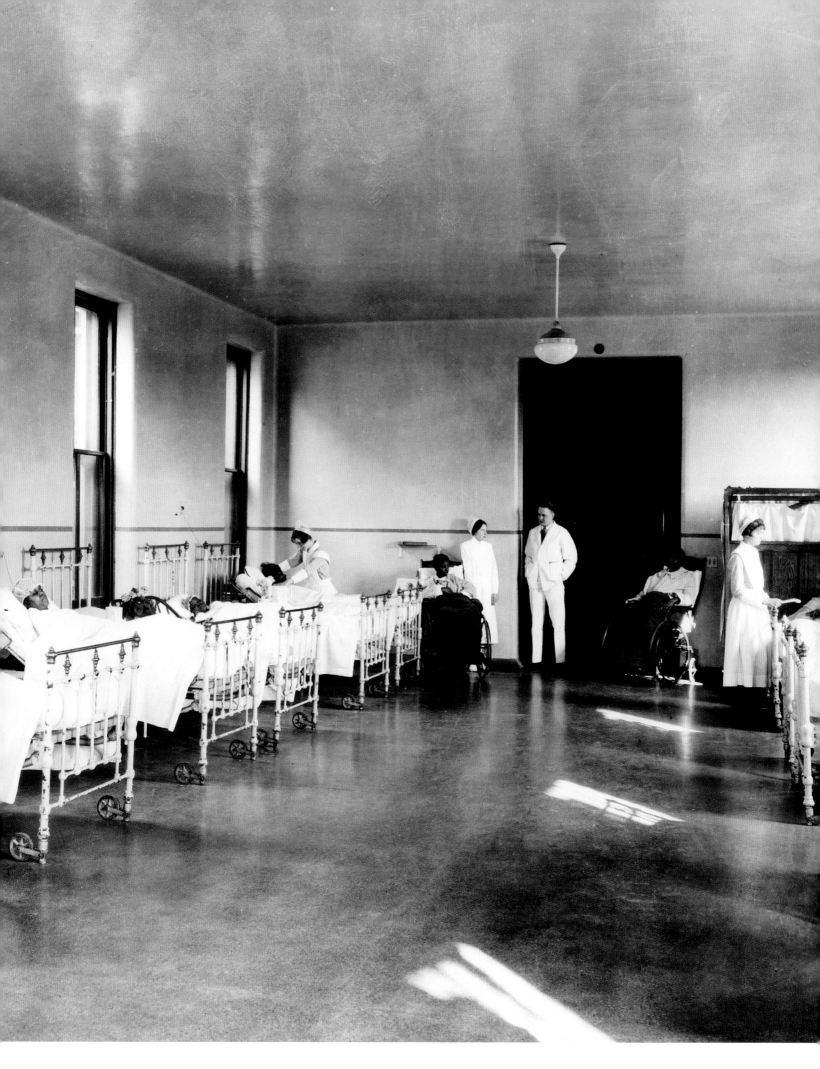

"I heard about the attack on Pearl Harbor. The campus was all upset; people were really frightened. Some of us were infuriated. I said, 'You know, it's going to be awfully difficult for me to settle down and be a student after this.' So I went down and enlisted."
WILBERT "BILL" LOCKLIN, B.S. '57

Twenty-three Hopkins men died in World War I, including six of the doctors and medical students who served (with Hopkins nurses) at Base Hospital 18 in France at left. On October 16, 1916, Johns Hopkins established the first Reserve Officers Training Corps in the United States. ROTC Company D marched on May 23, 1938, below, in front of Gilman Hall toward an uncertain future.

Two Hopkins units participated in World War II. The 18th General Hospital was based first in New Zealand, then went to Fiji and the India-Burma theater. The 118th General Hospital was based first in Sydney, Australia, at the Royal Prince Albert Hospital (where there is still a walk called the Johns Hopkins Parade). The 118th then moved into New Guinea (where doctors and nurses waited on a landing ship transport as a gangplank was positioned, above) and eventually to the Philippines.

Each hospital unit accommodated a patient
population of five hundred. Medical personnel
in the 118th unit cared for more than forty
thousand casualties. Occasionally there was
respite time; nurses gathered for a group
portrait that illustrated their exotic setting,
at far left. When Eleanor Roosevelt spoke
at Hampton House in 1945, at left, she had
just returned from the South Pacific and was
able to report to Hopkins nurses on the welfare
of their peers.

"Lynn Poole had *The Johns Hopkins Science Review* on television. People knew Johns Hopkins because of the *Science Review*, because it was all over the country and it was a great thing."
WILBERT "BILL" LOCKLIN, B.S.'57

April 11, 1954

Gentlemen:

    We enjoy all your television programs, we never miss any of them.

    We would like to see more on the subject of Atomic Energy for Peacetime Use.

Mr. & Mrs. Joseph Kiefer
102-21 213 St.
Queens Village, 9
New York

3-31-54

Dear Sir:

I have just watched your production on "the heart." I enjoyed it very much and believe what you are doing is of great benefit to mankind.

Thank you for the opportunity of witnessing such progress.

Yours truly,
June Gunderson
924-83 Street
Brooklyn 21, N.Y.

"Steve Muller thought that the *Johns Hopkins Magazine* was just great. One of his professors, when Steve was a graduate student, used to come up the stairs waving the magazine and saying that Johns Hopkins was the only university that thought enough of its alumni to send them a really good magazine. Steve never forgot that. He wanted a magazine in that tradition.

Steve said that he did not want an editor who stayed in her office, that when he was around on the campus, he wanted to see me talking to people, because he wanted the magazine to reflect the place. The role of the magazine was to hold up a mirror to the institution, to the people in it. It was aimed at the alumni, but the idea was to say, 'This is who we are. This is what you are a part of.'" ELISE HANCOCK

On May 7, 2000, five editors of the award-winning Johns Hopkins Magazine *gathered at Evergreen House to celebrate its fiftieth anniversary. Each held an issue emblematic of his or her era. Left to right: Ron Wolk, founding editor Corbin Gwaltney, current editor Sue DePasquale, Elise Hancock, and Bob Armbruster. Students began publishing the* News-Letter *in 1897 as a literary magazine; it had evolved into a newspaper by 1910. Over the years other publications, such as the* Standard, *left, have emerged, but none has lasted as real competition.*

The Johns Hopkins Science Review *was the first network television show ever produced by a university. Fans wrote appreciatively (far left above) to Public Relations Director Lynn Poole about the valuable information conveyed by the program, which aired from 1948 until 1955. Students began operating WJHU (far left c.1960) as an AM radio station in 1955. WJHU-FM went on the air in 1979; the university converted it to a professional, National Public Radio member station in 1985.*

As plans were being finalized for the Hopkins-Nanjing Center, President Steven Muller met with officials at Nanjing University, right. The center opened in 1986 and became a branch of the School of Advanced International Studies where U.S. and other international scholars could live and study with Chinese counterparts. Its fifty-thousand-volume library is the only open-stack library in China.

Before he was president of the United States, Woodrow Wilson (who earned his Ph.D. in 1886) served as president of the Johns Hopkins Alumni Association in 1889–90. At the close of World War I, President Wilson sent future Hopkins president Isaiah Bowman to France as his chief territorial advisor.

"Abel Wolman was head of the School of Hygiene and Public Health's Department of Environmental Health Sciences at the same time he had a position at Homewood and a career with the city. Abel was such an extraordinary person: encyclopedic knowledge of the field, highly respected, innovative, creative. So the School of Public Health claims ownership of him just as much as Homewood does, and he's somebody we all appreciate.

The design and establishment of water supplies was certainly his baby, which is some contribution to make. He was so broadly knowledgeable on the whole issue of both water and sewage, the importance of these to cities. As an engineer, he brought to public health a concern for the environment, whether it's air or water. He played a major role in advancing the science of the subject." D. A. HENDERSON, M.P.H.'60

"I consider Abel Wolman the archetype of Gilman's civic engineer. Civic engineering is a commitment to the idea that the engineer has a larger social responsibility than merely to his employer or his profession." PROFESSOR STUART W. "BILL" LESLIE

"The Nanjing Center started with a conversation the then-provost and the then-dean of SAIS and I had during one of our visits to the Bologna Center. I freewheelingly said, 'You know, we really ought to have a counterpart of this in Asia.' The dean of SAIS at the time was George Packard. He said, 'Well, probably in Japan.' And Dick Longaker said, 'Well, a lot of baggage in Japan. Maybe Hong Kong, maybe Singapore.' And we got to wherever we were having dinner and talked about something else.

There was a professor on the faculty, Chih-Yung Chien, and I learned from him that the then-president of Nanjing University was coming to the U.S. Would we be interested in having him at Hopkins? Yaming Kuang came, with his entourage, and I took the opportunity to have a conversation with him about collaboration with an American university for a joint center of Chinese and American studies. The Chinese would study in English with American professors, the Americans in Chinese with Chinese professors. He was very interested and encouraged me to pursue this. I think it's a hell of a good idea, and it's the kind of thing Hopkins can do because it's not huge and it's not flashy and it doesn't make a lot of headlines, but it continues to train Americans who really do understand China and Chinese who understand the United States." STEVEN MULLER

In 1986, far above*, Abel Wolman (with Mayor William Donald Schaefer at his side) held a proclamation declaring that the City of Baltimore had named its municipal building in his honor.*

Paul Nitze (on right, for whom the School of Advanced International Studies is named) welcomed Secretary of Labor Robert Reich to SAIS in 1994 as Dean Paul Wolfowitz watched.

181

The School of Continuing Studies developed the Police Executive Leadership Program in 1994, the first in the nation. Participants learned new ways to solve problems, plan strategically, foster creativity and trust, and establish and maintain integrity in their departments. In 1996 PELP joined a consortium of the most highly regarded law enforcement programs in the country. At right, adjunct professor Steve Vicchio (a professor of philosophy at the College of Notre Dame) lectured to officers representing numerous departments in the Baltimore-Washington area.

When the division modified its name in 1999 to become the School of Professional Studies in Business and Education, the change reflected a concentration on innovative courses in several professions as well as a renewed commitment to serving teachers at all stages of their careers.

"Stan Gabor was a visionary. He really dispelled the perception that you have to be a certain kind of person to attend Hopkins. He created the Police Executive Leadership Program, the Business of Medicine—giving business certificates to doctors to help them in their practices and to understand how health care is changing—and the program with teachers. Baltimore City's educational system is certainly in dire need of better teacher training. All these programs come through the School of Professional Studies in Business and Education because the other schools at Hopkins really don't have a place for that."
HELEN HOLTON, M.S.'95

"People from Peabody have insinuated themselves into the fabric of our lives. It's hardly possible to visit a school, a church, or a synagogue in Baltimore that doesn't have a Peabody musician in it, or several Peabody musicians. You can drive up Charles Street and tick off the organists and choir directors and church musicians who attended Peabody, who are currently on the Peabody faculty. It's hard to go to a symphony concert without running into Peabody people—Atlanta, National Symphony, New York Philharmonic, Boston, Berlin, they're everywhere. Obviously somebody's been doing something right for a very long time." ELIZABETH SCHAAF

Gerhard Samuels, music director of the Cincinnati Chamber Orchestra, led a rehearsal in North (later Griswold) Hall in 1982. Year after year audiences have thrilled to superior performances by Peabody students and visiting virtuosos.

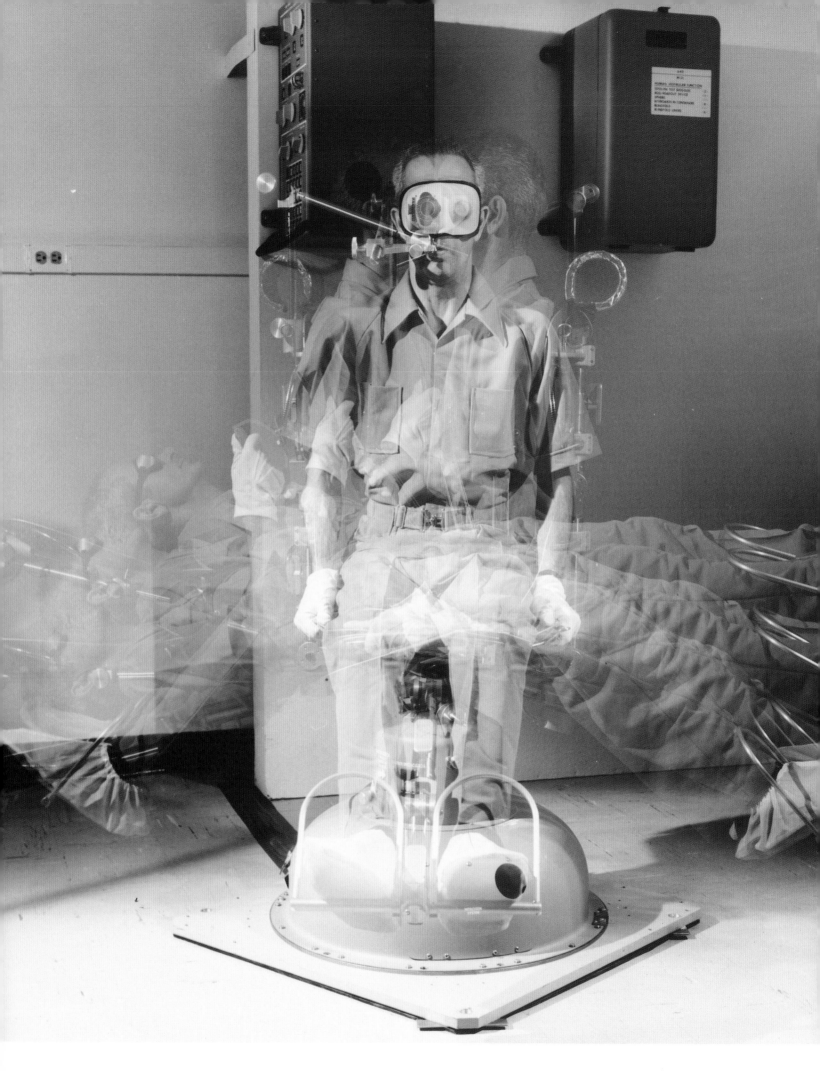

The Applied Physics Laboratory has helped solve some of the technological and engineering challenges posed by space travel. The chair being demonstrated, at far left, in 1971 was designed to increase stability during flights to the moon. Closer to home, starting in 1970, APL collaborated with the School of Public Health to investigate the causes, prevention, and control of unwanted fires, below. Studies revealed that most victims die from inhaling carbon monoxide rather than from burns. Promoting occupational health was the specialty of Anna Baetjer (relaxing after lunch, at left, with colleagues Roger Herriott, Paul Lemkau, and D. A. Henderson). Baetjer was a member of the public-health faculty for sixty years.

For the Good of the Country

ALEXANDER KOSSIAKOFF, PH.D.'38

Interviewed on March 14, 2000

James Van Allen (center of group) was a member of the team that organized the Applied Physics Laboratory in 1942. His rugged vacuum tube solved the last hurdle in the development of the proximity fuze. He later discovered the Van Allen radiation belt.

When the Applied Physics Laboratory started in 1942, Merle Tuve, the director, was a top physicist, and people like James Van Allen were physicists, as were many of the leaders in defense research in World War II. So it was natural for them to call this applied physics. For developing the proximity fuze, APL's first wartime task, it was lucky that they didn't understand engineering very well because they would never have attempted to build a little radio in the nose of an artillery shell accelerated at twenty thousand times the force of gravity. It was an incredibly difficult task, but they didn't know how hard it was going to be. They had a lot of faith in themselves, and it worked.

The laboratory was organized under the sponsorship of the Office of Scientific Research and Development. Its head, Vannevar Bush, was an engineer who was recruited by Franklin Roosevelt to organize universities and other laboratories to do research for the war effort. They set up laboratories, including APL, the Radiation Laboratory at MIT, laboratories at Cal Tech, Harvard, Columbia, Cornell, along with the Manhattan Project. Johns Hopkins was persuaded, I guess by Vannevar Bush, to undertake the management of a research effort that already had been started by the Department of Terrestrial Magnetism, under Merle Tuve, and become one of the universities that sponsored large-scale research for the government.

Luke Hopkins, a member of the Hopkins board of trustees, undertook to be personally responsible for the operation of APL on behalf of the university. He and Merle Tuve were sort of co-directors of the laboratory. Merle Tuve was the technical director, and Luke Hopkins ran the administration.

APL originally was housed in a made-over garage in the center of Silver Spring. Two miles north of APL, the laboratory built some structures where they simulated the combustion of ramjets—a noisy operation. As Silver Spring grew, the countryside filled with houses. The residents complained bitterly that there was too much disturbance. Actually, it was that laboratory whose noise eventually forced APL to move out of town into the country to Howard County.

When the war ended, most defense laboratories led by universities disbanded. Because the guided missile program was just getting started and the navy badly needed it, the navy asked Johns Hopkins to continue to be responsible for APL, and Hopkins agreed. Right after the war, the laboratory employed probably about eight hundred people, and the payroll was comparable to the total payroll of the university.

After World War I the country had turned against defense. The cold war following World War II changed public attitudes very strongly, so it became obvious that defense was going to be of national importance. Hopkins was from its beginning very public service oriented; the trustees felt that APL was a form of public service that they could support. In 1948, APL was designated a permanent division of the university, very much on a par with the Schools of Medicine, Public Health, Arts and Sciences, and Engineering. On the whole, the relationship has worked remarkably well.

I came to APL right after the war was over, along with my colleagues Ralph Gibson, Richard B. Kershner, and Frank T. McClure, who also were doing rocket work in the '40s. We arrived in the spring of 1946. The laboratory in 1945 had started a large program for developing guided missiles to defend naval ships against air attack. These guided missiles had to be supersonic, a lot faster than their targets. To reach supersonic speed, they had to be launched by a rocket booster. The physicists at APL knew nothing about rockets, so the four of us came as a rocket group, a so-called launching group, actually.

Our initial task was not to develop rockets ourselves, but to get places like Allegheny Ballistics Laboratory and Aerojet to develop booster rockets. The client was the United States Navy. Since proximity fuzes first went into production, the laboratory had been contracting with the navy directly rather than with the Office of Scientific Research and Development. The technical direction of the contracts between the navy and APL was vested in Johns Hopkins and APL, which gave the university and the laboratory the authority to coordinate the program and direct the technical work without at the same time having to

Employees at APL undertake assignments from clients as varied as the U.S. Navy, NASA, and doctors at the School of Medicine searching for technological solutions to medical problems. Cramped quarters, above in 1986, often yielded amazing accomplishments.

administer the financial end. That convenient pattern lasted until the '60s.

In the 1960s, many universities went through a very traumatic period. Across the country there was a strong student and, to some extent, public reaction against the Vietnam War and everything connected with warfare. All the universities that had anything to do with defense research were beset by student and faculty protests. At Hopkins, there was an activist group called the Committee for the Conversion of APL. The idea was: Here was this marvelous facility. Wouldn't it be nice if they converted their work from defense research to research for public good?

Fortunately, the university trustees were always close to APL. Right from the very beginning, the university set up a special trustees committee on the Applied Physics Laboratory. This gave the trustees a much closer look at what we were doing and who was sponsoring us. That connection was extremely important because it enabled the university to know what they had at APL and the degree to which they needed to support it. So there was really no severe threat, but in 1968 the staff of the laboratory asked for a confirmation of support that resulted in a formal mission statement signed by the trustees, and that's now the cornerstone of the relationship.

There's also a trust agreement between the government and the university that sets up a mechanism that would go into operation if the government no longer had any need for the laboratory or the university wanted to disassociate itself from the laboratory. When the contract was established with the navy, it was not a typical university contract but one based

on the cost principles of industrial contracts in which the contractor can earn a fee. Commercial contracts always have a fee associated with them. The purpose was to accumulate a stabilization and contingency fund where, if the government no longer needed the place, there would be enough funds to make a severance package for the staff. That enabled the laboratory and the university to acquire the land out in Howard County, to build permanent buildings, and to furnish them with regular facilities owned by the university but held in trust. If the government says, "We no longer require the services of the laboratory," it all reverts to the university.

The main mission of the lab since its beginning has been the defense mission, so ninety-five-plus percent of what we have ever done, including spacecraft, has been to that end. I claim that the GPS, the Global Positioning System, was built on the foundation of the Transit navigation system that the laboratory invented and built for the navy. Prior to the Transit, nobody thought that spacecraft could help position the location of somebody on the surface of the Earth. That was a totally novel idea back then in 1957. Astronomers ridiculed the thought.

When the Russians put up Sputnik, a couple of APL scientists decided that it would be fun to listen to the beep that it was emitting, so they set up a receiver with a recorder. As the satellite passed overhead, they heard the Doppler effect. When the satellite was approaching, the beep had a high pitch, and as it was receding, it dropped to a low pitch, so it made an S-curve on the plot. They said, "I wonder what we could learn by studying the

exact shape of that curve. If we assume that it was emitting a constant frequency, could we tell the orbit that the satellite was traveling in?" They went into the calculation and came up with an orbit about as good as the astronomers could do.

Frank McClure, who was the chairman of the APL research center and consultant to the strategic submarine system for the navy, realized this might be the solution to finding out where a submarine was on the surface of the Earth. If you knew exactly where the satellite was at all times and you recorded the beep, perhaps you could figure out exactly where the submarine was from the shape of that curve, just turning the whole thing inside out. The lab proposed to the navy and to the Advanced Research Projects Agency that "This could be a solution to the navigation problem, and we'd like to build a satellite and try it out." They gave us the start-up funds.

We quickly put up the first demonstration, and then the navy sponsored a program of developing this into an operational system over the next several years. The lab realized that these same satellites, equipped with instruments, could measure the Earth's magnetic field or x-rays emanating from space. So we succeeded in getting support from NASA to build scientific satellites.

We are an extremely flexible organization skilled in almost all of technology—devices of all kinds, spacecraft, undersea phenomena. We can compute anything. We are capable of undertaking almost any problem. We work best in teams because we're accustomed to doing that. Not so many people are good at that. So potentially we could apply ourselves to a variety of things. There's a temptation to spin off little companies, but I worry that if we fragment ourselves too much, we will lose some of the pride, some of the effectiveness that we've had.

I hope the laboratory remains mostly devoted to public service. The university is at its best when it's not trying to make money, when it's doing something for the good of the country, the good of people. Ninety-nine percent is that right now. APL is marvelously good at it, and I think most of the staff has stayed as long as it has because they were proud of what they were doing.

Alexander Kossiakoff is chief scientist and former director of the Applied Physics Laboratory.

"Going from being a member of the faculty to the dean's office is a sea change, because you constantly have to remind yourself that your job is to serve the faculty and the students and everyone else. You have to learn how to work top down, bottom up.

I learned a long time ago that if you're not in an administrative position, you really can't effect big change. On the other hand, the further you get from the problem you're trying to resolve, the harder it is to convince the people who are in the midst of it that you really are interested in changing it.

If you want to use a metaphor, it's the difference between being the first violinist or the concert pianist and being the orchestra conductor. Suddenly everyone who's playing in that orchestra is a better musician than you are on that particular instrument, but there is nobody who has a better sense of the big picture. Your job is to make sure people are playing the same symphony and that they're playing together."
DR. CATHERINE DEANGELIS

"Johns Hopkins can be quite demanding. One is expected to be a teacher, a scholar, a research person, as well as to make contributions to the enterprise as a whole, to the region and beyond. That's a high order once characterized to me by a person who left voluntarily to become a professor at one of the Big Ten universities. When I asked him why he was going, he said, 'Reds, I'm expected to teach as if I were at Swarthmore, to make research contributions as if I were at Cal Tech, Harvard, Yale, Chicago, and I'm expected to provide services as if I were at a community college. I'm not sure I want to meet that standard.'" PROFESSOR GORDON "REDS" WOLMAN, B.A. '49

The leadership of The Johns Hopkins University assembled around President William C. Richardson (in gold robe above) c. 1995 as his administration drew to a close. All nine divisions were represented by their deans or directors. Provost Joseph Cooper stood at Richardson's right.

An unusual gathering of trustees and senior Homewood faculty met in the boardroom of Shriver Hall c. 1960, at right. The subject of the conference is not known, but participants included some of the most respected personalities on campus.

AN ACADEMIC GROVE

"Although it will take time to develop the plans, I hope we shall all live to see the day when the simplicity, the timeliness, and the strength which characterized our founder's gift, will be also apparent in the structures which his trustees erect; and when that site, beautiful in itself and already well planted, may be, in fact, an academic grove, with temples of learning, so appropriate, so true, and so well built that no other ornament will be essential for beauty, and yet that in their neighborhood no work of art will be out of place."

DANIEL COIT GILMAN, 1876

"When I arrived in 1949, I was very impressed by the place. The interplay between the undergraduates, the graduates, and the faculty was really absolutely magnificent despite the rumors that it's always been a bad place for undergraduates. We were an excellent undergraduate school for the right kind of student, someone who had decided on his profession rather early and was interested in academic matters. That kind of person had all sorts of nurturing. The undergraduate student body was slightly bigger than the graduate student body. Undergraduates were treated very much like graduate students, and they were mentored from the time they came.

There weren't any special advanced courses for undergraduates. In chemistry, there was freshman chemistry, quantitative analysis, and organic chemistry. Then all of the advanced courses were joint with the graduate students, and those same graduate students might well be their lab instructors. That kind of interplay was really very good."
PROFESSOR JOHN GRYDER

The student who snagged a chair (far left) *in July 1958 by one of the elegant windows in the Gilman Hall library enjoyed not only extra light but also the serenity of his surroundings, a marked contrast to the rigors of academic competition in the lecture hall* (above c.1960).

In 1976 Abel Wolman took pleasure in recounting that, while a student, he had helped to survey the ground for Gilman Hall in 1913. Three days of ceremonies in May 1915 included the first graduation on the Homewood campus, the inauguration of Frank Goodnow as The Johns Hopkins University's third president, and the dedication of Gilman Hall, above.

Maryland and Latrobe Halls (far left) were planned to accommodate only the School of Engineering, but science departments occupied parts of the buildings until Remsen Hall was completed in 1924. Maryland Hall was originally called the Mechanical and Electrical Engineering Building and Latrobe was known as the Civil Engineering Building. In 1931 the trustees renamed both structures to recognize the generous role the state had played in the creation of the School of Engineering in 1912. Henry Latrobe was a prominent Marylander and chief engineer of the Baltimore & Ohio Railroad at the end of the nineteenth century.

On October 2, 1922, workers poured concrete for the floor of the first Alumni Memorial Residence, named to honor former students who had died in World War I. Each section of the building was subsequently designated to commemorate a prominent early faculty member or alumnus.

"Homewood House is one of the finest examples of Federal architecture in the world. In those days it housed the president; Dean Wilson Shaffer; Stewart Macaulay, the provost; and the director of public relations, Lynn Poole."
WILBERT "BILL" LOCKLIN, B.S.'57

The c.1925 aerial photograph of Gilman Hall, below, shows intricate botanical gardens in front of the greenhouse. The first segments of the colonnades that would connect Gilman, Mergenthaler, and Remsen Halls were already in place. Professor Reds Wolman recalled playing tennis on the one court that remained when the c.1945 aerial at far left was taken. Ames Hall filled that site by 1954. The photo also reveals the drive that bordered the bowl (later called the beach). On June 14, 1962, the day after ground was broken for the Eisenhower Library, fresh sod was laid in front of Homewood House, left.

"There were only three academic buildings when we arrived in 1925: Gilman Hall and the two engineering buildings, which have since been vastly enlarged. The Carroll mansion was here, and the Barn, which was really the stable that belonged to the Carroll mansion, and a powerplant to supply the electric power needed to run the operation. And in the distance, just one dormitory; and way far out was Homewood Field. Well, today the same piece of property looks like lower Manhattan.

The campus was very lovely, really, a lot of trees and shade and intriguing paths."
WILLIAM BANKS, B.A.'29

President Milton S. Eisenhower accepted congratulations from Albert D. Hutzler in 1965 when it was announced that the library would be named for Eisenhower. Hutzler had led the fund-raising campaign for the new building. In 1984 staff members were busy keyboarding data, an effort that eventually eliminated the card catalog and made its information available beyond the library.

"Milton Eisenhower was a great man who served eight presidents of the United States in both parties and had an extraordinary breadth of knowledge and service. He was the president of three major universities, all of which named buildings after him. Now, that says something." NEIL GRAUER, B.A.'69

"Milton Eisenhower was incredibly honest and honorable. We had a cigar box for petty cash in the office with stamps in it, and every time Dr. Milton would write Ike he'd fish in his pocket and take out whatever the postage was in those days.

He was a tireless perfectionist. Anytime a person phoned him or wrote him, Milton would answer immediately: 'I've referred the matter to Dean Shaffer, and if you do not hear from him in seventy-two hours, call me at this number,' and then he would carbon in Shaffer, and Shaffer would know damn well that he'd better fix whatever it was that needed to be fixed." WILBERT "BILL" LOCKLIN, B.S.'57

Evenings are usually busy in the Eisenhower Library. The decision to build most of the library underground reflected concern that the large structure might overwhelm Homewood House and Gilman Hall. Before the Eisenhower Library, the university's books were distributed among departmental libraries around the campus; it took five months to move one million books to the new repository.

"What is now the Eisenhower Room used to be the ladies' dining room. Women were not admitted in the other half of the building. For that matter, men weren't permitted in the ladies' side of the building unless they were accompanied by a lady. Clearly, it was a disadvantage for women faculty not to be able to eat at that big faculty table.

Bob Strider thought that it was bad that women faculty members couldn't come to the men's side, and he was on the board of the club. He decided to define women faculty members as not being ladies, and therefore they didn't have to eat on the ladies' side. That caused more trouble than making the school coeducational." PROFESSOR JOHN GRYDER

"When I came here, the faculty had lunch at the Hopkins Club and used it as the social center after seminars. Discussions would continue serially, going on from Monday to Thursday as people came back for lunch and continued to ventilate the idea that they were discussing. People really spent a large proportion of their social time pursuing intellectual ideas." PROFESSOR FRANKLIN KNIGHT

"I worked for three years in the faculty club parking lot. The night school students tried to use the parking lot; I sat at the top of the driveway and kept them out, for which I got thirty-five dollars in cash every week and dinner in the club kitchen. The cooks loved me, and they gave me sirloin steaks and slices of roast beef. The woman who ran the club wanted me to have peanut butter and jelly. For three years I had dinner there five nights a week, and the thirty-five dollars took care of my social life. It took care of my room as well. It was an enormous amount of money in those days. And the fact of the matter is, there was nothing to do. All I had to do was sit there under a streetlight with my slide rule, working on my physics problems. If it was raining, I had to have one hand holding up an umbrella. If they saw me, the night students wouldn't come in. I never even had to talk to anybody and turn them away. I was the BEWARE OF THE DOG sign and they didn't need a dog. It was a great job." MICHAEL R. BLOOMBERG, B.S.E.'64

The long table reserved for faculty and administrators (above left c. 1970) in the Johns Hopkins Club frequently served as information central on the Homewood campus.

A 1972–74 addition to Levering Hall (far left in 1975) that expanded the cafeteria's seating capacity also included a small theater and the Glass Pavilion (visible through the dome). The pavilion provided another venue for receptions, dances, and other community functions. Its balcony overlooked blossoming azaleas in 1996, above.

"We ran a coffee house upstairs in Levering Hall called the Room at the Top. We had Joan Baez there, and she stayed with us a week. Students were interested in what she was doing, and she just fitted in. She had just been discovered. The university didn't know who Baez was or how popular she was. The big concert we had in Shriver stopped traffic on the campus.

Later on, the name of the coffee house was Chester's Place."
CHESTER WICKWIRE

Chester Wickwire (at right teaching an outdoor class by the Give Peace a Chance *sculpture in 1971) came to Hopkins in 1953 as secretary of the YMCA; he was later named university chaplain. He used his office as a bully pulpit and urged students to become involved in social issues, especially by tutoring disadvantaged children. A champion of civil rights and a vocal opponent of the war in Vietnam, Wickwire worked with students to bring new voices to campus, particularly in the coffee house, above.*

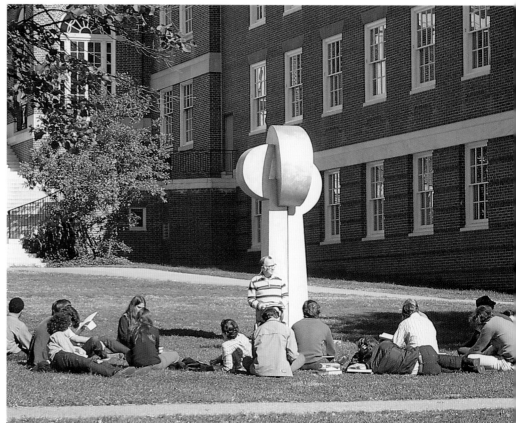

"The campus was a grand place. I lived down in south Baltimore, which was not a slum by any means, but it was crowded. It was row housing. The Hopkins campus is swell: beautiful quadrangles, beautiful buildings, and the old clock sounding off periodically. There's a feeling of spaciousness and luxury about it.

The library was in Gilman Hall. I could get a book, sit by these magnificent windows in a marvelous chair, looking out on the park. Boy, was I in heaven."
RUSSELL BAKER, B.A.'47

Springtime on the Homewood campus provides many lovely settings for relaxed conversation and study. The gardens bordered by the greenhouse, Nichols House, and the Johns Hopkins Club have been redesigned several times. In 1976 they were named the Decker Gardens to acknowledge the generosity of trustee Alonzo Decker and his family. Decker's father had met his business partner, Duncan Black, c.1910 when they both worked at a company started by Hopkins physics professor Henry Rowland.

Virtually no one travels on campus empty-handed. It is often books that are tucked into packs such as those at far left, or under an arm—even on a snowy January day in 1960, at left. Keyser (upper) and Wyman (lower) Quads were named in 1954 for the men who donated land for the campus.

The computer in the Eisenhower Library's new computing center where Bill Brand labored at 3 A.M. on February 13, 1991, had not crashed, but his friend apparently had, below.

"The library is definitely the place that you're going to find most students on almost any day of the week. The old joke about the library, since it's subterranean, is that you start out with the most normal, well-adjusted people at the top, and the deeper you go into the bowels of the library, the more you get these possessed-looking superannuated graduate students who have not seen natural light for six years." CHRISTOPHER NIEDT, B.A.'99

The Bloomberg Center (under construction below in 1988) encompasses 181,081 square feet (with 593 rooms) in the research section and 31,235 square feet (with 70 rooms) in the section devoted to instruction.

"In the late '80s, the hospital had been rebuilt; the School of Medicine had new buildings; we had an enlargement of the School of Public Health. SAIS got the Rome Building. But arts and sciences had buildings that were becoming outmoded in terms of modern science, and there was no money for that. My first plan was simply, since the endowment was earning a lot of money, to take some money from the endowment and put it into construction. But in October '87, there was this decline in the market and the endowment went down.

Roughly fifty cents of every dollar given to Hopkins is given to medicine. I gave a ruefully entitled speech on occasion called 'Nobody Ever Died of English,' which is, of course, part of the reason people give to medicine. The trustees, on my recommendation, passed a tax, which taxed all the divisions so that arts and sciences could have a construction program. Well, that violated the fundamental ethos of Hopkins, and obviously the biggest contributor to the tax was the School of Medicine. I don't blame them for being upset. I knew they'd be upset. I would, however, do it again because those buildings are worth their weight in gold. If we didn't have them, I don't where we would be in terms of quality in arts and sciences.

My thesis was both unarguable and unacceptable. You can't have a great university without a strong division of arts and sciences. That was unarguable. What was unacceptable was to take their money to achieve that." STEVEN MULLER

"People say Steve Muller got us into trouble by expanding too much. If Muller hadn't done that, we wouldn't have been in trouble a couple of years before everybody else, which let us get our house in order without losing a lot of faculty. I think Muller's problem was simply that after eighteen years as president, you invariably, every time you make a decision, alienate somebody, and eventually there are more alienated people than unalienated people. That catches up with everybody. Muller did a good job." MICHAEL R. BLOOMBERG, B.S.E.'64

"As a woman on campus, you felt like a standard-bearer for feminism, equal treatment, and equal consideration. Yet I was always aware that the majority of the support staff—the secretaries, the cleaning people—were women. I always felt a little uncomfortable proclaiming that we're pushing forward but at the same time taking for granted the fact that well, yes, all my courses are going to be completely and correctly registered because all the women in the registrar's office are handling it. The cafeteria food's going to be there on time and served right because predominantly there are women doing it.

We breeze through our four years at this place, grab our degrees, and then forge onward, and there's this whole cadre of people who work quietly in mundane jobs. They don't have the academic kudos and all the excitement; they're the people who make the place work. If one day all of those folks decided not to show up, the place would stop."
HELEN BLUMBERG, B.A.'73

"The only people who mattered at Homewood in 1938 were the president; Irene Davis, the registrar; Wilson Shaffer, the dean; Stewart Macaulay, the provost; and Henry Baker, the treasurer. There were no committees. Irene Davis meant so much to Johns Hopkins. She set the tone. Irene was committed to the institution; she understood it thoroughly, and she always worried about making it more national, more international."
WILBERT "BILL" LOCKLIN, B.S.'57

The Space Telescope Science Institute (seen across San Martin Drive in the construction photo) is the Bloomberg Center's neighbor, appropriate since Bloomberg is the home of physics and astronomy. Dunning Park provided a wooded approach, far left in 1984, to the other side of Homewood's largest building. The park features ten animal sculptures by Beniamino Bufano, which were donated by the artist's son and the Bufano Society for the Arts.

Participants on both sides of the table struggled through registration in pre-computer days, above.

205

"Hopkins is a small institution, but that in itself is an advantage. I worry that it's becoming too big, but there is such great depth and breadth and an atmosphere of collegiality and congenial scholarship, which makes it very easy to get involved in new things and new ideas." VICTOR MCKUSICK, M.D.'46

"You have to be able to allow good people to expand, and you can only do that if you have space. A very good person who really has a wonderful future in science says, 'Look, I've got to have another laboratory and more people to take advantage of all the new ideas I have,' and if you cannot do that, then he goes somewhere else. The better he is, or she is, the more offers they are going to have. If you can't supply the research-friendly environment, you are going to lose them." DR. RICHARD ROSS

In January 1998 the School of Nursing inaugurated the Anne M. Pinkard Building at 525 Wolfe Street. The state-of-the-art educational and research facility featured lecture halls, classrooms, seminar rooms, labs, social areas, and an auditorium.

Andre W. Brewster (chairman of the hospital board of trustees), university and hospital president Steven Muller, and Dr. Robert Heyssel, who succeeded Muller as president of the hospital, posed in 1983 under the portrait of the young Johns Hopkins.

FOLLOWING PAGES:

The East Baltimore campus in May 2000 embraced The Johns Hopkins Hospital and the Schools of Medicine, Nursing, and Public Health.

"You had to be an idiot not to realize the importance of nurses. Bob Heyssel and I began to talk about a nursing school run by the university. The university didn't need it as much as the hospital did and the hospital had more money than the university, so we worked out joint financing and established the School of Nursing.

Quite a significant number of Hopkins nurses bitterly resented and regretted the closing of their school, but I hadn't been involved in that. When it turned out that the president of the university was committed, with Dr. Heyssel's full help, to establishing a university school of nursing, my God, I got hugs and kisses, and people were very sentimental. Now they finally have their own building, which is gorgeous." STEVEN MULLER

"I was in a meeting that included people from the hospital and the School of Medicine, and comments were made about where they were going to move people from the second floor of the Phipps Building where the School of Nursing was based. I said, 'Excuse me. It sounds like something's happening to the Phipps Building.' They said, 'Yes.' I asked if the dean knew, and they said, 'No, we assumed you would tell her.' It was business as usual here, but it pointed out what happens when you don't control your own space.

We ended up in space that really didn't meet our needs. The reality was as stark as it could ever be that we had to have a space that belonged to nursing. We had a wonderful, wonderful strength in our alumnae. We had a real leg up as we started the campaign for the building because it represented a permanent presence to those nurses, something that meant more than they could put into words. The bricks and mortar give nursing education at Hopkins a permanency that it had never had before." PROFESSOR STELLA SHIBER

209

True to the Mission

PROFESSOR STELLA SHIBER

Interviewed on November 22, 1999

From the beginning nursing students had their own residence on the hospital grounds. Below far right, *student (on the left) and registered nurses gathered for a ceremony in Shriver Hall in 1963. Far right, student nurse Marc Dunbar administered medications in February 2000 as instructor Betty Jordan supervised.*

I was hired in November '62 as a brand-new, right-out-of-college, master's-prepared nurse to work in The Johns Hopkins Hospital's diploma program. The students had a number of classes, but the largest part of their time was spent working on the units with the patients. In the early '60s, there were not very many registered nurses assigned to the units. We had nursing students in large numbers on all the units on days, evenings, and weekends. It generally was about a forty-hour week. Classes were factored into that. There was a strong component of service, apprenticeship learning.

All of us pretty much came from hospital diploma schools. That was the legacy that we started this century with. Florence Nightingale and her group in London started schools of nursing that, by and large, were affiliated with hospitals. It quickly became essential that as hospitals grew in this country, they have a school of nursing affiliated with them, because that ensured a steady, very inexpensive labor force. That's really what enabled the hospital

industry to grow as it did in this country.

In the early days especially, there was great concern that nursing students were very close to being abused because they worked fifty to a hundred hours a week. They worked all shifts. They had, in the early days of our school, a half a day off a week. On the infectious disease units, nursing students were expected to move in and physically live with the patients on the unit for their tour of duty, three months or so. It was extremely hard, backbreaking work. But for some reason, and I guess part of that is still with us, nurses were a group of women who felt that this was a service that they were lucky to have—the honor of caring for sick and dying people—and they weren't doing it for any sort of reward in this life. Part of that, of course, comes from the ties of nursing with religious orders.

There was very little in the way of money available to send young women to college, especially women from working-class backgrounds. By and large, you could be a teacher, a nurse, or maybe a social

worker, and of the three, nursing was the one that usually working-class families would choose. You were told, "Don't worry. If anything ever happens, you'll always have something to fall back on." It was assumed that most of us would marry and have families and leave the labor force. But the hospitals didn't really care because they had a new class graduating every year.

Society began to change, so that gradually more and more of the hospitals closed their diploma schools. In many cases diploma schools moved into a college environment. You would have thought that Hopkins would have been the ideal place for that to happen because we were right here as part of an academic medical center and should have had all the resources to take a premier, wonderful school of nursing into a university setting. One of the concerns was how to integrate nurses into this all-male undergraduate university. And, second, how was this going to be paid for? Who would be able to support this?

All the way into the early '70s, the quality of the student who came to Hopkins always was outstanding. A number of the young women—and it was primarily young women—already had a university education. But it got to the point where it was very difficult to say to those young women coming to Hopkins, "You're going to be something special. You're going to be a Hopkins nurse." When they left, they had no academic credentials at all, and when they joined the work force, they were not really viewed as special.

When we got into the '70s and that transition to university education had not taken place, the decision was finally made, "We will close the nursing school rather than take an inferior candidate," which was heartbreaking to alumnae. It's just too bad that a place like Hopkins had to call a halt to nursing education and have a period of time pass when there was no nursing education at all because a viable way to do this could not be found.

Dr. Muller had taken the presidency promising that he would do what he could to see that nursing education came back. The School of Health Services was founded to educate an allied health professional. It seemed plausible that this might be the place to open a nursing education program. From the beginning, a number of nurse leaders at Hopkins were against that. They felt that was an inappropriate place to put nursing. The dean of

the School of Health Services was a physician; the overall mission was to educate a new kind of health care professional, which was not nursing.

The NEP, Nursing Education Program, opened as the second program in the School of Health Services, admitted two classes, and was about to admit the third class when the decision was made to close the school. So there were only three classes that graduated from the School of Health Services. They were, I must say, outstanding people. They were chosen, again, because they were the quality that Hopkins wanted. The faculty that were recruited to teach that group were outstanding. The classes have gone on to distinguish themselves. A number of them earned master's and doctorates and are in positions of leadership both here at Hopkins and in nursing generally.

So there were two periods when there was no nursing education at Hopkins at all. This school was officially declared a reality in '83, and I was hired to come back and to put the curriculum together, do the proposal for the Maryland Higher Education Commission as a new degree from Hopkins, and recruit the students. We admitted twenty-eight students in September 1984.

I think there's no question but that we have improved the education of the student. We now can say unequivocally that while the student is with us, the learning experiences are planned with the student's learning needs being utmost. When the students are on the clinical area, they certainly are providing care to patients—and it's a very high-quality care—but it's planned very carefully to support their learning needs.

We wanted to do something that was on the cutting edge, that was preparing

them for practice in the system that we were currently in and that was going to exist in the future. We had a computer course in '84, and I think we were probably one of the very first. We wanted our students to look at the policy arena and be aware of the impact that these decisions were going to have on their nursing practice. As a result of managed care and some of the other things that have happened in the last five to seven years, nurses are expected to be experts in terms of the clinical care of the patient, assessing and providing care and so on. Decisions about where a patient would receive care and what kind of care were being made by the insurance companies. There was no one at the table to represent the patient. The ideal person to represent the patient, of course, is the nurse because she's the one who's going to have the expertise to clinically assess needs and where they can best be met. To send the nurse into that kind of group without being able to understand the language and the economics was ridiculous.

So we planned the Business of Nursing Program. We were looking for people with at least a bachelor's who would have three to five years of experience, including some management experience. We would give them the ability to come to the table knowing what the patient's clinical needs

are, to put a dollar sign on those, and to tell the insurance companies or the hospital that this patient, when they're provided care at this level, you're going to save this much money. They could add to their repertoire the understanding that nursing is, in fact, a large part of a very large business. We offer this graduate certificate program together with the School of Professional Studies in Business and Education.

Growing out of that also is a joint degree program that combines our master's in nursing with SPSBE's M.B.A. It appears that it's going to be a very popular program. The nursing courses generally are here, and then students may go to Homewood or to the Downtown Center or Columbia, wherever courses are offered that they require.

So it's a very different world than any one of us could have envisioned in '84 when we were opening this school, but I think we have been very true to the mission of Hopkins. We stay on the cutting edge; we always are looking for the trend and we're ahead of it; we're preparing people for not just practice right now but for practice well into the future.

Stella Shiber is associate professor and associate dean for professional education programs and practice at the School of Nursing.

The Peabody Library that welcomed early Johns Hopkins students and faculty remains a sanctuary for scholars and an awe-inspiring site for events hosted by university divisions.

"The Peabody trustees asked for a building that would be 'capable of harmonious adjustment' because they knew that the institution would change over the years and the building had to be able to change with it. It's grown with us; we have these fabulous nineteenth-century buildings, and we have state-of-the-art electronic music and recording facilities with the latest digital equipment." ELIZABETH SCHAAF

Graduate students pursue a myriad of disciplines at the Villa Spelman in Florence, Italy, above. An annual spring seminar in Italian Studies drew participants from the Departments of Art History, History, and Hispanic and Italian Studies. Since 1984, a joint workshop on current problems in particle theory has been offered every three years by the University of Florence and Hopkins' Department of Physics and Astronomy.

Acquisition of the Rome Building (far left) in 1987 expanded the School of Advanced International Studies.

The Montgomery County Center (left) was dedicated in 1988 as an interdivisional facility providing classroom space for engineering, arts and sciences, business, education, and public-health courses.

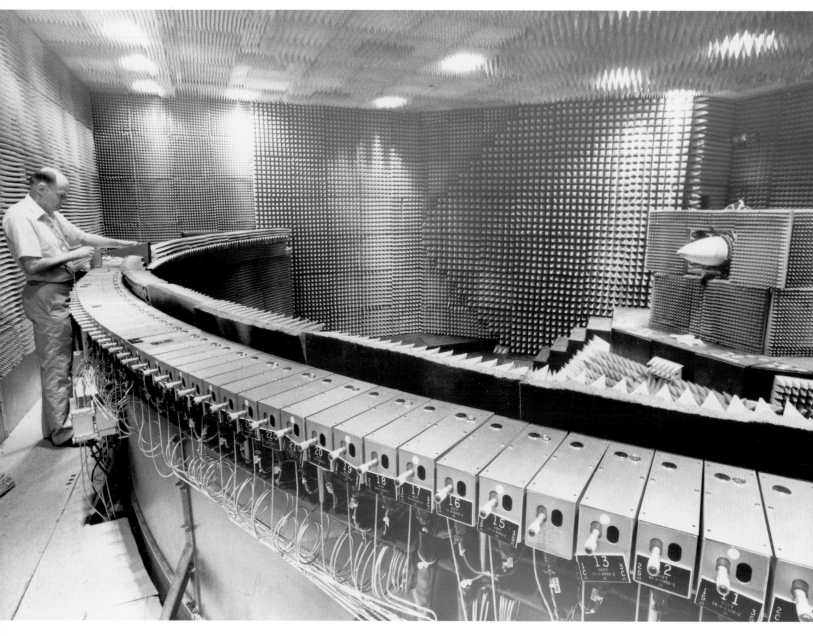

Charles Chalmers prepared to test a missile
guidance system in the Applied Physics
Laboratory's anechoic chamber in 1983,
above. The spikes giving the room its unusual
appearance were made of spongy material that
absorbed sonic and electromagnetic echoes and
reverberations. The number of buildings on
APL's Howard County campus has more than
doubled since the aerial at right was taken in
1964, but the labor force has remained steady
at about twenty-eight hundred. Academic links
between APL and Homewood began in 1963
when APL became the first off-campus site
for McCoy College classes. By 1985, far
right, strong educational programs benefiting
both divisions linked APL and the Whiting
School of Engineering.

THE BEST OPPORTUNITIES

Of this I am certain, that they are not among the wise, who depreciate the intellectual capacity of women, and they are not among the prudent, who would deny to women the best opportunities for education and culture."

DANIEL COIT GILMAN, 1876

got a job working in a lab. That was probably the single event that turned me toward medicine. My mentor helped me to see that there was life beyond the classroom and to realize that medicine was a lot of fun and that seeing patients was an end goal. I couldn't really see that when I was a college student, especially a freshman. He helped me get through a lot of the course work and keep focusing on my end goal. When I applied to medical school, he helped me decide where I wanted to go and helped me with the

The medical school and the hospital's nursing school always admitted women; the Faculty of Philosophy began admitting them as graduate students in 1907. The two women in the math department c.1916, above, helped pave the way for the student at far left.

Christine Ladd met the university's require-
ments for her Ph.D. by 1882, but the degree
was not awarded until 1926. She became
the first woman on the Faculty of Philosophy
when she lectured in logic and psychology
from 1904–09.

A glimpse into McCoy Hall on the downtown
campus reveals almost as many female scholars
as male. Thirteen women received advanced
degrees in 1911; one aspiring Ph.D. compressed
three years of work into two.

"Christine Ladd was truly extraordinary. She was probably the most important mind that
went through Johns Hopkins in terms of formal logic. Ladd did all the work for a degree;
it wasn't awarded. They finally got around to giving her a degree at the fiftieth anniversary in 1926.

Ladd is a fascinating figure because while she was here she did teach and she terrified
the graduate students. She was a much tougher mentor than her husband, Fabian
Franklin. The students would go over to their house and she would ask questions that
would stop them in their tracks. Christine Ladd is a special case because she probably
would have been barred not just because she was a woman but because of nepotism rules:
her husband was the chairman of the department."
PROFESSOR RICHARD MACKSEY, M.A.'53, PH.D.'57

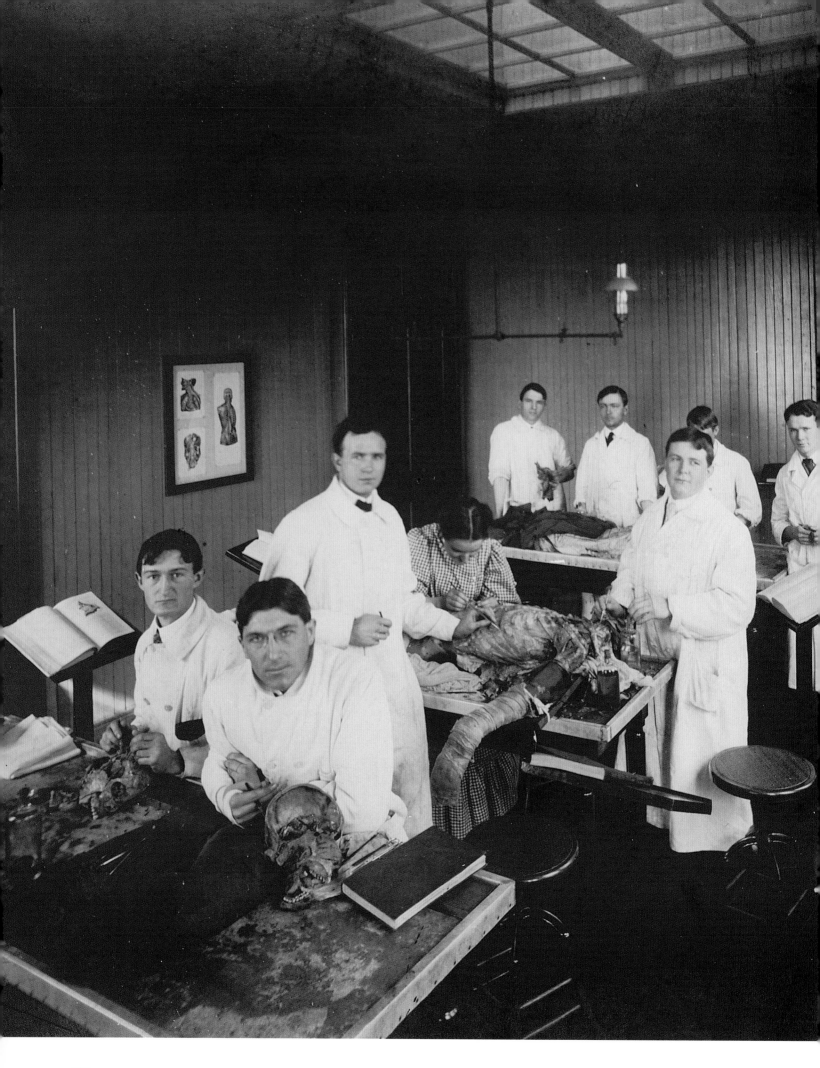

All of the medical students in this anatomy class paused for the photographer—except one diligent woman who continued dissecting a cadaver. Marjorie Lewisohn recalled three marriages in one medical class of couples who had met over the anatomy table.

The Women's Fund Committee, above, raised money for the establishment of the medical school through a national campaign. Miss Garrett, with the fan, made the largest individual contribution ($354,764). The terms of their gift stipulated high standards for applicants and the admission of women on the same basis as men.

"I wanted to be a doctor from the time I was ten years old. I thought I wanted to do research, but then I realized I was a people person and really wanted to practice medicine and Johns Hopkins had a wonderful reputation for that, too. They had Osler, Welch, Halsted, Kelly; the pupils of Osler were teaching me.

I was one of seven girls in a class of seventy, and they certainly welcomed us and gave us every chance. The generation before mine had had a hard time, but my generation was given every opportunity. Dorothy Reed Mendenhall was a pioneering woman doctor at Hopkins. She said that Sir William Osler told her, 'A nice girl like you should get married and go back home and not take the place of a man.' There was nothing like that in my day." MARJORIE G. LEWISOHN, M.D. '43

"I was in Boston giving a talk to the Hopkins alumni. I had been talking about the story of Mary Elizabeth Garrett and how the medical school got started by the women, and Mary Ellen Avery, who was a graduate and former faculty here, said, 'Dick Ross, don't tell that story anymore. Tell us what you've done for women lately.' That brought me up short. We did not do anything specific, but we watched women's enrollment rise from ten percent to fifty percent." DR. RICHARD ROSS

The School of Public Health provided educational and employment opportunities to women from its inception. Although their status was not high, females made up a third of public health's faculty just a year after the school opened. Women also worked in some of its laboratories, above c. 1926.

"Nursing students benefited because we had the best teachers in the medical school also teaching us. We went on rounds every morning and had the experience of watching the house staff and the medical students present, and then we were often called upon. We were the ones who had been there all night with the patients; we knew more about the patients' social environment or family situation.

You learned to answer concisely. That's part of the hallmark of a Hopkins education: you're expected to know why. Why is this patient here? Why didn't this patient take his or her medication? You were constantly being intellectually stimulated and challenged to understand what was going on with a patient and then what you were going to do and why you were going to do it." PROFESSOR MARTHA HILL, R.N.'64, B.S.N.'66, PH.D.'87

Five women doctors joined their male colleagues and the departmental secretary for a portrait of the Phipps Clinic staff in 1936–37.

"Katie Borkovich dressed in the old-fashioned way that people thought women doctors should dress. She wore women's suits that were like men's and a necktie and brown gripper shoes. She was a very fine physician and had an enormous practice. She was a very good role model and teacher because she was on the house staff when we were medical students.

We were lucky to have people like Katie, who was just a little older than we, and Dr. Carol Thomas, Dr. Ella Oppenheimer, Dr. Marion Hines, and Dr. Harriet Guild, a beloved pediatrician who took care of all the faculty's children, as role models."
MARJORIE G. LEWISOHN, M.D.'43

Anna Wolf, at left *with a student, arrived at Johns Hopkins for her nursing education in 1912. She returned in 1940 as the School of Nursing's director. Her sister, Eleanor, earned her M.D. at the School of Medicine.*

"I think that one of the great improvements at Homewood was when it finally went coed. Homewood was very much a masculine place in my day. Fortunately, Goucher was just down the street a few blocks; they hadn't moved out to the country yet. It sort of made up for the fact that we didn't have classes with women." WILLIAM BANKS, B.A.'29

"The girls from Baltimore who were working at Glenn L. Martin decided that when the war was over we would go to college, and we decided that Hopkins was the place for us. I thought I'd like to pursue mechanical drawing. I got as far as the algebra, trigonometry courses, but anything above that, forget it. It wasn't open. You had to go to day school, and day school wasn't open to women. I resented not being able to take what I wanted. Of course, that was a reflection on the times, because nobody else could either." ANNE E. CLARK, B.S.'49

"I suspect that when the university went coed that may have gentled the aspect a little bit. The graduate school in arts and sciences, mind you, was always coeducational, so there were always women on the campus, high performing ones. When I came back to Hopkins to teach, it was by then a coeducational institution. It seemed the most natural thing in the world that some of my best undergraduate students were women and odd to think that once this was an all-male bastion with no female voices in the room. It seemed so strange, as if you would have all dwarves or all one-handed people." JOHN BARTH, B.A.'51, M.A.'52

The Woman's College of Baltimore (later Goucher) opened in 1888, and Hopkins men quickly befriended their contemporaries. Goucher's first location was between the university's old and new campuses, so visits were frequent, as evidenced by the Goucher students who came to Homewood after a snowstorm in 1922, above far left.

Though their numbers were not large, female graduate students were a consistent presence at Homewood. Two women took a 1942 Romantic poetry course, at far left.

McCoy College offered the only chemistry classes available to undergraduate women in 1948, above.

Fair Exchange

HELEN HOLTON, M.S. '95

Interviewed on November 23, 1999

"The School of Professional Studies in Business and Education offers tremendous opportunities, setting the pace for the involvement of business in the educational community and of education in the business community. SPSBE makes education a two-way street: the professors learn from their students, the students learning from each other and the professors. With Hopkins' traditional entrepreneurial atmosphere and outreach, it could develop business programs that are absolutely leading edge in what businessmen are going to need to be educated about over the next decade."
E. MAGRUDER "MAC" PASSANO JR., B.S.'67, M.L.A.'69

I've known about Johns Hopkins since I was a little girl because my grandmother received her Ph.D. from Hopkins. Growing up in Baltimore, it's kind of difficult to not know about Johns Hopkins, either the university or the hospital.

In the early 1990s, I came across this ad about a leadership development program at Hopkins for African-American professionals. My first thought was, "Oh, I certainly am not qualified to be in this program," because Hopkins always carried with me a certain level of prestige. You didn't just go to Hopkins; you had to be selected by Hopkins. The next year I decided I would apply. What did I have to lose?

A couple of times before, I had attempted to start a master's program and I just didn't like the notion of going to work all day and then going to class at night. When I saw this program, one of the things that drew me was that the classes were on Saturday. I said, "Well, I could give up a whole Saturday two or three times a month and do this."

I'd have fifteen graduate credits—I could figure out what I was going to do with those later, but I'd have some advanced learning. I'd been working professionally for a number of years, watching younger people get their M.B.A.s, and I needed something to update my academic credentials, so to speak, in the workplace.

Well, the Leadership Development Program was one of *the* most wonderful experiences of my life. It's a nine-month program, from September to May, and you go through the program with a cohort group. Some of the people that I went through this program with are some of my closest friends today, and though we're now spread out around the country, we still make a point of staying in touch. They're like extended family.

I first met Dean Stanley Gabor when the program began its first major change—they were bringing in a new program director. Now, here you have a program created for African-American professionals that had a majority of African-American instructors inside this university that really did not have a large African-American population, period. This was the largest concentration of African Americans in all of Hopkins, and they had selected a white female to head this program.

We decided, "Absolutely not. No, you won't." And so we requested an audience with the dean and the president of the university. Well, it happened to be Homecoming weekend, and Stan Gabor and President Richardson came and had lunch with us. We invited alums from the first two classes that had completed this program to talk about why this was not the right person to head up this program. What came out of that was she would become a higher-level program director and they would select an African-American director of this program. One of our classmates was on the selection committee. It was a very productive meeting. We, that class, had the ability to impact change. So that's where I first met Stan Gabor.

Well, it was such a wonderful program I decided, "I'm already in this mode, back in academia, so I'll complete my master's at Hopkins." I was taking a course on Homewood campus, and I remember this day as if it were yesterday. I'm walking past Shaffer Hall and Stan is coming out of Shaffer Hall and he calls to me by name! And I thought, "This is incredible." And I was so

"I strongly supported the Evening College and encouraged its expansion. Under Stanley Gabor we got a very entrepreneurial dean. They're making more money than ever and doing a lot of good things. One of the great entrepreneurial feats of Stanley Gabor was to have, in effect, an M.B.A. program, not as a business school but as part of the School of Continuing Studies. The other thing that will always be with us is education, which is really why we now have this very unglamorous but quite a descriptive title of the School of Professional Studies in Business and Education." STEVEN MULLER

in awe of that, because here he is, a dean who sees thousands of students, and he remembered me by name. I just thought that was really special. It meant a lot to me.

The summer before my last semester, I got a phone call that Hopkins was going to enter the National Black MBA Association student case competition for the first time and asking me if I'd like to interview to get a spot on the team. The director of the Leadership Development Program was Dr. Jo Ellen Gray. I interviewed and she said, "We are also looking for a coach for the team."

I said, "I took a strategic management course and I thought that the instructor was phenomenal." She worked us hard. Half a dozen people dropped the course once they saw the syllabus because it was the first summer session course and people were like, "Hey, I need my credits. I want to get through this, but clearly, this woman's a taskmaster." But I appreciated it because it taught me a lot, and so I suggested that Tina Rodriguez would be a wonderful person to coach this team.

So for about six weeks leading up to the competition, we lived at Tina's house. We worked during the day and then we were at Tina's every night doing research, we were in the library, we were putting together this presentation. This was the first time that Hopkins put themselves out nationally for this competition.

Jo Ellen Gray went with us to San Francisco. There were two rounds in the competition. There were five groups, and then four or five schools in each group. We competed, and then they announced the winners of each of the five at lunch the next day. We were selected to go into

the final round. We were really prepared. We anticipated questions they would ask; we already had slides prepared to address their questions.

They announced third place, they announced second place, and then it was down to Hopkins and Cal Tech. And we won. We came in first in the nation in this case competition. It was just incredible. I remember Jo Ellen calling Stan that night, it must have been one in the morning here, to tell him that we had won.

It was a real big win for Hopkins, far beyond what anyone could have imagined, because it was a first and we got national recognition for doing this. Two of us were graduates of the Leadership Development Program and so it lent more credibility to the program, and it was a wonderful, wonderful time. I wasn't even on the city council yet; I was just a consultant working and pursuing my master's. We all received job offers from Fortune 500 companies.

Then around '95, '96, I received a letter inviting me to be a member of the Alumni Council, and once again I was honored. It was there that I learned so much more about Hopkins and its schools. Basically all I knew about was the School of Continuing Studies; I knew there was a medical school and undergrad arts and sciences. It was through the Alumni Council that I learned about the other schools of Hopkins as well as meeting alums from the '40s and '50s and learning about the different alumni groups throughout Hopkins. Hopkins is so much more than what the average person would ever come to know through matriculating, working there, or just being in Baltimore.

In the School of Professional Studies in Business and Education the average age of students is mid-thirties. You're getting people who have been in the workplace, career changing, empty-nesters, all sorts of people that decide they want to go back to school. And now there are so many programs being offered that there's really something for everyone, and so it makes for a dynamic mix in the school. SPSBE graduates more students than any other school in Hopkins.

My experience at Hopkins has been wonderful. I loved going to Hopkins. I am very proud to be an alum of Hopkins.

There's no way that I could talk about my life as an adult and where I am today without Hopkins being a part of it. I grew exponentially during the time I went to the Leadership Development Program. It was during that time that I left corporate America and decided I wanted to take more risks with my life and the direction of my future and to have an impact. The Leadership Development Program helped me touch that part of myself, to step out on faith and be bigger than my fears. I owe a lot to Hopkins for helping me to be more of me, more my own person. There's a saying "Fair exchange is no robbery." Yes, I bring a lot to Hopkins, but Hopkins has certainly brought a lot to me.

Helen Holton represents the Fifth District on the Baltimore City Council.

Twenty-one freshmen and sixty-nine transfers, the first undergraduate women registered at Johns Hopkins, arrived in September 1970 and immediately plunged into university life. Some became cheerleaders, below. Some were elected to offices in student government and other extracurricular activities.

"Probably the class of '74, which would have been the first class with women who were there all four years, was the first time that there was a sense of, 'Okay, we're here to stay. Things are being equalized.' When it got to the point where nobody looked twice to see women in class, that's when things had finally sunk in. I'd venture to say that if you talked to women undergraduates now, it's no big deal, it's nothing." HELEN BLUMBERG, B.A.'73

It did not take long for women to form inter-collegiate sports teams and begin their own winning traditions as Hopkins student-athletes who excelled both in the classroom and on the playing field.

"Going to Hopkins as one of the first undergraduate women was very strange. I don't think that anyone was really ready for us on the campus. We didn't have campus mailboxes for the first semester; they forgot. Housing for upperclass women was in McCoy Hall, which was graduate apartments. They stuck us in little nooks and crannies that were single rooms. Of course, the bathroom situation was pretty grim, too.

Within an undergraduate student body of twenty-five hundred, we definitely stood out. There were some freshmen, but the majority were transfers. The guys felt that the standards had been lowered to get a quota of women and that we were there for one of two reasons, the first being that we were going to beat them out of medical school, the second that we were going to marry them. I heard from a lot of my women friends who were in the pre-med courses that if you happened to be taking a course and there were no other women, guys would stand in the back of the hall rather than sit next to you. You felt like a cross between Typhoid Mary and Gypsy Rose Lee. On one hand, you were supposedly going to take their futures away because you were going to beat them out of medical school; on the other hand, you were this feminine wile personified who was going to bewitch them. That first year was very, very difficult." HELEN BLUMBERG, B.A.'73

The Committee on Coeducation that recommended the admission of undergraduate women presumed the new arrivals would have different interests than their male counterparts, but one of the first coeds told Johns Hopkins Magazine *that her peers were "very career-oriented. The profile of the women students is like the profile of the men." Few arrangements were made to prepare for their arrival, but the women appreciated a tea given by faculty wives that gave them the opportunity to meet female graduate students. In 1971 there were 235 female undergraduates, and in subsequent years their numbers grew.*

231

Affiliation with the Peabody Institute in 1977 brought benefits throughout The Johns Hopkins University. Highly gifted Peabody students and faculty joined the Hopkins family and welcomed their colleagues to the Mount Vernon Place campus for classes in performing arts and music history. Medical archivist Nancy McCall noted that she has made many friends with people from East Baltimore who also take courses at Peabody "thanks to the university's generous tuition remission benefits."

From the first year of the university's College Courses for Teachers in 1909 through McCoy College, the Evening College, the School of Continuing Studies, and today's School of Professional Studies in Business and Education, women of all ages have been major beneficiaries of a multitude of course offerings. Many are part-time students who work by day and take classes in the evening, on weekends, or during the summer. This family shared the proud accomplishment of a 1985 Hopkins graduate.

"Milton Eisenhower was president of Johns Hopkins and Dwight Eisenhower was president of the United States. Milton invited Harold Macmillan to be the speaker at our graduation and he accepted. I got permission from the schools to let my children go. It was quite a ceremony. The next day their teachers asked my children to report on it, so my younger child said, 'Oh, yes, the president of the United States and the prime minister of England both came to see my mother graduate.'" MARGARET SPARROW, M.A.T. '58

Charles L. Fulton
J.H.U. class 1889
Alumni Day, May 14, 1955
In his 89th year

A GENEROUS AFFILIATION

"What are we aiming at? An enduring foundation; a slow development; first local, then regional, then national influence; the most liberal promotion of all useful knowledge; the special provision of such departments as are elsewhere neglected in the country; a generous affiliation with all other institutions, avoiding interferences, and engaging in no rivalry; the encouragement of research; the promotion of young men; and the advancement of individual scholars, who by their excellence will advance the sciences they pursue, and the society where they dwell."

DANIEL COIT GILMAN, 1876

"The first five years of his presidency Steve Muller brought Hopkins, which was really a community of collegial scholars, from the nineteenth century into the twentieth century. He did major fundraising. We had the Hopkins Hundreds to raise $100 million."
MARJORIE G. LEWISOHN, M.D.'43

"Campaigns were somewhat new at that time. Hopkins Hundreds was a dramatic venture for Johns Hopkins, and Muller showed tremendous guts in getting that started. Relative to its mission and reputation and what Hopkins had accomplished, it was one of the most under-endowed universities in the country, so that was the justification for the $450-million campaign that started in 1982–83.

A campaign has a tremendous secondary benefit, and that's the groundswell of enthusiasm—getting people to think about Hopkins, working together collegially, having a mission in mind. It gets people internally to be thinking about *their* Johns Hopkins."
MORRIS W. OFFIT, B.A.'57

Charles L. Fulton made quite an impression when he and his steed represented the class of 1889 at Homewood Field in 1955. Alumni have always been enthusiastic advocates of the university. In the early 1970s they joined with corporations and foundations to contribute to the Hopkins Hundreds capital campaign. On May 20, 1976, national chairman Alonzo G. Decker Jr. announced the campaign's success— a grand total of $108.9 million.

The interplay between Johns Hopkins and the neighbors of its various campuses has been stressful at times. Today lectures, concerts, plays, Spring Fair, and the university's strong support of community organizations have significantly improved relations. As the world grows more complex and the university's influence continues to expand, Baltimore's traditional gatherings, such as the Easter Parade, at left on Charles at 28th Street in 1921, have become charming memories.

Alumni began organizing just ten years after the university had been founded, and for some years graduates held a breakfast before Commemoration Day events. In 1919 alumni initiated a fund for the first residence hall at Homewood. Linking reunions with lacrosse games began in the 1930s; the custom was resumed after World War II and provided a spirited focus for homecomings (such as the one in 1967, above) for more than fifty years.

"They called Charles Street America's Champs Élysées because it was beautiful with all those trees and roads going up on each side. There was an Easter parade on Charles Street every year. When I was a little child I expected elephants—of course, it was just people driving by and walking home after church. When I was a teenager and started dating, we always went to the Easter parade. We saw everybody we knew dressed in their finest. Girls had white gloves and hats on, and the boys always gave a corsage."
MARGARET SPARROW, M.A.T.'58

"We were a great institution of higher learning, but Milton Eisenhower expanded Hopkins in so many ways and gave the alumni someone to rally around. Steve Muller took us international and big time. Then we had such a solid guy in Bill Richardson, and now to back him up with Bill Brody—the advances that are taking place at Hopkins are really tremendous." ROBERT SCOTT, B.A.'52

Reunion-goers joined with students to support the Blue Jays in 1985, far above. Meals at the Hopkins Club in the 1950s were dress-up affairs for alumni and faculty families, above.

The university's seventy-fifth year attracted many banner-waving alumni to Homewood Field in 1951. Conrad Gebelein directed the band, as he had since 1930.

"I remember going to the Hopkins Club, which was the faculty and alumni dining club. Going for dinner was *the* most special thing to do when I was a little kid. If it was still light when we got there, we could look at the pond in front of the president's house and see if the goldfish were visible. So my first sense of Johns Hopkins wasn't so much as an educational institution; it was a nifty park in the middle of the city.

The treat was that you got to have sherbet in the middle of the meal and it didn't count as dessert. All the staff seemed to know my dad, which made me feel special, and they fussed over children. Because it was a club as opposed to a restaurant, chances were my dad, who had graduated in 1935, would know virtually everybody in the dining room. He later became director of alumni relations." HELEN BLUMBERG, B.A.'73

"One of Mother's sisters married a Hopkins man. He's the one who started the Senior Alumni. When I came back to Baltimore, he got me to join. We would go to lunch at the Hopkins Club and then to the Barn for plays or go on trips. Now we have about three meetings a year at Evergreen House. Last meeting, the place was packed—there was no room for another seat." MARGARET SPARROW, M.A.T.'58

University trustees met at the Applied Physics Laboratory on October 13, 1980, above. Some trustees have been nominated by alumni since 1959, and since 1971 the board has elected a graduating senior from a small pool of candidates nominated by the undergraduate student body.

"When Milton Eisenhower became president, the board of trustees at Hopkins was a little local club. It was the blue-stocking crowd of Baltimore and a prestigious organization with which to be associated. I think there was one Jew on the board, no blacks, no women. Milton wanted women on the board and he wanted younger people, so we created the Young Trustees.

Steve Muller expanded the board in terms of women and geography and minorities. He had a sense of a much larger board and one that was more representative of the institution. We started by adding people from places where we had larger concentrations of alumni, particularly New York and Washington." ROSS JONES, B.A.'53

"The State of Maryland was so interested in obtaining young men who understood civil and mechanical engineering to work for the state and help build bridges and roads that they subsidized many scholarships at Hopkins. I think the big utilities—the gas and electric company and the telephone company—probably did the same thing because they needed electrical engineers. So a very large percentage of the students at Hopkins were on scholarships." WILLIAM BANKS, B.A.'29

"When Theodore McKeldin was governor, he gave a talk in a course that my father taught called Legal and Social Aspects of Engineering. My father's office was on the fifth floor of Ames Hall. The governor arrived with his state patrolmen, and my father said, 'Governor, you seem quite breathless.'

The governor said, 'Well, Abel, I had to walk up the four flights of stairs.'

My father said, 'Why did you have to do that? There's an elevator right here.'

And the governor said, 'Well, we were standing in front of the elevator and a student came along and said the elevator is only for the faculty, so we walked upstairs.'" PROFESSOR GORDON "REDS" WOLMAN, B.A.'49

The Johns Hopkins University's centennial year of celebration in 1976 culminated on February 22, Commemoration Day, at a special ceremony in the Lyric Opera House, far left.

Thomas D'Alesandro Jr., mayor of Baltimore, addressed those gathered at the laying of Shriver Hall's cornerstone in 1953, below. Governor Theodore R. McKeldin sat in the corner on the mayor's left, next to university president Detlev Bronk.

The Peabody Orchestra performed at the Hall of Columns in Moscow in November 1987, above. Steven Muller recalled that "the cold war was still very much alive. As their closing number, they played 'Stars and Stripes Forever' and all the Russians clapped. It was a great moment." Six months before the Moscow trip, Muller had watched as Lieutenant Governor Melvin Steinberg "struck a note" at the groundbreaking for a new building at the Peabody (far right above). Steinberg later played a key role in securing state support for the institute.

Evergreen House and its carriage house often provide elegant settings for university functions, far right in 1971. The estate was the gift of former trustee John Work Garrett.

"An orchestra, to a music school, is its varsity team. It's a wonderful opportunity for young people to learn. It's a metaphor for life—the idea of people coming from quite different backgrounds, working together toward the same goal, learning not only your own part but knowing what everybody else is playing because you have to fit your part into the fabric of the whole, accepting the fact that there are a few times when you're in the forefront but more time when you're in the middle ground and probably most of the time you're in the background, depending on your instrument, but that it's all of equal importance. It's teamwork, subservience of individuality in the service of the good of the community, of the whole. It's a wonderful experience for them. They can go away from a concert or a good rehearsal walking on air, taller than when they came in—empowered, in a sense. The orchestra is a powerful tool of the Peabody." LEON FLEISHER

"Peabody was going down the tubes, and I thought that was disgraceful. I asked myself what would happen if we stepped in there. How could we do that? Peabody had an art collection, most of which was on loan to the Baltimore Museum of Art. We needed to have a campaign for Peabody and we also knew that no campaign would succeed without a tremendous starting kick. We also thought—correctly, thank God—that the state, particularly the Baltimore people in the legislature and the governor, had an interest in seeing Peabody survive. We knew that the Baltimore Museum of Art, which is city-owned, did not want to give up its Mary Cassatts and its other Peabody paintings. When people said, 'How can you do this?' we'd say, 'Well, I guess we'll have to sell the art collection.' Well, we did sell it. We sold it to the state for $15 million, which constituted enough of an initial kick so that we raised some money, and the institute is now solvent. It's a glorious asset for Hopkins. It helps us in all kinds of ways and it's a first-rate conservatory."
STEVEN MULLER

Chewing Gum and String

BARBARA BONNELL, M.A.'54

Interviewed on July 12, 1999

Involvement in the community has taken many forms, from an undergraduate who tutored a local child, above, to a faculty member and a student from the School of Nursing who interviewed a resident of East Baltimore, at far right, with a community health worker.

When I was president of Family and Children's Society, the executive director called me one day. "Barbara, we have gotten a contract late in the game to try to help relocate or give counseling to people who have to relocate from one of the apartment houses that Hopkins has bought."

I said, "Well, thank goodness. I can't imagine what was going on in their minds to think they could simply purchase two apartment houses without having made plans for how people were going to be relocated."

The executive director said, "Well, you know Hopkins. They're in their own ivory tower. They have no concept of what their decisions can do in terms of the world outside their boundaries."

Now I have been very pleased to see the Homewood campus become more sensitive to the fact that it is part of a community. I do not expect a president of Johns Hopkins University, with all the complexities that that involves, can be knowledgeable about the communities around it, but I can expect a president to

have on staff people who can apprise him of that.

Ross Jones, vice president, was largely responsible, with a wonderful woman named Dea Kline, for organizing the Greater Homewood Community Corporation some thirty-one years ago. A group at Union Memorial Hospital and a group at Maryland Casualty were convened by Ross to help put up a little money and to create leadership initially, to create an umbrella organization of residents and businesses and institutions in the area to try to improve the quality of life. Over time, the Greater Homewood program for adult literacy and English as a Second Language became known citywide as a premier program.

About five years ago, Ross came to me, representing Union Memorial Hospital at that time, and said, "Barbara, I think that there should be a survey done to show the needs in Greater Homewood, that they are far beyond literacy, that they include crime and drugs and failing schools and vacant housing."

I said, "Well, why don't you do it?" He

smiled at me. I said, "Look, you've got the Institute for Policy Studies, you have the resources, you have the money. Why don't you just go ahead and do it?" He looked at me, and I said, "Oh, yes, you're looking for cover, Ross."

He said, "Exactly."

I said, "You're worried that if Hopkins does a wonderful study, it will be viewed with suspicion and hostility, 'Here is Hopkins trying to get some benefit rather than the community.'"

He said, "Yes. Would Union Memorial be willing to put up half the amount to pay for the study and to really become involved in it?"

I said, "I think that's a wonderful idea, and clearly this is bigger than Hopkins and Union Memorial. It's going to affect a much larger area."

The Institute for Policy Studies had a wonderful sociologist, Patricia Fernandez-Kelly, who used her graduate students to do a spot analysis. She said, "I am finding that many of the problems which affect Greater Homewood do not begin at 25th Street; they go much farther south. To balance that out, I think we ought to go north of University Parkway or Cold Spring Lane to the city line because there you will incorporate a number of the very well-educated, affluent people who have positions of power in city government or in the business community who could bring those resources to bear to help the southern area."

Within about a year and a half, we had a very comprehensive analysis of data showing crime statistics, under-performing schools, vacant housing, the racial and employment demographics. And at that point we thought we had a working plan.

Ross spoke to a good friend of his, Tim Armbruster, head of the Goldseker Foundation, and Tim said, "You need to take the study out to the neighborhoods and ask people to react and even revise drastically what the scientific study shows."

"Well," he said, "That costs money and staff, and we don't have that."

Tim Armbruster said, "Well, the Goldseker Foundation thinks this is important and we're going to support this."

It was the Hopkins connection. I know it was Ross Jones as an individual whom Tim Armbruster trusted and realized could bring greater resources, not only financial resources but a moral commitment, to the process. I see Ross Jones as being the moral wellspring of all of this.

Goldseker came up with the money and provided a staff director from the Development Training Institute to create a series of community meetings over a summer, and from that came about a plan which was adopted by the community. It represents the thinking of fifteen hundred people, not only in large meetings but in smaller subcommittees, resulting in thirty-two recommendations that were boiled down to five critical areas and a $32-million, five-year master plan.

There are volunteers and support from everywhere implementing that master plan. I mean volunteers from the College of Notre Dame, Loyola, and Hopkins leading the parade. Volunteers from the neighborhoods. Volunteers from the business communities. We don't have an organization, I like to say, at Greater Homewood; we have a movement and we are going to transform this area over the next five years.

Also in the last nearly two decades there's been a wonderful director of Volunteer Services, Bill Tiefenwerth. Bill has a remarkable understanding of the dynamics of the community, its problems and its strengths. He's been placing students as volunteers, matching the interests of the students with the community needs.

I cannot tell you what a difference it makes to have young people who are Hopkins students going to communities and saying, "We're your neighbors at least for four years." I can remember a young man standing up at a community meeting. He was handsome and articulate and attractive, and I thought, "Boy, I wish everybody at Hopkins could see who your representative in the community is today. You'd be very proud of him. This is Hopkins at its best."

"I remember a very good course called Cities Under Stress. The professors piled everyone on two buses and took us on a tour of Baltimore neighborhoods like Druid Hill, Highlandtown, and Canton. They gave us everything from histories about how the towns had been built up and what immigrant communities lived there to current efforts at revitalization. Juniors and seniors had never been exposed to these areas of the city."
CHRISTOPHER NIEDT, B.A.'99

In an area on Greenmount Avenue in the 2300 block, Hopkins students are involved. One of the Greater Homewood board members said, "There's an old rec center I think I can get opened if we can get some volunteers and some paint." Well, that was arranged. We got some battered old computers donated, where volunteer students from Hopkins could come and tutor children after school.

So this was a triumph in my mind, a real triumph. What I didn't know was that one of the students who was tutoring the children would stay at the center and type e-mail to Bill Gates. Now, students often do not understand all the restrictions that are out there, that we adults know, that make it impossible for anybody to reach Bill Gates, that make it impossible to do a lot of things. And so this young man for a month would write an e-mail to Bill Gates every night saying, "These kids are terrific, but this is a bunch of junk I'm trying to teach them on. I can keep it going with chewing gum and string, but this is a worthless bunch of junk. If we had some decent equipment, we could really do a terrific job with these kids." Well, at the end of a month or six weeks, there was a call from Seattle that said, "Mr. Gates has received your e-mail and you are to be the recipient of one hundred thousand dollars of state-of-the-art equipment." Now, you can imagine what that has done to that group of people.

I'll tell you one other Hopkins story. Last year we recruited a student from Hopkins, Anand Das, who was interested in the whole welfare-to-work movement. His job with Greater Homewood has been to create job fairs and to bring people together who had not really considered going out into the work force. Anand belonged to a fraternity at Hopkins. In my day, fraternities were places where young men drank excessively and did unspeakable things to the neighborhood. Well, times have changed, I gather, and fraternities are really wonderful outfits, at least the fraternities that I know about today.

Anand's idea was to see if he could start a basketball program after school. And you would have each fraternity adopting a group of students so that you could get a

rivalry going. But the point wasn't just to occupy these kids after classes but to bring them to Hopkins to show them what a college environment was and what it would mean to you, where you could go rather than doing drugs or sitting at home watching television after school, that there really was a great deal more to life, and that university campuses were not elitist and white, that indeed there was great diversity.

This new dimension that Hopkins is exhibiting both at Homewood and in East Baltimore of becoming *the* community leader is a thrilling one. Hopkins is now the major private employer in Baltimore

Hopkins purchased the Cambridge Arms Apartments (where F. Scott Fitzgerald had lived in the 1930s) in 1966, transformed it into a residence hall, and renamed it Wolman Hall.

City, and it recognizes what that means. So do all the political forces. The opportunity for Hopkins to really apply its knowledge and its students and its faculty to the laboratory right at its front door—namely its community—offers enormous promise both for the university and for the community.

Barbara Bonnell was president of Greater Homewood Community Corporation in 1998 and now serves on its board of directors.

"I came from a high school where people wanted to become professionals, wanted to get good-paying jobs. They weren't interested in being scholars. Hopkins might encourage people to be achievement oriented and committed to doing well and getting into good med schools so it can look good for Johns Hopkins University, but at the same time, if you want to have long, drawn-out conversations about what it means to be college educated within the world today and what one should do with that college education and what is our place as students within the larger scheme of things, you have people who are very intelligent who are willing to think about that with you." CHRISTOPHER NIEDT, B.A.'99

Student hangouts like P.J.'s Pub on Charles Street, left in 1991, offer a place to relax and solve the world's problems, if not one's own. Good coffee in a friendly setting (above in Gilman Hall) is now easy to find at Homewood and in East Baltimore.

Fraternity houses like Delta Phi, far above at 105 East 32nd Street in the 1930s, are places where students can escape campus stress. In recent years fraternities and sororities have become active in Greater Homewood community projects.

"There is an unbroken chain from the very beginning: Osler, Halsted, Welch, Kelly. They picked their successors, and then they picked their successors, and they picked their successors. So all the way, we are seeing the same heritage of excellence—the phrase Tommy Turner likes to use—that the original people had."
DR. RICHARD ROSS

"Johns Hopkins helps define where the cutting edge is. We're always pushing and stretching. To be in an environment where creativity and vision are rewarded is very, very exciting. No one in government or industry or any other academic institution has yet been able to make me an offer that I would seriously consider because I can't imagine why I would leave.

Today's science is not about nursing and medicine and public health; it's about urban health, and urban health is about more than the care of individual people in terms of disease or even prevention. It's about economic opportunity. It's about the problems of poverty and racism. It's about issues of nutrition. It's about what's a healthy community. That kind of discussion is not the exclusive purview of any part of this university; it's going to take the whole university."
PROFESSOR MARTHA HILL, R.N.'64, B.S.N.'66, PH.D.'87

Kelly Gebo remembered that before they started their medical internships, Victor McKusick escorted her cohort up hundreds of steps to the top of the Billings Building dome. "Dr. McKusick sprinted up those steps and we were all panting." McKusick had established the tradition many years before; the group at right made the climb in 1986. "The view is amazing," Gebo recalled. "You have to get a view of the whole city to appreciate where the patients are coming from."

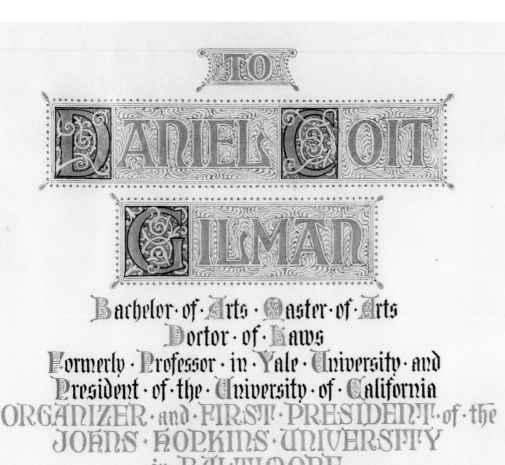

TO DANIEL COIT GILMAN

Bachelor · of · Arts · Master · of · Arts
Doctor · of · Laws
Formerly · Professor · in · Yale · University · and
President · of · the · University · of · California
ORGANIZER · and · FIRST · PRESIDENT · of · the
JOHNS · HOPKINS · UNIVERSITY
in · BALTIMORE
on · the · occasion · of · his · retirement · from · the · presidency

* * * * *

Presented · on · Commemoration · day · the · twenty-second · of · February
in · the · year · of · Our Lord · nineteen · hundred · and · two

*When Daniel Coit Gilman (far right) retired in 1901, he left a university and
a hospital that had achieved national renown. On Commemoration Day 1902,
grateful faculty and alumni gave him a beautifully illuminated manuscript with
the signatures of more than a thousand graduates from throughout his twenty-
five-year administration. The next day Ira Remsen was inaugurated as the university's second president.*

251

CHRONOLOGY

1795

May 19: Johns Hopkins is born at Whitehall, his family's tobacco plantation in Anne Arundel County, Maryland.

1867

August 24: Johns Hopkins incorporates both his university and his hospital.

1868

The Peabody Academy of Music opens under the direction of Lucien H. Southard with 148 students. In 1857 George Peabody had proposed the establishment of an institute in Baltimore to comprise a library, art gallery, academy of music, and a lecture series. Peabody attended the dedication of the institute's first building on October 25, 1866, and declared, "I never experienced from the citizens of Baltimore anything but kindness, hospitality and confidence." The building was completed in 1861, but the Civil War deferred the institute's opening.

1870

June 13: The first meeting of the trustees for the university and hospital is held under the charters of 1867. Galloway Cheston, Baltimore financier and philanthropist and one of the original trustees of the Peabody Institute, is elected president of the university's board of trustees.

1873

March 10: In his letter to the trustees of The Johns Hopkins Hospital setting forth the principles they are to follow, Hopkins states that the hospital must provide for "the indigent sick of this city and its environs, without regard to sex, age, or color, who may require surgical or medical treatment, and who can be received into the Hospital without peril to other inmates." The letter also directs that the hospital should accommodate four hundred patients and that a school of nursing and a school of medicine should be established in conjunction with the hospital.

December 24: Johns Hopkins dies at his residence at 81 Saratoga Street in Baltimore at the age of 78. The funeral, conducted according to the form of the Society of Friends of which Mr. Hopkins was a member, is held December 26 from his home; he is buried in Greenmount Cemetery. The Baltimore *Sun* estimates his estate at $8 million, including $2.25 million in stock of the Baltimore & Ohio Railroad Company and $1 million in bank stock. In an editorial, the *Sun* compares Hopkins' gift of the proposed university and hospital to those of George Peabody and Moses Sheppard and says of Hopkins, "It is gratifying to see a man who had thus successfully labored turning his attention ere life's close to great schemes of beneficence, by which an undoubted good is to result which cannot be interred with his bones. The good which such men do lives after them, blossoming and bearing fruit for the improvement and happiness of future generations."

1874

The Peabody Academy of Music becomes the Peabody Conservatory of Music.

October: University trustees write to Daniel Coit Gilman, president of the University of California in Berkeley, requesting that he consider the presidency of Johns Hopkins. Gilman travels to Baltimore and meets with the trustees on December 29. He tells them that he would create a major university devoted to research and scholarship. Trustees elect him president the following day.

1875

Daniel Coit Gilman begins his term as first president of The Johns Hopkins University.

1876

February 12: At the annual meeting of the board of trustees of the Peabody Institute, Judge George Brown makes the motion, which the trustees adopt, that "In view of the establishment of The Johns Hopkins University in our community, and of the wide field thus opened for the advancement of the intellectual & moral welfare of our people; and, desiring to establish, at the earliest date, affiliation with it in promoting the educational interests of the State: Resolved, That the Board of Trustees of The Peabody Institute convey to the President & Trustees of The Johns Hopkins University this expression of interest & good will; suggesting that this Institute being, within its scope, an educational element of the State, should be in sympathy with the university, and by interchanges of courtesy, and cooperation, assist in its high educational aims."

February 22: Daniel Coit Gilman is inaugurated as first president of The Johns Hopkins University during ceremonies at the Peabody Institute at which the Peabody Orchestra performs. An editorial in the *Gazette* proclaims, "We consider this one of the most important events in the recent history of the city. Baltimore, which has so often been reproached as a big provincial town, is about to become the seat of a great university—a city set on a hill, a center of light."

September 12: Thomas Huxley delivers the university's opening address and sparks controversy among those who see his writing as subversive of religious faith.

October 4: The first lecture at the new university is given this day at 5 P.M. by Professor Basil L. Gildersleeve on Greek lyric poetry. Classes for students begin the next day. The faculty consists of Gildersleeve (classics), James J. Sylvester (mathematics), Ira Remsen (chemistry), Henry A. Rowland (physics), and Henry Newell Martin (biology). The university is located a few blocks west of the Peabody Institute, on the west side of North Howard Street near Centre Street.

1878

Professor James J. Sylvester edits the first issue of the *American Journal of Mathematics*, and it is published "under the auspices of" the Publication Agency of The Johns Hopkins University. The *New York Times* says, "Johns Hopkins University ought to become the highest court of appeal in theoretical science and philosophy. Looking to occupy a position of this kind, it is very appropriate that so important a step as the foundation of a journal of pure and applied mathematics should be taken by the Baltimore university."

Summer: Dr. William K. Brooks of the biology department opens a laboratory on the Chesapeake Bay, the first undertaking of its kind by a university and the first such laboratory south of New England. By 1880 The Johns Hopkins University Marine Zoological Laboratory has moved to Beaufort, North Carolina.

September 30: Peabody Library occupies a new building designed by Edmund G.

Lind, who also designed the original building. The central well is sixty-one feet high, with six levels of stacks supported by cast-iron pillars. Fifteen percent of the library's holdings are not duplicated in the Library of Congress.

1879

Professor Ira Remsen edits the first issue of the *American Chemical Journal*, which is published by the publication agency.

June: George W. McCreary, A. Chase Palmer, and Edward H. Spieker receive the first bachelor of arts degrees granted by The Johns Hopkins University.

1880

Basil L. Gildersleeve edits the first issue of the *American Journal of Philology*, which is published by the publication agency.

1881

April 22: Alexander Graham Bell lectures to a large audience in Hopkins Hall on his experiments with the transmission of sound by using rays of light instead of wires.

1882

June 3: The first Peabody graduates receive their diplomas.

December: Herbert B. Adams, associate professor in history, edits *Studies in Historical and Political Science*, the first monograph series published by The Johns Hopkins University publication agency.

1883

January 30: In an address before the YMCA of Baltimore, John Work Garrett criticizes his fellow trustees for spending "enormous sums in the City of Baltimore and not at Clifton Park," Johns Hopkins' country estate, where both men had expected the university to locate. Clifton is gradually whittled away by condemnation: in 1879 for a reservoir, in 1892 for a railroad right-of-way, and finally the remainder of the estate in 1895 for a public park. A close friend, neighbor, and colleague of Johns Hopkins, Garrett also takes issue on several occasions with the emphasis on graduate study and research which, he implies, prevents the university from doing much for the young men of the region, whom Mr. Hopkins had wanted to aid.

May 1: The Druids Club of Baltimore defeats the newly formed Johns Hopkins lacrosse club 4–0. This is the last official game until 1888, when Hopkins enjoys its first win, a 6–2 victory over the Patterson

Kelly Miller became the first African-American student at Johns Hopkins when he entered the graduate program in mathematics in 1887. Miller completed his degree at Howard University.

Club. From 1888 Hopkins teams play every season except 1944, when athletics are curtailed by World War II.

December 3: The Baltimore *American* notes, "Whenever there is a lecture at Johns Hopkins University upon a plain, everyday topic of practical importance, the audience consists almost exclusively of men; but when a speaker gets up to talk about abstruse psychological subjects, such as are discussed by Mr. Stanley Hall, there is always a large number of ladies present. The same singularity is noticed at the Peabody lectures when profound themes are elucidated."

1884

The Johns Hopkins Glee Club gives its first concert. Woodrow Wilson sings first tenor. Wilson receives his Ph.D. in 1886; in 1913 he becomes the only U.S. president to hold an earned doctorate.

1885

May 4: University trustees adopt the official seal presented by Stephen Tucker of London. Tucker describes the seal as symbolizing "an heraldic picture of a University situated in the State founded by Lord Baltimore." The seal carries the motto "Veritas vos Liberabit" (John 8:32) and the legend "The Johns Hopkins University: Baltimore: 1876."

1886

The Proficiency in Applied Electricity course to train students for engineering positions opens under the leadership of Louis Duncan. The course was requested by local industry, especially the Baltimore & Ohio Railroad. The program is offered within the department of physics led by Henry A. Rowland, under whom Duncan obtained his Ph.D. Duncan tells President Gilman that he sees the course as teaching "electricity as a science and in its practical application." Hopkins offers the course for thirteen years and certifies ninety-one students, almost all of whom become practicing electrical engineers.

April 26: A resolution is offered for formation of an alumni association at the observance of the tenth anniversary of the university at Mount Vernon Place Methodist Church.

1887

Kelly Miller, the first African-American student to enroll at Johns Hopkins University, begins his studies for a graduate degree in mathematics with the encouragement of Simon Newcomb, professor of mathematics. Miller is obliged to leave two years later when the university's economic crisis prompts a twenty-five percent increase in tuition. Some years later, Newcomb and President Gilman recommend Miller for a faculty position at Howard University, his undergraduate alma mater, where he serves for many years as professor of mathematics and dean of arts and sciences.

1888

April 10: The hospital is completely finished inside and out except for the gas fixtures.

November 13: Daniel Coit Gilman and the Reverend J. F. Goucher give addresses at the opening ceremonies for the Woman's College of Baltimore. The *Sun* deems the new school "one of the most comprehensive of its kind in the world, and a fit companion for The Johns Hopkins University."

1889

May 7: About six hundred people attend ceremonies formally opening The Johns Hopkins Hospital. Mrs. Daniel Coit Gilman, writing to her daughters, describes the occasion: "Of course the great event of the week has been the opening of the hospital. The day was superb and all the buildings in apple pie order; grounds ditto. The exercises were in the administration building and a band of twenty-five instruments was in the third gallery. There was plenty of bunting and flowering plants and ladies in their gay dresses and it was a very pretty scene. Mr. Francis King made an excellent little address and Dr. Billings a very sensible one and Papa touched the popular heart as usual. I think all the speeches struck a very high note. There was no self-glorification, no mere spread eagle and empty oratory but a tone of earnest responsibility in the presence of a great trust. I think everyone must have been struck with it."

September: The failure of Baltimore & Ohio Railroad stock creates a crisis in the university's finances. Professors accept reduced salaries and fees are increased. President Gilman says the 1889–90 school year will begin as usual.

October 9: The Johns Hopkins Hospital's School of Nursing formally opens. Miss Isabel Hampton, first superintendent of nurses, speaks on the role, training, restrictions, and duties of nursing. The next day, an editorial in the Baltimore *American* says the training school for nurses "is destined to be in the coming years scarcely less important and useful than the development of the more imposing science of medicine and surgery, of which it is rapidly growing to be the twin companion. Without careful nursing, medicine and surgery are crippled agencies in the preservation of health and life, and with careful nursing it is often possible to preserve both without their assistance."

1890

March: Eight thousand books bequeathed to Johns Hopkins University by John W. McCoy are being readied for use. The collection concentrates on illustrated folios of geography and topography and engraved reproductions of the fine arts. Mr. McCoy, a Baltimore businessman, left his pictures and statues to the Peabody Institute.

April 13: The New York *World* runs an article with the headlines: "SOBER JOHNS HOPKINS. IT IS A UNIVERSITY OF MANLY YOUNG MEN. DUDES ARE SELDOM FOUND THERE." The text continues, "Johns Hopkins University is a steady-going place, containing few dudes and no students who lead the sumptuous lives that characterize the Harvard men. The classes are made up largely of manly fellows who mean business and who have little time to devote to college frivolity."

May 2: Five Baltimore women organize the Women's Fund Committee. M. Carey Thomas, Mary Elizabeth Garrett, Mary Gwinn, Elizabeth King, and Julia Rogers intend to raise the money needed to establish the School of Medicine with the condition that the school will accept women with the same high qualifications as male applicants. Women in Baltimore, Boston, Philadelphia, Washington, New

York, Chicago, San Francisco, and other cities contribute to the fund.

November 25: Professor William K. Brooks warns that unless oysters are deliberately planted, they will die out.

1891

The Johns Hopkins University lacrosse team wins its first national title in the Intercollegiate League. The win is followed by championships in 1898, 1899, and 1900. Hopkins then withdraws from the league to become a charter member of the Intercollegiate Lacrosse Association.

The Publication Agency of The Johns Hopkins University becomes The Johns Hopkins University Press and remains under the direction of Nicholas Murray, who is also librarian of the university.

May 15: Peter Ilyich Tchaikovsky performs at the Peabody Conservatory.

June 5: Dr. William Osler, physician-in-chief of the hospital, addresses the first class to graduate from The Johns Hopkins Hospital's School of Nursing and tells the new alumnae, "Practically, there should be for each of you a busy, useful, and happy life; more you cannot expect; a greater blessing the world cannot bestow. Busy you will certainly be, as the demand is great, both in private and public, for women with your training. Useful your lives must be, as you will care for those who cannot care for themselves, and who need about them, in the day of tribulation, gentle hands and tender hearts. And happy lives shall be yours, because busy and useful; having been initiated into the great secret—that happiness lies in the absorption in some vocation which satisfies the soul; that we are here to add what we can *to*, not to get what we can *from*, life."

October 1: Classes begin for the university's sixteenth year. Two days later, the Baltimore *American* reports that Miss Florence Bascom, daughter of the ex-president of the University of Wisconsin, will "take part" in the geological department, "giving special attention to the course in geography conducted by Professor Williams." Bascom's admission will not be as a "member proper" of the university; she will not pay tuition; she will not appear on the roster of students. Johns Hopkins sometimes allows this if no like instruction is offered at women's schools. Thus, Bascom's admission "marks no change in the general attitude of the university towards the admission of women to its courses."

December 16: McCoy Hall, a new academic building, is being planned by archi-

tects. To make room for the new structure, Levering Hall will have to be moved by jackscrews westward to Eutaw Street. The following July the trustees agree to the design and award a contract. The move of Levering Hall begins the week of August 12.

1892

March 15: Dr. Henry Hurd recommends that a separate ward for colored patients be built, and the hospital trustees vote that his motion be referred to the executive and building committees. The Baltimore *American* reports that the building will be erected to the east of the isolation ward on the east end of the hospital. It will have a center wing of three stories and north and south ward wings of two stories, with accommodations for fifty-six patients, men on the first floor, women on the second. Nurses will occupy the third floor of center wing. "Special care will be taken to see that the heating and ventilation apparatus is as perfect as possible. A sun balcony will be erected on each floor on the east side, for convalescents, while a sun bay-window will be constructed at the south end of the south wing. On each floor there will be a dining room, kitchen, lavatory and bath-rooms. . . . The building will be fireproof throughout."

November 1: The National Academy of Sciences meets this week at the physical laboratory of Johns Hopkins University. Hopkins professors Rowland, Remsen, Brooks, and Williams present half of the papers at the meeting. Public attendance in Baltimore is unprecedented.

December 22: Mary Elizabeth Garrett announces that she will give more than three hundred thousand dollars so that the Women's Fund Committee can meet its goal to open the medical school. Garrett stipulates that not more than fifty thousand dollars may be spent on buildings and the main building shall be known as the Women's Fund Memorial Building. The school must be a four-year graduate school for men and women, who are to be admitted without distinction between them. She also requires the creation of a committee of six women "to whom the women studying in the medical school may apply for advice concerning lodging and other practical matters, and that all questions concerning the personal character of women applying for admission to the school and all non-academic questions of discipline affecting the women studying in the medical school shall be referred to this committee, and by them be in writing reported for action to the authorities of the university." University trustees accept

Garrett's gift and her conditions on December 24. An editorial statement in the *Sun* says, "The women of the country are to be congratulated upon finding so generous a champion as Miss Garrett has proved to be, and the university has no less cause to be congratulated. All will wish for the success of this important step toward the education of women in a profession where equal opportunities with men have been so long denied them."

1893

June 13: Florence Bascom becomes Johns Hopkins University's first female Ph.D. The *American* notes that Miss Bascom is "very modest" and did not attend the ceremony to receive her diploma.

October 2: Dr. William H. Welch, professor of pathology in the university and the hospital's pathologist, reviews the credentials of applicants to the School of Medicine, five of whom are graduates of Johns Hopkins University. All of the applicants, including three women, are admitted and classes begin.

1894

Sisters Marian and May Garrettson Evans open the first music school for Baltimore children, the forerunner of the Peabody Preparatory School.

October 8: About a thousand people inspect the new McCoy Hall, which is lighted by electricity. The building also features two large electric elevators, said to be the first in Baltimore. Classrooms, offices, and lecture rooms are on the second and third floors, and a library with thirty thousand volumes is on the fourth.

1895

October 11: President Gilman meets with students to talk football and rouse interest in the sport. The *Sun* reports that Baltimore businessman Edgar Allan Poe, former coach of the Princeton team and of at least one former disastrous Johns Hopkins team, chides, "You must keep abreast of the other colleges. Foot-ball is today recognized as the typical college sport, the national college game. And you ought to be ashamed to have it said that such a great university as this is has no team to represent it." Poe contends that "nothing develops a man's character more, quickens and makes more perfect his self-reliance, makes him think quickly and act promptly, develops his muscles, his brain, his courage, his courtesy. It is the safest and most legitimate outlet for animal spirits among young men."

December 19: Professors and graduate students who have been members of chapters in other colleges organize the Johns Hopkins University chapter of Phi Beta Kappa Society. The Hopkins chapter is to be called Alpha of Maryland. Daniel Coit Gilman is elected chapter president and eighty-six men who have received bachelor's degrees from Johns Hopkins (of the more than four hundred total) are selected for alumni membership.

1896

May 20: William Bullock Clark, professor of organic geology and the state geologist, sails with six scientists for the Eastern Shore on an oyster navy boat. They will do preliminary work on the state geological survey.

October 14: The statue *Christus Consolator*, the gift of William Wallace Spence of Baltimore, is unveiled in the rotunda of the hospital by Emily Riggs, four-year-old great-granddaughter of the donor. The figure is a copy of a statue created by Danish sculptor Bertel Thorswaldsen.

1897

June 15: The first class graduates from The Johns Hopkins University School of Medicine. The fifteen graduates include Mary Packard of Bayonne, New Jersey, one of the three women who had entered with the class.

James M. Thompson and Edgeworth Smith establish the *News-Letter* to give undergraduates news on campus. The trustees had initially opposed the idea of a campus paper, but they eventually allow four issues to be published at the end of the 1896–97 school year. They give formal approval the following year. The paper is printed every two weeks of the school year for the first twelve years and is largely literary in character, with articles written by both faculty and students. In 1909 the *News-Letter* becomes a six-page weekly newspaper.

1898

November 4: A course of lectures in history especially for teachers in the Baltimore public and private schools begins at 8 P.M. The next morning a scientific course for teachers begins in the geological lecture room of Hopkins Hall. Each course will have twenty lectures.

1899

March 22: Members of an expedition from the medical school meet in Chicago

to begin a journey around the world. They will go to Hong Kong and Japan and will set up headquarters in Manila to study tropical diseases.

June 2: More than one hundred alumni, faculty, and graduate students join the new Johns Hopkins Club.

1901

February 5: Local newspapers announce the proposed gift of 151.75 acres of land on Charles Street as a new site for The Johns Hopkins University. Donors William Wyman and William Keyser stipulate that $1 million in endowment must be raised.

June 11: Daniel Coit Gilman gives his farewell address as president of Johns Hopkins. Gilman congratulates the university on the selection of Ira Remsen as its next president.

1902

February 22 and 23: The Johns Hopkins University belatedly celebrates its twenty-fifth anniversary and inaugurates its second president. Woodrow Wilson, of Princeton University, presents Daniel Coit Gilman with a testimonial gift from the alumni that contains the signatures of more than a thousand graduates. The Peabody Orchestra plays the processional.

November 6: Frederick Law Olmstead Jr. views the grounds of the future Homewood campus with President Ira Remsen.

1903

Henry Phipps, an iron and steel magnate, donates ten thousand dollars for the establishment of a tuberculosis clinic at The Johns Hopkins Hospital.

Dr. and Mrs. Christian Archibald Herter of New York give twenty-five thousand dollars to found a lectureship in medicine "designed to promote a more intimate knowledge of the researches of foreign investigators in the realm of medical science." The first lecture at the opening of the 1903–1904 academic year is given by Dr. Herter on the "Influence of Pasteur on Medical Science." Forty years later, Dr. Herter's nephew becomes one of the founders of the School of Advanced International Studies.

1904

February 7: The hospital loses seventy investment properties, most of them warehouses, in the Great Baltimore Fire. The buildings had yielded one-half of hospital's annual endowment income, which helps fund its free dispensary. This work is now threatened. The university does not hold its regular Commemoration Day exercises on February 22 because of the fire's enormous impact on the city. In May the hospital receives a letter from John D. Rockefeller Jr. stating, "In view of the high character of work which the hospital and medical school are doing in medical instruction and research, including the training of nurses, which work he understands will otherwise be materially curtailed because of the losses, my father will give five hundred thousand dollars to Johns Hopkins Hospital."

February 17: Poet William Butler Yeats visits the university and lectures to the English seminary on drama.

October 4: A portrait of Mary Elizabeth Garrett painted by John Singer Sargent of London is unveiled in the rotunda of the hospital and will remain there for several days for inspection by the public before being given a prominent place in the institution.

October 5: Dr. William S. Halsted performs the first operation in the new surgical amphitheater. A team of residents handpicked by Halsted to assist him includes Joseph Bloodgood, Richard H. Follis, James Mitchell, Harvey W. Cushing, Hugh H. Young, and J. M. T. Finney.

1905

February 22: Dr. William Osler delivers a farewell address at the Commemoration Day celebration before leaving for England to become regius professor of medicine at Oxford University.

May 17: The Baltimore *News* describes "New Wyman's Park" in "North Baltimore," which has not yet formally opened. The park is nearly a mile long, but narrow, located along east bank of Stony Run from Merryman's Lane to 29th Street, with frontage on Charles Street for one block. The park circles around to the rear of the proposed site of The Johns Hopkins University. "It is a very rough and heavily wooded territory" famous for chestnut expeditions. The park board is building a drive that will emphasize the land's natural beauty.

June: Pathologist William H. Welch, surgeon William S. Halsted, and gynecologist Howard A. Kelly of the original medical faculty meet their former colleague William Osler in London and sit for a portrait by John Singer Sargent. Mary Elizabeth Garrett will bear the expense of the painting.

June 5: Florence Sabin is promoted to

John Singer Sargent's portrait of four distinguished members of the original medical faculty, The Four Doctors, *provided a dramatic background for Professor John C. French's English literature class in McCoy Hall c.1915, shortly before the Faculty of Philosophy moved to Homewood from its original downtown campus. French wrote* A History of the University Founded by Johns Hopkins.

associate professor of anatomy. The following week the Baltimore *News* comments that "the appointment of a woman to a position of this rank in an institution of such distinction as The Johns Hopkins Medical School, and other than a college for women, is without parallel among American universities, in the Eastern section of the country at least." Dr. Sabin received her medical degree from Johns Hopkins University in 1900; in 1917 Sabin becomes the first woman at Johns Hopkins to be appointed to a full professorship.

1906

April: Professor Henry A. Rowland's multiplex telegraph is used by the Italian government to transmit messages from Naples during eruptions of Mount Vesuvius. For a time, these are the only telegraphic messages to get through.

May: John Singer Sargent's *The Four Doctors* is the centerpiece at a private showing before the opening of the 138th exhibition of the Royal Academy. The New York *Sun* reports that the painting is considered to be "the noblest work of art that has been hung in the Royal Academy since Sir Joshua Reynolds was president of it, and the most important and impressive of its type that has been painted by any man since the seventeenth century drew its curtain across the art of Holland."

May: University trustees approve a four-year undergraduate plan, although a bachelor's degree can still be secured in three years. The sub-freshman class will become freshmen and regular freshmen will become sophomores. Twenty courses are required for graduation.

1907

January 19: *The Four Doctors* is unveiled in McCoy Hall.

April 9: Registrar Thomas Ball announces that women "who have taken a baccalaureate degree at any institution of good standing" may be eligible to be admitted to graduate school at Johns Hopkins University. President Remsen observes, "It was simply a matter of justice—I should say of justice and common sense." The *News* notes that previously there have been "other special students from time to time."

May 28: The new athletic field is finished at Homewood and stands for spectators are being constructed. All should be ready by October for football games. Medical students are not expected to compete any longer since Homewood Field is so far from the hospital.

1908

The Johns Hopkins University lacrosse club plays its first game on Homewood Field under coach William C. "Father Bill" Schmeisser and shares the national championship with Harvard this year.

May: The university trustees approve a master of arts degree that will be granted when a Ph.D. is impossible or unnecessary. The M.A. degree is especially suited to public school teachers.

June: A generous gift from philanthropist Henry Phipps permits the hospital to establish America's first clinic for the treatment of mental illness and endows a professorship of psychiatry at the university.

September 17: Fire damages McCoy

Hall. Sargent's portrait *The Four Doctors* is protected when newspapers are rolled up and placed behind it to keep it away from the wall.

October 9: Botany professor Duncan S. Johnson announces that the regular work of his department will move to the Homewood campus since the new botanical gardens and greenhouse are ready.

October 13: Daniel Coit Gilman dies at the home of his sister in Norwich, Connecticut.

1909

June: President Remsen announces that the university will offer college courses for male and female teachers from public and private schools in cooperation with the Woman's College of Baltimore. Classes will start in October and continue to June; they will allow teachers to continue their professional duties and still attend classes.

November 20: Johns Hopkins University beats traditional rival St. John's College 18 to 0 in their first football game at Homewood Field.

1910

April: A campaign to raise the $2 million to build necessary buildings and move the non-medical portion of the university to Homewood is announced.

The Carnegie Foundation issues a report on education by Abraham Flexner that singles out Johns Hopkins as a leader in medical education. Five years later, Flexner notes that Hopkins, "fortunate in its freedom from all entanglements, in its possession of an excellent endowed hospital, and, above all, in wise and devoted leadership, set a new and stimulating example precisely when a demonstration of the right type was most urgently needed."

1911

February 22: The university board of trustees president, R. Brent Keyser, announces that construction on Homewood campus will begin next summer with the building of a hall dedicated to the memory of Daniel Coit Gilman.

May 8: Newspapers announce that faculty at the medical school will no longer be allowed to have private medical and surgical practices and must devote all their time to research and teaching. The change will severely restrict the income of popular physicians and the university is proposing to pay larger salaries.

June 13: So many degrees are awarded that recipients no longer fit onto the stage

of the Academy of Music. Four women have earned Ph.D.s, six M.D.s, and three M.A.s. The next day, the *Evening Sun* remarks, "Many people are waking up to the fact that the Johns Hopkins is a coeducational institution, and announcing their discovery to their friends in accents of amazement."

July: The Peabody Conservatory initiates a summer program in cooperation with Johns Hopkins University. The university also offers summer school for teachers of both sexes. Students have access to all the resources of the university. Classes include social hygiene, physics, education, English, German, manual training, chemistry, domestic science, biology, mathematics, Latin, French, and history.

1912

April 4: The governor of Maryland signs a law to fund "a school or department of applied science and advanced technology" at The Johns Hopkins University, establish scholarships, and give Hopkins enough money to build at Homewood. The law authorizes a bond issue of six hundred thousand dollars to construct buildings and provide equipment and to furnish fifty thousand dollars per year for maintenance. Hopkins is to give 129 scholarships of free tuition to "worthy men of this State" to the school of advanced technology or "courses preparatory thereto." The following month, the trustees agree to the state's conditions. In 1913 the school enrolls its first students, including Abel Wolman (although a number of students were admitted the previous fall to take mathematics and physics courses preliminary to their engineering studies). The first undergraduate engineering degrees are awarded in 1915. The department becomes the School of Engineering, with John Boswell Whitehead as its dean, in 1919.

September: Announcement is made that a new hospital building named for Charles L. Marburg (whose heirs gave one hundred thousand dollars in 1907) will be constructed for the use of private patients.

October 14: The *Sun* reports that Dean J. Whitridge Williams says that the number of medical students will be limited so that facilities will not become overcrowded. This year there are 355 medical students; almost fifty applicants have been turned away. Williams says that a limit on the number of students is "essential to the preservation of high ideals and of proper methods of teaching and that further expansion cannot be expected until those interested in the advancement of medical education add materially to its endowment and to that of Johns Hopkins Hospital."

November 20: The Harriet Lane Home for Invalid Children opens.

December: The first issue of Johns Hopkins *Alumni Magazine*, a quarterly designed to keep alumni "in closer touch with their alma mater," is published.

1913

January 14: The *Sun* writes that Robert W. Wood, head of the physics department, has developed "invisible-ray photography" and has used ultra-violet rays to take pictures of the moon. Professor Wood intends to make a series of ultra-violet and infra-red photos of planets.

February 10: The *American* announces that Johns Hopkins is the third U.S. hospital to be equipped with an x-ray machine. A few nights earlier, physicians Howard A. Kelly, C. F. Burnam, Frederick Baetjer, and Leonard Roundtree worked all night in a lab to set up the machinery. In order to work without tiring, "it was agreed that the radio-rays be turned on for light, and in this manner a new virtue of the radium was discovered—that where the rays shone there was no sleep to be had, for the light is visible even when the eyes of those about it are closed." By the time Dr. Baetjer dies of heart disease in 1933 at the age of 58, he has lost all his fingers and undergone more than one hundred operations as a result of his x-ray experiments.

1914

The Peabody Conservatory initiates the first formal music education program in Maryland, a model for later programs at other colleges in the state. Graduates will be awarded school music curriculum certificates.

September 28: A wagonload of books (part of the engineering library in the physics lab on Monument Street) arrives at the new Mechanical and Electrical Engineering Building at Homewood. The engineering department faculty will move in soon. Students will be able to watch turbines and other large equipment being installed in the coming months.

October 5–8: The twenty-fifth anniversary of the hospital is observed.

October 9: James Buchanan "Diamond Jim" Brady makes a surprise visit to East Baltimore to inspect the new urological building for which he provided funds. He is so pleased with the nearly completed building that he draws up a new will to provide money for its maintenance and improvements. The *American* reports that, "as usual, Mr. Brady wore a princely array of diamonds."

October 15: Librarian M. Llewellyn Raney announces a unique arrangement for the new library in Gilman Hall. Some universities have all books in one-large room under control of one librarian; others separate books by subject in accessible reading rooms. In the past, Johns Hopkins has used the latter system. Raney proposes to gain the advantages of both systems by designing the library in two stacks from basement to top floor, each resting on its own foundation. Each stack will have nine decks, two on each floor except the top floor, which will have only one. Books belonging to various departments will be placed on the same level as the classrooms and offices of that department.

1915

May 20: Rain forces into Gilman Hall the enormous crowds attending the inauguration of Frank Goodnow as third president of the university.

May 21: Henry Carter Adams, the first person to receive a Ph.D. from The Johns Hopkins University (because of the alphabetical order of graduates in 1878), dedicates Gilman Hall, and General George W. Goethals, the army engineer who managed the Panama Canal's construction, dedicates the new engineering building before an immense crowd. President Woodrow Wilson was expected, but could not leave Washington.

1916

February 11: Peabody faculty members and Peabody-trained musicians form the core of the Baltimore Symphony Orchestra as it plays its first concert. Baltimore's is the only municipal symphony orchestra in the United States.

June 13: Dr. William H. Welch announces that The Johns Hopkins University has received a grant from the Rockefeller Foundation to establish a school of hygiene. Welch will be its director and Dr. William H. Howell will head the physiological department.

October 16: The first Reserve Officer Training Corps in the United States is established on the Homewood campus.

1917

March: Members of the junior engineering class at Johns Hopkins University build two flag staffs in front of Gilman Hall as memorials to Bob Layfield, a Hopkins quarterback who died in the spring of 1915 as a result of injuries received in a football game in 1914.

Thirty-two medical students are among those who serve at the Johns Hopkins

Engineering students put their education to work in 1917 when they created a memorial to their classmate Bob Layfield, who had died from injuries incurred in a football game. The two flagpoles they erected in front of Gilman Hall were lopped off some years later, but the bases remain, along with plaques commemorating Layfield.

Base Hospital 18 in Bazoilles-sur-Meuse, France. They spend their senior year attending lectures and rounds with their professors and tending to the wounded in a thousand-bed facility built early in the war by the French government. By late 1917, the base hospital is filled with American victims of gassing as well as battle and bomb casualties. As the war progresses, the base becomes an evacuation hospital with the operating room in use around the clock. Tents are erected to handle the overflow of patients. Two medical students and two Hopkins nurses die from diseases contracted in the hospital. The remaining thirty students receive their medical degrees in April 1918 while still in France.

October 5: The *Sun* comments in an editorial that "The Johns Hopkins University is meeting a very present need in continuing the night courses in technology which were begun last year. The public response to this opportunity and privilege ought to be even greater at this time than it was twelve months ago. Higher education is suffering from the shock and disarrangement of war."

1918

October: The School of Hygiene and Public Health opens in the physical laboratory of the old downtown campus with Lieutenant Colonel William H. Welch as its director. Welch is on active duty as a member of the surgeon general's staff in Washington. The student body consists of persons ineligible for military service, among whom are two South American physicians, three women, one public-health instructor, and one medical student.

October 7: All classes at Homewood are suspended because of an influenza epidemic. Courses affected include the Students' Army Training Corps, college courses for teachers, and night courses in business economics and for technical workers. SATC classes resume in a few days.

1919

May 23: Charles H. Bochau of the Peabody Conservatory faculty conducts the first concert by the Johns Hopkins Orchestra. Sixty musicians are joined by members of the glee club.

June 18: Alumni gathered in Baltimore for a reunion decide to fund a residence hall for the Homewood campus to be named in honor of all the Hopkins men who gave their lives or participated in the late war.

Alumni, faculty, and friends of the university gathered in 1922 to watch senior class president Gibson Colby Engel break ground for the first residence hall on the Homewood campus.

November 28: A fire at the downtown campus virtually destroys McCoy and Levering Halls and many adjacent houses. This is declared the worst fire in the city since 1904. A few weeks later, on January 3, fire strikes the hospital's pathology building on the southwest corner of Wolfe and Monument Streets. The *Sun* reports, "When the flames leaped into the air and the word spread over the city that the hospital was afire hundreds of relatives and friends of patients hurried to the scene in taxicabs, automobiles, and trolley cars."

1921

February 22: Franklin D. Roosevelt, former assistant secretary of the navy, speaks at the annual Alumni Association dinner following Commemoration Day events at the Lyric.

December 23: An anonymous donor endows the Department of Art as Applied to Medicine at the School of Medicine. Max Brödel has headed the department since its inception.

1922

After several years of studying nutrition-related issues, Elmer V. McCollum and a team of researchers at the School of Hygiene and Public Health discover vitamin D.

February: The Rockefeller Foundation gives $1 million to erect new buildings for the School of Hygiene and Public Health and $5 million toward its endowment.

May 5: Professors Arthur O. Lovejoy, Gilbert Chinard, George Boas, and others interested in the exploration of ideas by scholars in various fields convene the first formal meeting of the History of Ideas Club.

June 12: Alumni break ground for the new residence hall at Homewood. Students occupy Alumni Memorial Residence in September 1923.

September: Registrar Thomas R. Ball indicates that the university will not bar student use of automobiles. "Some of the students waste a good deal of time riding about in automobiles, but this holds good for the public in general. Automobiling for pleasure is indulged in to an unnecessarily great extent."

1923

January 7: The Tudor and Stuart Club forms, thanks to a generous gift from Sir William and Lady Osler. The Oslers want the club to serve as a memorial to their son Edward Revere Osler, who was killed in the war in 1918. The *Sun* notes that the

Oslers see the benefaction as a "grateful recognition of the happy years" they spent in Baltimore. They hope the club will promote study of English literature of the Tudor and Stuart periods and promote "good fellowship and a love of literature among the members."

February 9: Undergraduates vote 232 to 37 against what the *News-Letter* calls "female intrusion into the undergraduate body." The coeducation issue arose the previous fall when some women students in the College for Teachers had asked for equal status and the same degrees as men in undergraduate school.

April 23: Interclass rivalry results in the arrest of one student after a near riot at a downtown hotel; four sophomores are arrested for suspicious behavior while attempting to kidnap a freshman.

October 13: Professor Knight Dunlap of the psychology department publishes preliminary results of three years of experiments on the effects of smoking. His study indicates that accuracy of work is negatively affected by smoking, but speed is not. Smoking may have a negative affect on thought processes, but accuracy may also be decreased by deprivation of smoking.

November 9: Students ignite the annual bonfire in preparation for the football game with St. John's. The *Sun* reports, "A tackling dummy in the uniform of St. John's was cremated noisily in the rear of the engineering buildings on campus." Revelers then march down Charles Street and serenade Goucher girls.

November: Ichiro Ohga, a graduate student from Japan, sprouts rare lotus seeds in the plant physiology lab behind Gilman Hall. The *Sun* notes that the seeds were found "under layers of peat, some of them 15 feet deep, in the bottom of what once was a pond on the edge of the Gobi Desert." It is speculated that the seeds may be five hundred years old.

December 4: The Baltimore *News* announces that a railway test set, designed by Professor William B. Kouwenhoven and built by Westinghouse Electric and Manufacturing Company, will soon be in operation in Machinery Hall. The model will be used for lab tests by students in electrical engineering and for research. "The outfit consists of two 25-horse power railway motors, the same as those used in one-man trolley cars." The newspaper comments that "such test sets are comparatively rare in this country. In most of the technical schools where they have been installed the high voltage required to operate the sets has rendered them unsafe for experiment."

1924

January 9: The Women's Clinic is dedicated at the hospital, made possible by a generous gift from Mrs. Lucy Wortham James of New York. Gynecologist Thomas S. Cullen and obstetrician J. Whitridge Williams (former dean of the School of Medicine) direct the new clinic.

Florence E. Bamberger becomes the first woman appointed a full professor (in education) in the Faculty of Philosophy.

August: The chemistry department finally makes the move to the Homewood campus. The *Sun* reports, "Highly flammable metals, acids and other substances, including gas explosive material" have been moved from old chemical laboratories on the downtown campus to the new chemistry building. A special police escort guarded the truck. The newspaper notes that in recent years the old building vibrated so badly from streetcars and trains

Over the years an intense football rivalry grew with St. John's College, which was a military school in 1925 when the team's fans from Annapolis helped to pack the stands for this game at Homewood Field.

that experiments had to be made in the middle of the night to keep vibrations from interfering with chemical reactions. Ira Remsen, the university's first professor of chemistry and its second president, will have an office in the new building. After Remsen's death in 1927, the building is named in his honor and his ashes are interred in a wall there.

1925

February 21: President Frank Goodnow announces his proposal to eliminate the first two years of the undergraduate program, award no bachelor's degrees, and raise the whole university to the level of a graduate school.

August 12: The School of Hygiene and Public Health begins the move to its new building at East Monument and Wolfe Streets.

October: The *Sun* reports that until a new structure can be built for it at Mount Vernon Square, the Peabody Preparatory School is moving into the old physical laboratory at 301 West Monument Street, "which is all that remains of the group of buildings where The Johns Hopkins University first came into being." The Prep moves to Leakin Hall in 1926.

1926

The Tudor and Stuart Club hosts poet Robert Frost, who reads to a crowded assembly.

The State of Maryland authorizes the Peabody Conservatory to grant bachelor of music degrees.

The *Sun* interviews William "Billy" Stewart, who has been custodian of the chemistry department since its opening in 1876, on the occasion of his seventy-first birthday. Stewart reminisces, "I liked those days when the classes were small and everybody knew each other by name. Now there are too many students to get acquainted with all of them. Lots of them speak to me and I know only their faces. I don't care at all for those flapping trousers and falling down socks worn by some of the fellows. In the early days most of the men dressed plainly and naturally. Some of them wore wing collars and gaiters to classes, but they were never undignified. There was none of this modern foolishness and swagger in dress. Once they tried the cap and gown for seniors, but that didn't last long. There wasn't much hazing of the new students in those days, as there is now. The fellows didn't seem to have time for that sort of thing. Bicycles were popular then. I still can remember Dr. Ira Remsen, head of the chemistry department, riding down the avenue on his bike. In the early days there wasn't any prohibition law to prevent a man from taking a drink in peace if he wanted to. I can recall the old Saturday night club, where graduate students and professors used to meet every week to discuss learned subjects over their beer."

February 22: At fiftieth-anniversary Commemoration Day exercises, the university awards a Ph.D. to seventy-nine-year-old Christine Ladd-Franklin, who earned the doctorate in 1882. Ladd was the first woman to teach in the Faculty of Philosophy when, from 1904 to 1909, she lectured in logic and psychology. The belated granting of the degree to the

Until Shriver Hall opened in 1954, Johns Hopkins had no large auditorium. The Peabody Institute often hosted commencements and formal occasions such as this Commemoration Day assembly.

brilliant scholar provokes *Sun* columnist Anne Kinsolving to ask, "Is Johns Hopkins University now conferring an honor upon Mrs. Christine Ladd-Franklin, or is Mrs. Christine Ladd-Franklin conferring an honor on Johns Hopkins University?"

April 26: The Department of Art as Applied to Medicine mounts an exhibit at the Baltimore Museum of Art at 101 West Monument Street.

September 30: In his annual report, President Goodnow acknowledges that the university cannot adopt his new plan without more endowment to replace the income that will be lost by not having freshmen and sophomores. "We can and should, however, always keep in mind the ultimate goal which we are striving to reach," he says.

October 21: An eight-story residence for nursing students opens at the corner of Broadway and Monument Street. The building is named Hampton House to honor Isabel Hampton, the first superintendent of nurses.

1927

March 19: Plans for the construction of a library for medical and public-health students and the hospital are announced. When the library is built, it houses the Department of the History of Medicine (later called the Institute of the History of Medicine) and William H. Welch becomes the department's first director. The *Alumni Magazine* notes, "There is a room for a secretary, but there is no secretary. Dr. Welch's associates are wondering what he is going to do about that. He has not, throughout his life, engaged a secretary. He prefers to conduct all correspondence himself."

March 22: Sophomores storm the National Guard Armory in Annapolis where the freshman class is holding its banquet. Police and fire departments arrive and ten students are jailed on charges of destroying state property, malicious mischief, and rioting; four are taken to the hospital. The melee causes three thousand dollars in property damage in the armory. The Student Council passes a rule that fighting is not allowed from two hours before a banquet until an hour after.

1928

June 23: In postseason competition, the Johns Hopkins lacrosse team beats University of Maryland 6 to 3 and earns the honor of representing the United States at the 1928 Olympics. Hopkins beats the Canadian team 6 to 3 in Amsterdam on August 6. The *Alumni Magazine* reports, "The game developed into an unusually rough affair, which greatly amused the spectators, most of whom had never witnessed a lacrosse game before." The next day Hopkins loses to the English team 7 to 6.

June: The Institute of Law is established as an independent school of the university; its purpose is to foster research into the law. Unable to secure an endowment following the financial crash of 1929, the institute closes in 1933.

1929

The portrait *The Four Doctors* is moved to the new Welch Medical Library.

May 7: The fortieth anniversary of The Johns Hopkins Hospital is celebrated. The hospital that opened with 250 beds now has 743. During the hospital's first year, 1,825 patients were treated; during the past year, 11,697 were treated. In forty years, the hospital has administered to 947,000 patients in wards and 3,250,000 in the dispensaries.

July 1: Joseph Sweetman Ames takes office as fourth president of the university.

October 6: Professor John C. French presides at the dedication of Levering Hall. The basement accommodates a cafeteria, kitchens, a soda fountain, student publication offices, and a barber shop. The main floor has a lobby paneled in black walnut, a parlor, a library, and a great hall in the rear. The YMCA conference room, a meeting room, and a faculty dining room are on the second floor.

October 15. The William H. Wilmer Ophthalmological Institute, the first in the United States associated with a university, is dedicated. The institute is under the direction of Dr. William Holland Wilmer of Washington, D.C.

1930

President Ames asks Mary Willard Berry, wife of Dean Edward Berry, to establish the Women's Faculty Club to promote social contacts among faculty members, some of whom live a distance from the Homewood campus. The name of the organization changes after the death of Mary Berry in 1939 to the Mary Willard Berry Club of The Johns Hopkins University. During World War II, members serve as a Red Cross group, as grey ladies, nurses aides, and air raid wardens. Membership in the club is offered to wives of the medical school faculty in 1948. In 1951 the name again changes to the Woman's Club of The Johns Hopkins University.

April 13: Nineteen memorial windows in the main reading room of Gilman Hall are dedicated to the memory of Francis T. King, one of the first trustees. Given by King's daughter, Mary King Carey, the windows feature stained-glass decorations against a clear background; the designs are printers' marks and watermarks employed by early printers and papermakers.

October: The Walter Hines Page School of International Studies opens on the Homewood campus with John Van Antwerp MacMurray, U.S. diplomat to China for the past five years, as its director. The president's report notes that the school is a research institution, "not one for students looking for degrees or certificates."

1931

February 1: Dean Edward Wilber Berry tells the *Sun* that he favors removing Johns Hopkins from intercollegiate sports and making all sporting competitions intramural. "The degree to which intercollegiate gladiatorial combats have developed in this country and the substitution of the aim of winning for the aim of sport for the sport's sake have caused both the public and the institution to lose sight of or subordinate the true value of athletics for physical improvement, recreation and training in all the manly virtues—physical, mental, and moral."

The first Turtle Derby is run in a large circle on the hospital's tennis court with turtles that are descendants of those kept in the early days of the hospital by Benjamin Frisbee, doorman at the hospital from 1889 to 1933. Contestants are released from a large wire sterilizing cage positioned in the middle of the circle. The first turtle to cross the outer line wins. Each department sponsors a contestant and contributes to the purse. The first winner is "Sir Walter," pride of the brain surgeons, who takes this year's cash prize. Races in following years attract several thousand spectators and more than fifty brightly painted, cleverly (and sometimes raunchily) named entries, some of them from Hopkins men in other states or countries. In the 1933 race, a large grey rabbit wanders slowly toward the circle's edge while "Panic II," the entry of the Phipps Clinic, trudges steadily outward and wins, thereby reinforcing the lesson of the tortoise and the hare. Future races are broadcast over national radio and featured in newsreels. Proceeds are contributed to charitable causes.

1932

September: An agreement between The Johns Hopkins University School of Hygiene and Public Health and the Baltimore City health department establishes the Eastern Health District in a one-square-mile area of the city near Johns Hopkins Hospital. The district becomes a base for broad public-health and research programs conducted with financial support from the Rockefeller Foundation and the U.S. Public Health Service. Public-health nurses are trained and graduate students in the School of Public Health gather data for thesis research. Residents of the Eastern Health District are contacted individually and information is collected on living conditions, general health, and diseases, especially tuberculosis and diphtheria. Child health studies and epidemiological studies on infectious and chronic diseases are important components of the research. In 1936 Dr. Thomas B. Turner and his staff conduct a study of syphilis that results in papers of national import.

1933

February 24: As the national depression worsens, the faculties of philosophy, engineering, public health, and medicine join with administrative officers of the university to voluntarily contribute a portion of their salaries to help avoid a university deficit. The *Sun* observes, "The money itself is extremely important to the university at this juncture; but we doubt that even the money will be as important, in the long run, as this demonstration that the members of its staff believe in it so strongly that they are willing to back their belief with hard cash."

1935

April 12: Students at Johns Hopkins, Morgan, and Goucher hold antiwar meetings on their respective campuses. The largest group is at Hopkins. Thirty Goucher girls march to a rally in front of Levering Hall protesting the ROTC and war spending. Demonstrations continue into 1938. Margaret Sparrow, a Goucher student at the time, recalls that she and her friends "knew there was a war coming. The ROTC at Hopkins was full. We didn't go to the peace march. It's not that we didn't want peace, but we didn't want

During the late 1930s students on many campuses held rallies for peace; this was one of several held at Homewood. At the same time hundreds of students trained in the ROTC for the coming war.

Hitler taking over. The peace marchers made a lot of noise, but they were always in a minority."

July 1: President Ames retires and is succeeded by geographer Isaiah Bowman.

1940

The Peabody Conservatory receives funding from the Carnegie Foundation to underwrite music training for teachers in Baltimore's public schools. Peabody's music education department administers the program.

1942

Johns Hopkins personnel staffs two five-hundred-bed military hospital units in the Pacific during World War II. General Hospital Unit 18 spends two years in Fiji, then moves on to the India-Burma theater. General Hospital Unit 118 is based successively in Australia; Papua, New Guinea; and the Philippines and treats more than forty thousand patients.

John W. Garrett dies and leaves the university his substantial library, which includes many rare and valuable books, his Asian and other collections, and his home, Evergreen House (about a mile north of the Homewood campus)—all without an endowment. Prior to her death in 1952, his widow, Alice Warder Garrett, establishes the Evergreen House Foundation and bequeaths to it her important collection of early twentieth-century paintings and an endowment, the income from which helps to maintain the house and its programs. Evergreen House is restored in the late 1980s and opens for daily public tours and for meetings and special events.

Commemoration Day and commencement exercises are canceled. President Isaiah Bowman says elimination of the public events is a "war emergency measure." Summer classes begin in June as part of the university's accelerated program during the war.

March 10: The Applied Physics Laboratory (APL) is established to research and develop a radio proximity fuze (VT fuze) that will explode a warhead near its target. Merle A. Tuve, who has been working on the problem since 1940 for the Carnegie Institution's Department of Terrestrial Magnetism and the National Defense Research Committee, is APL's founder and first director. President Bowman and university trustees agree to manage the lab and sign a contract with the government's Office of Scientific Research and Development. Trustee Luke Hopkins becomes the university's liaison with the laboratory. The

The SS Johns Hopkins *was christened on February 28, 1943. The Liberty ship was one of many launched in World War II to transport cargo.*

lab's first location is a renovated garage on Georgia Avenue in downtown Silver Spring, Maryland—its USED CAR sign remains as camouflage.

1943

January 5: Gunners aboard the USS *Helena* south of Guadalcanal fire shells equipped with APL's new VT fuze at the enemy for the first time. Although there is no way to be sure that the fuze has actually worked as planned, the targets are destroyed and credit is given to the fuze

by antiaircraft control officer Commander R. L. Cochrane on the *Helena*, who says, "I am convinced that both planes were shot down by the influence projectiles because of the phasing of the bursts that were visible." Later generations of the fuze are used successfully in Europe by U.S. and British forces. A third of the U.S. electronics industry becomes engaged in fuze production and more than twenty-two million are produced.

September 17: Christian A. Herter, Paul H. Nitze, William Yandell Elliott, Joseph C. Grew, Halford L. Hoskins, and John Lockwood (representing the Rockefeller Foundation) meet in Washington, D.C., to discuss the founding of a graduate school in international studies to be based in Washington. Later in 1943, the School of Advanced International Studies (SAIS) is established by the Foreign Service Educational Foundation.

1944

June 14: The U.S. Army 3312th Service Unit, ASTP (Army Specialized Training Program), arrives on the Homewood campus under the direction of Lieutenant Colonel Harry M. Gwynn. His command includes 344 men at Homewood, 160 students at the School of Medicine, and the ROTC department. Additional men are expected to join. Students take courses in engineering, German, French, and Italian.

October: Classes begin at SAIS in the mansion formerly used by the Gunston Hall School for Girls on Florida Avenue,

Some of the Hopkins doctors who served in the South Pacific during the Second World War tried to recreate the feeling of home when they dubbed their quarters the Maryland Club. Hopkins nurses and doctors staffed two military hospital units and treated thousands of patients.

N.W. Halford L. Hoskins, former dean of the Fletcher School of Law and Diplomacy, is first director.

November 29: Dr. Alfred Blalock performs the first "blue baby" operation after careful collaboration with pediatric cardiologist Dr. Helen Taussig and laboratory technician Vivien Thomas. One grateful mother later recalls her son's surgery, "All of a sudden the rosy complexion of his face struck me. His lips were bright red. . . . The following day he was sitting up in his bed. The blood circulation in his lungs was fully restored by a miracle of intelligence and skill, intense work, and exacting attention which Professor Blalock and his assistants accomplish every day."

1945

APL's Forest Grove Station in Montgomery County, Maryland, houses equipment that simulates on the ground the conditions faced in the air by APL's new supersonic ramjet engines.

1946

The conclusion of World War II and passage of the GI Bill of Rights creates a huge influx of veterans into the student body. Russell Baker recollects, "My Hopkins career was split by the war, and it was quite a different place when I came back. Suddenly there were a lot of people there, and most of them were wearing fragments of old military uniforms. Many of them had been in combat. It was a very mature group of people and so much more fun than it had been before. These were people who weren't impressed by the professors. They were constantly challenging and arguing, and the professors loved it. They hadn't had such a good time since they were in college."

Remembering the camaraderie among doctors from the two hospitals serving in North Africa during World War II, John Boland, dean of Guy's Hospital medical school in London, proposes to Alan Chesney, dean of Hopkins' School of Medicine, that the two institutions exchange doctors "to maintain the friendship, cooperation, and exchange of ideas which has been one of the better things which has come out of this War." Alfred Blalock becomes one of the first Hopkins doctors to take advantage of the opportunity and introduces his "blue baby" operation to England. In subsequent years, hundreds of physicians and administrators participate in the program.

February 5: Igor Stravinsky lectures to students and faculty at the Peabody Conservatory.

1947

McCoy College becomes a separate division for evening programs, offering degrees in arts and sciences, business, education, and engineering. The school is named for John W. McCoy, a Hopkins benefactor and Baltimore business and civic leader. By 1959, McCoy College offers a B.S. in nursing in cooperation with The Johns Hopkins Hospital's School of Nursing.

April 1: APL director Lawrence R. Hafstad establishes the Research Center of the Applied Physics Laboratory to conduct fundamental research in areas of present or potential importance. Over the succeeding years, the Research Center collaborates with the Johns Hopkins Medical Institutions on biomedical research and with the School of Public Health on investigations of the causes, prevention, and control of unwanted fires. In 1979 the Research Center is named to honor President Emeritus Milton S. Eisenhower.

1948

The university establishes the Chesapeake Bay Institute as a joint enterprise of the Chesapeake Biological Laboratory, the Virginia Fisheries Laboratory, and the U.S. Navy.

March 26: The Applied Physics Laboratory becomes a permanent division of the university, underscoring Johns Hopkins' commitment to research and its application for the public good. Ralph E. Gibson is named director; he holds this position until 1969.

October 19: Photographs that give humans their first look at the curvature of the Earth are made by APL cameras sixty miles up in a V-2 rocket launched at White Sands Proving Ground, New Mexico. The high-altitude research program, which had begun in 1946, also determines the intensity of cosmic rays, reveals the nuclear processes at the edge of our atmosphere, and investigates the extent of the solar spectrum.

December 17: Lynn Poole, the university's first director of public relations, initiates *The Johns Hopkins Science Review*, a television program that explains and demonstrates technical ideas to the general public. The first pilot program went on the air in March and was broadcast from Remsen Hall with the scientists explaining their work on camera and Lynn Poole acting as the host. The program, which is the first weekly network series produced by a university, becomes a national favorite and wins several prestigious awards before its demise in 1955.

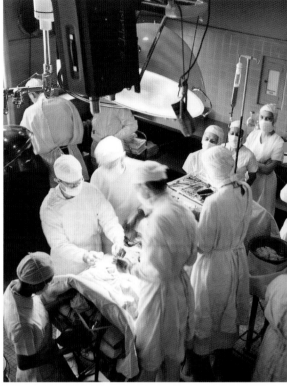

Television cameras loomed overhead on February 28, 1947, while Dr. Alfred Blalock performed surgery on the heart of a "blue baby." Nurse Olive Berger administered the anesthesia, as she had for other blue baby operations since 1944.

1948–1949

Three strains of the poliomyelitis virus are verified at Johns Hopkins. This verification is a step in the development of the Salk vaccine. In 1957 three Hopkins scientists, Dr. David Bodian, Dr. Isabel Morgan, and Dr. Howard A. Howe, are honored for their work by election to the Polio Hall of Fame.

1949

January: Biophysicist Detlev Bronk takes over the presidency of the university at the retirement of Isaiah Bowman.

1950

The School of Advanced International Studies affiliates with The Johns Hopkins University as a graduate division. Ownership of SAIS's buildings, library, and equipment is transferred to the university by the Foreign Service Educational Foundation. Philip Warren Thayer remains as dean, a position he has held since 1948.

April: Corbin Gwaltney edits the first issue of *Johns Hopkins Magazine*, which features top quality photographs and stimulating stories geared to alumni and friends of the university, a revolutionary concept for an alumni magazine.

1951

February 22: President Bronk inaugurates a plan enabling students to move at their own pace and breaking barriers between separate disciplines to create a "community of scholars." Bronk proposes "to make this a university in which the sharp distinction between undergraduates and graduates will be eliminated, . . . in which students will be given the opportunity to progress as rapidly as they are able." Under this New Plan, as it is called, any undergraduate student may take any course he is qualified for, even those at the graduate level. Bachelor's or master's degrees will not be required before working for a Ph.D.

1952

December: Owen Lattimore, director of the Walter Hines Page School of International Relations since 1938 (with a leave of absence from 1941 to 1944 to serve as an advisor to Chiang Kai-Shek), is indicted by a federal grand jury on seven counts of perjury following investigations by congressional committees and accusations by Senator Joseph McCarthy that Lattimore is the top Soviet agent in the United States. University trustees grant Lattimore a leave of absence with pay. Some people feel that Lattimore should be fired outright prior to a verdict. The charges against him are dropped in 1955 and Lattimore returns to Johns Hopkins to teach history until 1963.

1953

April 16: The Walter Hines Page School of International Relations at Johns Hopkins closes in a reorganization of the university. President Detlev Bronk says that the closing of the school is an "attempt to simplify Johns Hopkins' academic structure."

September: Lowell Reed, recently retired from a distinguished career as a professor of biostatistics and dean of the School of Hygiene and Public Health, takes over as university president when Detlev Bronk resigns to become the first president of Rockefeller University.

1954

The completion of Shriver Hall provides the Homewood campus with its first large auditorium. In 1939 Alfred Jenkins Shriver, a local lawyer, left the university the residue of his estate to build a lecture hall. In accordance with the conditions of his will, the building's walls are adorned with murals depicting the Hopkins class of 1891 (Shriver's class), ten philanthropists of Baltimore, ten famous beauties of Baltimore (as chosen by Shriver), the

original Faculties of Philosophy and Medicine, the original trustees of the university and hospital, and Baltimore clipper ships.

The first building at APL's new site in Howard County, Maryland, is dedicated. Lee A. DuBridge, president of the California Institute of Technology, says at the occasion, "Whenever you find a highly successful group, I suggest you seek the causes for its success not in the organization chart, not in the budget book, not by counting uniforms or rank, but by finding a man or small group of men who have created the spirit of the place and who know how to preserve that spirit." By 1982 the initial 290-acre complex has been expanded to 365 acres and APL buildings encompass one hundred thousand square feet of floor space. Field testing often takes place off-site.

February 22: Johns Hopkins University receives a silver and ebony mace, the gift of the late historian Douglas Southall Freeman, at Commemoration Day ceremonies. Professor C. Vann Woodward makes the presentation to Carlyle Barton, president of the board of trustees. The *Evening Sun* explains that the mace depicts in silver the "role of the arts and sciences in man's cultural development since ancient times." The mace will be carried at all future university processions and will be at the president's side during official functions.

1955

February 22: SAIS inaugurates its new campus in Bologna, Italy, as an American graduate school where future leaders of the U.S. and Europe can study together and learn to cooperate, without national bias, toward common goals. C. Grove Haines is the Bologna Center's organizer and first director (from 1955 to 1972).

May 11: Ames Hall, the new engineering building, is dedicated by Governor Theodore R. McKeldin, who declares that the structure embodies "the lasting shadow of a series of men whose impact on the university, the state, the nation, and the world will live on beyond their mortal stay on earth." The building is named for Joseph Sweetman Ames, fourth president of the university, a physicist and pioneer in aeronautical science. Ames Hall cost $1.5 million in state-appropriated funds.

1956

July 23: Milton Stover Eisenhower, brother of the current U.S. president, is elected the eighth president of The Johns Hopkins University.

December 13: Plans are announced for the construction of a new house for the university's president in the woods at the west end of the botanical gardens. This is the site designated for the president's house in the original campus plan. President Eisenhower expresses his pleasure: "I look forward to living on the Homewood campus so I can meet with student and faculty groups for discussions of mutual interests in an informal atmosphere." In 1972 the residence is renamed Nichols House to acknowledge the generous gift of trustee Thomas Nichols, which helped fund its construction.

1957

The Washington Center for Foreign Policy Research is established at SAIS for the discussion and study of U.S. foreign policy by both academics and government officials. The center undertakes government-sponsored research projects, holds weekly roundtable discussions with notable guests, and helps attract distinguished scholars to the faculty. In 1980 the center is reorganized as the Johns

Just six years after the School of Advanced International Studies opened its center in Bologna, Italy, in 1955, this modern five-story building became its new home, evidence of the European program's success.

Theodore Wyatt, second in command of the Applied Physics Laboratory's space program, described features of one of the lab's early satellites to visitors c. 1959.

Hopkins Foreign Policy Institute with all SAIS professors as members.

1959

Almost seven thousand students are enrolled in McCoy College, more than twice the combined enrollment of the other divisions of the university.

February 13: The Carnegie Institution of Washington, D.C., announces that, after forty-three years, it will move its East Baltimore operations to a new building on the Homewood campus. The Carnegie's areas of interest have changed over the years from anatomy and embryology to biochemical research.

September 17: Engineers from the Applied Physics Laboratory watch as their first satellite, the Transit 1-A, is launched from Cape Canaveral, Florida; it does not achieve orbit. In a second attempt, the Transit 1-B achieves an orbit on April 13, 1960, but it takes another year of experiments before an APL satellite reaches its projected orbit on June 29, 1961.

1960

July: William B. Kouwenhoven, professor emeritus and former dean of the School of Engineering; James Jude, a resident in surgery; and Guy Knickerbocker, an electrical engineer and instructor in surgery, report in the *Journal of the American Medical Association* that they have developed a process to keep the inert or fibrillating heart pumping blood by performing closed chest massage. Professor Kouwenhoven's defibrillation machine has been in use since 1957, but this new technique will enable trained persons to provide the life-saving therapy without machines or surgery. The procedure becomes known as cardiopulmonary resuscitation, or CPR.

July: Hundreds of children on the East Coast catch fireflies for researchers at the university's McCollum-Pratt Institute. The scientists are interested in the two chemicals that produce light in the fireflies, luiferin and luciferase, which also influence the energy output of cells. Hopkins researchers hope to obtain a million bugs this year because they are sending the chemicals to labs all over the world. Children receive thirty cents for every one hundred fireflies they deliver. Ten-year-old David Vogel says, "Of course the money makes a difference, but mostly I just like going out there and catching 'em."

1961

April 27: A modern five-story building for the Bologna Center of SAIS is dedicated on Via Belmeloro, a short distance from the center's original building. President Milton S. Eisenhower, SAIS dean Francis O. Wilcox, and past and present rectors of the University of Bologna participate in the ceremonies.

November: The Johns Hopkins University Press "publishes" the work that will become a bestselling release in subsequent years: an eighteen-inch plastic replica of a human skeleton that quickly gains the moniker Mr. Bones. The likeness is the result of three years of painstaking work by Leon Schlossberg, a renowned medical illustrator on the faculty.

1962

McCoy College introduces a Master of Liberal Arts Program for adults seeking to broaden their knowledge, perspective, and insights through studying the great ideas of civilization. The program draws lecturers from the Faculty of Philosophy as well as leading experts from cultural and other academic institutions in the region. The M.L.A. program is the first of its kind and is widely copied by other colleges and universities. In 1999 the program moves to the School of Arts and Sciences.

1963

McCoy College establishes an educational center at APL. Advanced technical courses leading to a degree have been taught at APL since 1958; this new center recognizes their popularity. The faculty is drawn largely from APL staff, but the students are generally not APL employees. In 1982, the APL center comes under the auspices

Ross Jones, right, and board chairman Charles S. Garland welcomed former President Dwight Eisenhower to a trustees meeting at SAIS in Washington on October 7, 1963, as Milton S. Eisenhower, then president of The Johns Hopkins University, nudged his brother toward the door.

of the G.W.C. Whiting School of Engineering.

May: The Maryland Department of Education authorizes the Peabody Conservatory of Music to grant the doctor of musical arts degree. Students have been enrolled in the program since the fall of 1962.

October: The School of Advanced International Studies moves to its new eight-story building at 1740 Massachusetts Avenue, N.W. President Milton Eisenhower actively solicited funding for the building, which came largely from the Ford and Rockefeller Foundations. In 1986 the building is named to honor founder and trustee Paul H. Nitze and his wife for their "lifelong dedication to public service, to education, and to SAIS."

1964

November 7: The new university library is formally dedicated. It is large enough to house library collections from across the campus and also provides space for future acquisitions. To keep the enormous building from overwhelming the older, small buildings on campus, the architects place four and a half of the structure's six levels underground. The following April, university trustees vote unanimously to name the library for President Milton S. Eisenhower.

1965

McCoy College becomes the Evening College and Summer Session. The name change accompanies a shift in continuing studies courses to the graduate level as a response to the changing requirements of students. Community colleges now fill the needs of most part-time undergraduates.

1966

The merger of the School of Engineering Sciences and the Faculty of Philosophy creates the School of Arts and Sciences.

The Peabody Library becomes a department of the Enoch Pratt Free Library system.

1967

July 1: Former ambassador to Brazil and assistant secretary of state Lincoln Gordon assumes the presidency of the university when Milton Eisenhower retires.

July 28: Johns Hopkins' new oceanographic vessel, *Ridgely Warfield*, named for the former director of the Institute for Cooperative Research, is christened. Funding for the 106-foot catamaran comes in part from the National Science

Steven Muller's inauguration in 1972 followed an unusual series of events. Lincoln Gordon, right, had resigned abruptly the year before, shortly after naming Muller as provost. Trustees asked Milton Eisenhower, left, the university's enormously popular president from 1956 to 1967, to step in as interim president until a successor could be chosen. Muller, center, served as president until 1990.

Foundation, and its operation is supported by the Office of Naval Research. A seven-person crew and eleven scientists can live aboard at sea for thirty days. Hopkins teams plan to use the vessel to study problems associated with the spectrum of motion in the ocean. Don Pritchard of the Chesapeake Bay Institute says, "If we're ever going to understand how the ocean responds to forces driving it, we must understand this motion."

1967–68

The university's student-operated radio station, WJHU-AM, broadcasts to dormitory residents for 235 days during the 1967–68 academic year. Programs include coverage of all away football and lacrosse games. During the riots in early April 1968 following the assassination of Martin Luther King Jr., the station remains on the air for almost sixty continuous hours to keep students informed with news bulletins and police and university announcements. The station, still run by students, switches to FM in 1979. In 1985 the university converts WJHU-FM to a professionally operated National Public Radio member station.

1968

May: The *News-Letter* announces the formation of the Black Student Union, "an informal coalition of Negro students" who want more black freshmen admitted (and more representation in the admissions office) and more black professors. Spokesmen Bruce Baker and John Guess say the association will "attempt to deal on the student level with the problems of race relations at Hopkins and within the Baltimore community."

1969

May: The Committee on Coeducation assembled by President Lincoln Gordon submits its majority report recommending that "coeducation at the undergraduate level be instituted without delay, that is, by the fall of 1970." The report suggests that coeducation will increase the potential pool of applicants from which to choose students, increase student body diversity currently biased toward natural sciences, improve the intellectual and social environment, and stop the discrimination that denies admission to qualified women. "The committee also believes that undergraduate coeducation is economically feasible as well as educationally desirable."

October 15: Some three thousand people gather on the Homewood campus for a rally before marching downtown in support of the Vietnam Moratorium. A Student Council resolution asks President Gordon to officially close the university for the day. Gordon refuses, saying "to suspend operation would violate the institutional neutrality of the university on matters of public policy."

October 30: The Academic Council recommends that women be admitted to the undergraduate divisions of The Johns Hopkins University by the following September; the trustees make the policy official with a formal resolution on November 10.

1970

April 16–30: Students hold demonstrations to protest university governance, American policy in Southeast Asia, and the presence of military recruiters on campus. President Lincoln Gordon offers to hold a referendum on the recruitment issue. Administrators secure a court injunction forbidding the occupation of campus buildings and other disruptions of university activities. Students hold a vigil on the lawn in front of Homewood House and some faculty join students in a two-day strike of classes. An agreement between the administration and the students ends the strike on April 23. The administration agrees to suspend recruitment until a referendum of full-time students and faculty on April 30. Seventy percent of those eligible to vote participate; the vote is 1,183 against recruitment, 1,121 for reinstatement of recruitment.

May 5: A memorial service is held for students killed during anti-war demonstrations at Kent State University.

September: The first full-time female undergraduates—transfer students and freshmen who can commute from home—arrive on campus.

1971

March 12: President Lincoln Gordon submits his resignation; Milton Eisenhower assumes the position as interim president on April 5. On that day Steven Muller, recently appointed as provost, also takes his new post. The prevailing opinion is that the budget deficit will be Eisenhower's biggest challenge and he calls a university-wide faculty meeting to urge the restoration of fiscal integrity.

President Milton Eisenhower lends his support to the formation of a credit union to benefit faculty and staff. On May 14th, in accordance with Federal Credit Union membership regulations, seven members deposit five dollars each into an account at the Maryland Credit Union League. The Johns Hopkins Federal Credit Union becomes fully operational on October 1, 1971, when the payroll deduction system goes into effect. The closing statement for the first year shows 744 members and assets of fifty-one thousand dollars. By 2000, there are more than twenty-three thousand member accounts with assets in excess of $99 million, making it one of the largest credit unions in Maryland.

As director of the Centennial Planning Office, electrical engineering professor emeritus Ferdinand Hamburger Jr. recognizes the university's need for an archival repository and oversees the establishment of what is later named the Ferdinand Hamburger Jr. Archives. The Hamburger Archives is the official archival repository for university administration, all Homewood divisions, and the School of Advanced International Studies.

1972

February 1: Steven Muller takes office as president of the university. Later this year, he also becomes president of The Johns Hopkins Hospital, the first person to hold both offices since Daniel Coit Gilman. Muller relinquishes the hospital presidency in 1983.

Spring: Students mount a festival on the Homewood campus that they call 3400 on Stage. In subsequent years the event becomes known as Spring Fair.

October: A new women's locker room opens in the Newton H. White Jr. Athletic Center. Undergraduate women on campus now number 375.

1973

February: President Steven Muller announces the launch of an ambitious capital campaign to raise $100 million for the Johns Hopkins Institutions. In 1976, as the university celebrates its centennial, national chairman and trustee Alonzo G. Decker Jr. announces the successful culmination of the Hopkins Hundreds campaign, which has raised $108.9 million.

February 22: The Milton Stover Eisenhower Medal for Distinguished Service is presented to G. Wilson Shaffer, who received his B.A. and Ph.D. degrees from Hopkins. The citation notes Shaffer's vigorous support for student athletics. "He installed an imaginative program of physical education" in 1934 and was a staunch advocate of free admission to athletic events. Shaffer founded the Psychological Clinic in 1936. He became dean of the College of Arts and Sciences in the 1940s and was appointed dean of the Homewood schools in 1948.

The last class in the hospital's School of Nursing graduates. The Johns Hopkins School of Health Services attempts to revive nursing education in 1975, but the school closes in 1979.

The Evening College opens a satellite branch at Columbia, Maryland. Almost three hundred students enroll in the eleven courses offered at the new site. Over the next twenty-five years the Columbia Center moves three times to ever-larger quarters to serve a growing demand for part-time graduate education in the greater Baltimore/Washington region.

1974

March 7: Fifteen naked students streak around the Homewood campus and through the Eisenhower Library. A few nights later about three hundred people watch a well-publicized "Streak for Cancer" that raises four hundred and fifty dollars. The new Hopkins Cancer Research Center turns down the money, but the American Cancer Society happily accepts it. Faculty members express hope that a noon-time streak through the Johns Hopkins Club will occur soon.

1975

April: University trustees adopt the third balanced budget in a row. Severe cuts (especially in the administration), tuition increases, state aid, and the generosity of donors help to achieve the goal of fiscal stability. President Muller asks the faculty to consolidate overlapping academic programs.

September 10: President Emeritus Milton S. Eisenhower speaks at opening ceremonies for The Johns Hopkins University's centennial celebration.

1976

February 20–22: The university celebrates the centennial of Gilman's inauguration with a special Commemoration Day convocation and symposia on expansive themes such as cosmology, the responsibilities of the critic, international health, and the impact of natural sciences on society. Northrop Frye, Linus C. Pauling, and S. I. Hayakawa are among the speakers. The Baltimore Symphony Orchestra performs "A Song of Celebration," composed by alumnus Hugo Weisgall with lyrics by poet John Hollander, at a special concert at the Lyric.

May 21: Dr. Helen Brooke Taussig receives the Milton Stover Eisenhower Medal for Distinguished Service at the centennial commencement ceremony. The citation notes her part in kindling the idea for the "blue baby" operation that "provided the impetus for cardiac catheterization and, eventually, open-heart surgery." The citation concludes, "the astounding progress of cardiac surgery in the last thirty years began with Taussig and Blalock." Vivien T. Thomas, another prominent member of the blue baby team, is honored with a doctor of laws degree. Thomas was Dr. Alfred Blalock's laboratory technician for many years and "earned a reputation as an outstanding surgical assistant and research associate, contributing ideas as well as operative and manipulative techniques," according to the citation that accompanies his honorary degree. During the first blue baby operation in 1944, "He stood behind Dr. Blalock as the operation proceeded, offering suggestions and answering questions put to him by Dr. Blalock."

Robert D. H. Harvey and the Honorable Harrison L. Winter were witnesses in 1977 as Hopkins president Steven Muller and Peabody director Richard Franko Goldman signed papers formalizing the affiliation of the two institutions..

1977

July: The Johns Hopkins University and the Peabody Institute formally affiliate after a century of friendly association. Peabody faculty member Leon Fleisher recalls, "The fact that Hopkins extended its umbrella over our sodden heads was a sign that we had a value to an institution as far-reaching and powerful as Hopkins. It gave us security. Everybody's heads were lifted and backs were straighter. Hopkins has been most judicious in the affiliation. They've not tried to impose or micromanage. And I think that Hopkins has benefited also. Students from Hopkins come to study at Peabody. It's a recognition that music is one of those human activities that most ennoble the spirit, which I think is one of Hopkins' goals."

1978

May 17: The Alan Mason Chesney Medical Archives is dedicated in conjunction with a special meeting of the Johns Hopkins Medical History Club. The archives is named to honor the author of a three-volume history, *The Johns Hopkins Hospital and The Johns Hopkins University School of Medicine: A Chronicle.*

September: SAIS graduates Hermann Eilts, ambassador to Egypt, and Samuel Lewis, ambassador to Israel, are members of the U.S. delegation headed by President Jimmy Carter during negotiations that lead to the Camp David Accords.

October: Daniel Nathans and Hamilton Smith, professors of microbiology at the School of Medicine, are awarded the Nobel Prize in Medicine or Physiology (with Swiss microbiologist Werner Arber) for their work on site-specific restriction enzymes. Their work paves the way for future research to decipher the construction and function of genes. The *News American* congratulates the Nobel laureates and their colleagues, "That this is a community of great intellectual ferment and excitement is amply proved by the honor accorded these men and the Hopkins."

1979

The G.W.C. Whiting School of Engineering is established as Johns Hopkins University's first named division with a gift from the estate of George William Carlyle Whiting, co-founder of the Whiting-Turner Contracting Company. Engineering studies gain momentum from the restoration of a separate division.

Professor Julian Stanley founds the Office of Talent Identification and Development, renamed the Center for Talented Youth in 1981. Its mission is to provide encouragement to highly able pre-collegiate youth by engaging them in programs that provide academic stimulation.

May: The Women's Medical Fund Memorial Building is torn down to make way for a modern preclinical teaching center. The demolished building, the first devoted to the School of Medicine, was built in 1894 to house the anatomy department.

Daniel Nathans' delight was apparent as he read news accounts of the 1978 Nobel Prize for Medicine or Physiology, which he shared with colleague Hamilton Smith and Swiss microbiologist Werner Arber.

1980

The SAIS Student Association requests that the division's commencement ceremony be held in Washington instead of at Homewood.

1981

April 30: The university signs a $40-million contract with NASA and AURA (Association of Universities for Research in Astronomy, Inc.) to establish the Space Telescope Science Institute at Homewood. The institute will become the world center of research in optical astronomy where scientists will receive information from the Hubble Space Telescope transmitted to them from the Goddard Space Flight Center.

1982

American Impressionism, an exhibition organized by the Smithsonian Institution Traveling Exhibition Service, features paintings from the Peabody's collection. The exhibition opens in Paris and travels to cities in Eastern Europe.

July: The Peabody Library leaves the Enoch Pratt Free Library system, which managed the library when the Peabody could not afford its maintenance, and officially becomes the George Peabody Collection of The Johns Hopkins University.

1983

The Johns Hopkins University School of Nursing opens as a degree-granting division, fulfilling the long-held dream of nursing alumnae for university affiliation. The first year is used for staff and student recruitment and planning. Twenty-eight students are admitted in September 1984.

The School of Public Health and SAIS establish a three-year degree-granting program in international health services.

October 8: The newly renovated Miriam A. Friedberg Concert Hall is dedicated at the Peabody Conservatory. Sidney Friedberg funded the renovations as a memorial to his wife, whom he had met while they were both students at Peabody.

December 13: A rally at Levering Hall calls for the university to convert the Applied Physics Laboratory to non-military research. Speakers include Professor Emeritus Jerome Frank and Chaplain Chester L. Wickwire. Leaders of the movement contend that the development of nuclear weapons is contrary to the humanitarian traditions of the university and a threat to humanity. Edward L.

Cochran, assistant director at APL, says that by and large APL's programs are not nuclear and are more in the nature of fleet defense.

1984

The Dome Corporation is established as a for-profit joint venture of the university and the Johns Hopkins Health System. Dome is involved in venture management and development of property around the hospital.

The Johns Hopkins Hospital acquires the Baltimore City Hospitals on Eastern Avenue. For a time the complex is named the Francis Scott Key Medical Center, but it becomes known as the Johns Hopkins Bayview Medical Center.

The Evening College and Summer Session becomes the School of Continuing Studies.

The Campaign for Johns Hopkins is launched with a $450-million goal. It concludes in 1989, having exceeded that objective with gifts totaling $644 million.

1985

The School of Medicine drops the Medical College Admissions Test as a requirement for applicants in an effort to encourage students to pursue broader educational opportunities before entering medical school.

The Peabody reaches the $12-million goal of its first campaign after its affiliation with Johns Hopkins and becomes a division of the university.

June 17: The School of Continuing Studies announces that it will revive its Master of Arts in Teaching Program for science teachers. The M.A.T. program began in 1950s with the support of the Ford Foundation.

October 20: The university reveals plans for a $209-million expansion in its facilities. The program will add six new buildings, upgrade dormitories, install a computer network, and expand classrooms and laboratories. Construction will take place at Homewood, in East Baltimore, and at APL. SAIS and Peabody will acquire and renovate existing buildings. The work is to be financed by a bond issue.

1986

September 10: The Hopkins-Nanjing Center for Chinese and American Studies opens in a new building constructed for that purpose on the campus of Nanjing University in the People's Republic of China. The center was established as a joint partnership between the two univer-

The inauguration of the Hopkins-Nanjing Center for Chinese and American Studies in 1986 marked the culmination of years of planning.

sities with the intention of training an equal number of American and Chinese postgraduate students each year in economics, history, political science, and international relations. The center features the only open-stack library in China.

1987

Spring: SAIS acquires more office and classroom space when it moves into a second building on Massachusetts Avenue. The newly acquired building is named for Benjamin T. Rome, a generous benefactor to the school.

Spring: The School of Continuing Studies opens its Downtown Center to accommodate the growing number of professionals in downtown Baltimore seeking advanced degrees and enhancement of their skills and training. The center has eight classrooms, two computer labs, an executive conference room, and a 222-seat auditorium as well as an on-site library, bookstore, and academic advising services.

The Center for Metropolitan Planning and Research becomes the Institute for Policy Studies. Originally established in 1968 as the Center for Urban Affairs, the institute is devoted to solving social problems through research and teaching. In 1992 the institute begins awarding master of arts degrees.

Following twelve years of meticulous research, an archaeological excavation, and a full-scale restoration, Homewood House, one of the finest Federal residences in America, is reopened to the public as a museum. The house was built by Charles Carroll of Carrollton, the last surviving signer of the Declaration of Independence, as a wedding present for his son, Charles Jr., when he married Harriet Chew of Philadelphia. Homewood's collections of eighteenth- and nineteenth-century furnishings and decorations include pieces originally owned by the

Carroll family. Robert G. Merrick, who lived in the house while a graduate student, funded the restoration.

November: The Peabody Symphony Orchestra performs at Tchaikovsky Hall and the Hall of Columns in Moscow.

1988

September 26: The Montgomery County Center in Rockville is established to allow executives in high-tech industries the opportunity to earn advanced degrees part-time. Engineering, arts and sciences, business, public-health, and education courses are offered.

December 6: Janus, the Eisenhower Library's online catalog, is demonstrated to students, faculty, and staff. Horizon, a graphical-based program, replaces Janus on January 1, 1998.

The School of Continuing Studies opened a satellite facility in downtown Baltimore in 1987 and celebrated by offering a series of special programs to entice business people to stop by. A new Downtown Center is scheduled to open in January 2001.

1990

The George Peabody Medal, the highest honor granted by the Peabody Institute, is awarded to outgoing university president Steven Muller "for his immeasurable contribution to the renaissance of Peabody as one of the top conservatories of music in the world."

July: William C. Richardson takes office as the university's eleventh president. Former board chairman Morris W. Offit recalls, "We had enormous financial problems in the late '80s and early '90s. The crises forged a bond among us because we had to work very hard. We worked through it, and we did it not only efficiently and very professionally but with dignity. Bill Richardson was probably the best crisis manager in the country. We could not have had a better president at that particular time. He worked eighteen hours a day, seven days a week. There were a lot of complaints that he only gave Hopkins five years. I think he gave Hopkins ten years, considering the amount of work that he did. I have nothing but enormous respect for Bill Richardson's contribution."

Lieutenant Governor Melvin A. "Mickey" Steinberg announces that the state will give $15 million to the Peabody if the institute can raise the same amount by September. The goal is reached. As part of a five-year aid package, the state acquires Peabody's art collection for the people of Maryland.

Rowland Hall is renamed for Zanvyl Krieger, who provided a large gift to renovate the building for the Krieger Mind/Brain Institute after the physics department moved to the Bloomberg Center. The Mind/Brain Institute, first proposed in 1987, brings together scholars and researchers from multiple disciplines to promote a synthesis of experimental and theoretical studies of the way in which the human brain controls and initiates human behavior. Krieger Hall also houses the Departments of Mathematics and Cognitive Science and Homewood Academic Computing.

December: Hopkins astrophysicist Sam Durrance flies on the space shuttle *Columbia* with the Hopkins Ultraviolet Telescope, which features diffraction gratings like those originally devised by Henry A. Rowland, the university's first professor of physics. The telescope gathers information in the far ultraviolet portion of the electromagnetic spectrum of hundreds of distant astronomical objects. More than two dozen faculty, staff, and students are involved in the HUT project, which was conceived by astrophysicist Arthur F. Davidsen of the Department of Physics and Astronomy. During the flight, Davidsen's team monitors Durrance's progress at the NASA Marshall Space Flight Center in Huntsville, Alabama. Durrance flies a second HUT mission in March 1995.

1992

June: The Chesapeake Bay Institute and its field laboratory near Shady Side, Maryland, close because of budget cuts.

1993

June 23: The Peabody Inn opens in four restored townhouses and provides lodging for an Elderhostel program that draws four thousand people annually for courses in music and dance.

Members of the Peabody Orchestra took in the sights of Moscow between their performances at the Hall of Columns and Tchaikovsky Hall in 1987.

1994

Astronomers from across the nation gather at the Space Telescope Science Institute to watch pictures of the collision between comet Shoemaker-Levy 9 and Jupiter taken by the Hubble Space Telescope.

September: Campaign chairman Michael R. Bloomberg announces the Johns Hopkins Initiative and its goal to raise $900 million; one third of this amount has been pledged already.

November: For the first time in the 101-year history of the School of Medicine, this year's incoming class of 120 students includes more women than men. According to Catherine DeAngelis, vice dean for academic affairs and faculty, women compose forty-three percent of last year's class and fifty-three percent of this year's. About thirty percent of the medical faculty are women, slightly above the national average.

November: Jerome A. Alston, Helen Holton, and Blair V. Johnson, students in the School of Continuing Studies' graduate business program, win a national student case-study competition in San Francisco sponsored by the National Black MBA Association.

1995

The Johns Hopkins University Press launches Project MUSE in collaboration with the Milton S. Eisenhower Library to offer the full text of the press's scholarly

journals via the World Wide Web. By 1999 MUSE publishes online forty-six JHUP titles in the humanities, social sciences, and mathematics.

May 31: President William C. Richardson leaves Johns Hopkins University to become president and CEO of the W. K. Kellogg Foundation. He is succeeded by Daniel Nathans, Nobel laureate and professor of molecular biology and genetics, as interim president.

June 13: The report of the Joint Trustee Committee on Governance (involving trustees of the university and the hospital) recommends the creation of the Board of Johns Hopkins Medicine to coordinate and serve the complementary interests of the Johns Hopkins Health System and the School of Medicine, allowing them to respond to the healthcare marketplace in an integrated way.

July: The Harry and Jeanette Weinberg Foundation pledges $20 million to the hospital to support construction of a new cancer treatment center. The new facility opens in 2000 and is named in the Weinbergs' honor.

October 1: The School of Arts and Sciences is named to honor alumnus Zanvyl Krieger, who has committed $50 million (on the condition that $50 million in matching money is raised) in an effort to increase the endowment of the school.

December 4: The Applied Physics Laboratory announces the establishment of the Institute for Advanced Science and Technology. The new institute builds on the thirty-year association between the Johns Hopkins Medical Institutions and APL, which has seen the development of more than a hundred specialized medical devices, including rechargeable pacemakers and implantable medication-dispensing systems.

1996

June 6: Groundbreaking for the School of Nursing's new building takes place on Wolfe Street across from the hospital. With fifty-seven thousand square feet of usable space, the Anne M. Pinkard Building nearly doubles the amount of space available to the school before the new facility's opening in January 1998.

September: It is announced that a Center for Central Asian Studies will open at the Paul H. Nitze School of Advanced International Studies in Washington. The center will concentrate on six historically Muslim republics in a core area bounded by Turkey, Iran, Afghanistan, and Russia.

September: The G.W.C. Whiting School of Engineering offers a minor in entrepreneurship and management to give students business and management training in addition to their engineering courses. "I think we're answering what seems to be the loud and clear message that's coming from the engineering community. We're near the leading edge on this," Roger Westgate, associate dean for academic affairs, tells a professional journal.

The School of Hygiene and Public Health expanded into its new eight-story building on East Monument Street in 1996, greatly increasing its ability to explore a wide range of local, national, and international health concerns.

September 1: William R. Brody takes office as the thirteenth president of The Johns Hopkins University. From 1987 to 1994, Dr. Brody was Martin Donner Professor and director of the Department of Radiology, a professor of electrical and computer engineering and of biomedical engineering at the university. During the same period, he was also radiologist-in-chief at The Johns Hopkins Hospital.

1998

Peabody Ventures, a for-profit company headed by Dr. Geoffrey Wright, is established to market intellectual properties developed by the Peabody computer music department.

September: After a seventeen-year restoration, the magnificent Renaissance tapestry *Scipio's Triumphal Entry into Rome* is rehung in the Peabody's renovated North Hall, now Leith Symington Griswold Hall.

October: University board chair Michael R. Bloomberg announces a gift of $45 million to the Johns Hopkins Initiative which, combined with his previous commitment of $55 million, brings his total contribution to that campaign to $100 million, the largest in Johns Hopkins' history.

1999

An independent economist's analysis shows that Johns Hopkins and its affiliates generate $2.41 billion in net new income in Maryland this year. Spinoff spending adds an additional $2.74 billion for a net impact of $5.15 billion on the economy of the state.

Hopkins researchers receive fifty-six patents and file for an additional 199. Fourteen new companies have been created in Maryland to commercialize Hopkins inventions.

February 5: The School of Continuing Studies, which will be renamed the School of Professional Studies in Business and Education effective July 1, renews Hopkins' commitment to downtown Baltimore by signing a lease as the sole tenant of a new facility in the former Hamburger's building at Charles and Fayette Streets. The graduate division of business and management will consolidate its classroom and office space at the new facility, which is expected to open in January 2001.

May: The School of Public Health receives a commitment of $20 million from the Bill and Melinda Gates Foundation to create the Institute for Population and Reproductive Health.

June 24: More than four hundred Homewood employees and friends crowd into the Schafler Auditorium in the Bloomberg Center to watch a broadcast of the liftoff of the Far Ultraviolet Spectroscopic Explorer at Cape Canaveral, Florida. Scientists downstairs in the Bloomberg Center take control of the mission, which they have designed for NASA, once FUSE achieves orbit.

December 31: Peabody Artist-in-Residence Forrest Tobey conducts a "virtual orchestra" in the world premier of "Anthem for the Millennium," by Whiting School and Peabody graduate Charles Kim, during the countdown to midnight in New York's Times Square.

2000

February 14: Near Earth Asteroid Rendezvous (NEAR) succeeds as the spacecraft, developed and operated for NASA by the Applied Physics Laboratory, enters its orbit around Eros, an asteroid named for the Greek god of love. Kishin Moorjani observes, "This is a tremendous feather in the cap of the space scientists at APL. It's absolutely breathtaking to see something that was fired off from this little Earth so far ahead of time rendezvous with an asteroid hundreds of millions of miles away. It gives you great faith in the laws of physics—and great admiration for the people who do this sort of work, from the people who calculate these orbits to engineers and scientists who actually put the equipment together. What we learn from this will have a great effect on our knowledge of the way the universe came about."

March: The Johns Hopkins Center for Gun Policy and Research, established in 1995 at the School of Public Health, plays a significant role in the Maryland General Assembly's passage of the Responsible Gun Safety Act.

After a year's work and input from literally hundreds of people, a new master plan for Homewood is adopted. The plan is intended to guide campus development and construction for decades. An anonymous donor jump-starts implementation of the plan, financing a six-month blitz on twenty-four acres of open space in the heart of campus. New brick, marble, and granite paths replace asphalt roads and walkways; cars and trucks are diverted from the center of campus. The result will be a safer, more functional, more serene, and far more attractive Homewood. New master plans for the East Baltimore campus, the Applied Physics Laboratory, and the Peabody Institute also are being developed.

WHO WE ARE

Only degrees earned or titles held at The Johns Hopkins University or The Johns Hopkins Hospital have been cited with the narrators' names. Unless noted otherwise, interviews were conducted by Mame Warren in Baltimore, Maryland.

RUSSELL BAKER, B.A.'47, is the author of several best-selling books, the host of *Masterpiece Theatre*, and a retired columnist for the *New York Times*. He was interviewed at his home in Leesburg, Virginia, on July 13, 1999.

WILLIAM BANKS, B.A.'29, is the retired president of Lord Baltimore Press. He was interviewed on July 16, 1999.

JOHN BARTH, B.A.'51, M.A.'52, is professor emeritus in the Writing Seminars and the author of books of fiction and nonfiction. He was interviewed on October 29, 1999.

ERNEST A. BATES, B.A.'58, is a neurosurgeon and chairman and CEO of American Shared Hospital Services in San Francisco. He was interviewed on October 11, 1999.

MICHAEL R. BLOOMBERG, B.S.E.'64, serves as chairman of The Johns Hopkins University Board of Trustees. He is founder and president of Bloomberg LP. He was interviewed in New York City on November 17, 1999.

HELEN BLUMBERG, B.A.'73, is a librarian at the Enoch Pratt Free Library. She was interviewed on October 13, 1999.

BARBARA JOHNSON BONNELL, M.A.'54, is the director of information at Baltimore Development Corporation and former president of Greater Homewood Community Corporation. She was interviewed on July 12, 1999.

PROFESSOR GRACE BRUSH is a paleobotanist in the Department of Geography and Environmental Engineering of the G.W.C. Whiting School of Engineering at Johns Hopkins. She was interviewed on July 6, 1999.

DR. BENJAMIN CARSON is a professor of neurological surgery, oncology, pediatrics, and plastic surgery at the Johns Hopkins School of Medicine, director of pediatric neurosurgery at The Johns Hopkins Hospital, and author of the best-selling autobiography *Gifted Hands*. He was interviewed on December 17, 1999.

LOUISE CAVAGNARO served in the administration of The Johns Hopkins Hospital from 1953 until 1985, when she retired as an assistant vice president. Since 1985 she has volunteered at the Alan M. Chesney Medical Archives. She was interviewed on July 19, 1999.

ANNE E. CLARK, B.S.'49, pursued a professional career and studied electronics, computer software and programming, and construction administration after completing her degree at McCoy College. She was interviewed on November 24, 1999.

PROFESSOR DONALD COFFEY, PH.D.'64, is a cancer researcher and the Catherine Iola and J. Smith Michael Distinguished Professor of Urology. He also holds appointments in the Departments of Oncology and Pharmacology and Molecular Sciences and is a member of the principal professional staff at the Applied Physics Laboratory. He was interviewed on May 9, 2000.

DR. CATHERINE DEANGELIS is on leave from her position as vice dean for academic affairs and faculty at the Johns Hopkins School of Medicine while she serves as editor of the *Journal of the American Medical Association*. She was interviewed on November 15, 1999.

LEON FLEISHER is a world-renowned pianist and holds the Andrew W. Mellon Chair in Piano at the Peabody Conservatory of Music. He frequently conducts the Peabody Orchestra. He was interviewed on September 23, 1999.

KELLY GEBO, B.A.'91, M.D.'95, M.P.H.'00, is a fellow in the Department of Medicine at the Johns Hopkins School of Medicine. She was interviewed on August 31, 1999.

JACK G. GOELLNER was director of The Johns Hopkins University Press from 1974 to 1995.

NEIL GRAUER, B.A.'69, is a media relations and marketing representative at the Johns Hopkins School of Professional Studies in Business and Education and a freelance writer. He was interviewed on July 8, 1999.

PROFESSOR JOHN GRYDER joined the Department of Chemistry at The Johns Hopkins University in 1949. Now professor emeritus, he was interviewed August 10, 1999.

ELISE HANCOCK is an acupuncturist and the former editor of the *Johns Hopkins Magazine*. She was interviewed on October 31, 1999.

JUDGE JOHN HARDWICKE has served as the chief judge in Maryland's Office of Administrative Hearings since 1989. He taught courses in business law from 1955 (at McCoy College) to 1998 (in the School of Continuing Studies). He was interviewed on December 6, 1999.

MINNIE HARGROW began working in the Levering Hall cafeteria in 1946. In 1981 she became the attendant in the Office of the President and has served Presidents Muller, Richardson, Nathans, and Brody. She was interviewed on September 20, 1999.

D. A. HENDERSON, M.P.H.'60, directed the smallpox eradication program for the World Health Organization from 1966 to 1977. He is University Distinguished Professor, director of the Center for Civilian Biodefense Studies, and former dean of the School of Hygiene and Public Health. He was interviewed on December 21, 1999.

PROFESSOR MARTHA HILL, R.N.'64, B.S.N.'66, PH.D.'87, is on the faculty and director of the Nursing Research Center at the Johns Hopkins School of Nursing, where she specializes in the prevention and treatment of hypertension in urban African Americans. In 1997 she became the first nurse to serve as president of the American Heart Association. She was interviewed on March 30, 2000.

PROFESSOR FREDERICK HOLBORN is a senior adjunct professor of American foreign policy at the School of Advanced International Studies. He was interviewed on December 10, 1999.

HELEN HOLTON, M.S.'95, represents the Fifth District on the Baltimore City Council, serves on the Johns Hopkins Alumni Council, and chairs the Alumni Council's Community Service Program. She was interviewed on November 23, 1999.

RICHARD JAMES JOHNS, M.D.'48, founded the Johns Hopkins School of Medicine's program in biomedical engineering in 1966. He retired as director of the Department of Biomedical Engineering in 1991, but he continues as University Distinguished Service Professor. He was interviewed on April 5, 2000.

ROSS JONES, B.A.'53, retired in 1999, becoming vice president and secretary emeritus of The Johns Hopkins University. He is chair of the 125th Anniversary Celebration Planning Committee. Ross Jones was interviewed on June 18, 1999.

PROFESSOR FRANKLIN KNIGHT joined the faculty in 1973 and is the Leonard and Helen R. Stulman Professor of History. He recently served as president of the Latin American Studies Association. He was interviewed on July 21, 1999.

ALEXANDER KOSSIAKOFF, PH.D.'38, served as director of the Applied Physics Laboratory from 1969 to 1980, after which he became its chief scientist. He was interviewed on March 14, 2000.

PROFESSOR STUART W. "BILL" LESLIE concentrates on the history of science-based industry and twentieth-century American science in the Department of History of Science, Medicine, and Technology at The Johns Hopkins University. He was interviewed on January 5, 2000.

MARJORIE G. LEWISOHN, M.D.'43, is a physician in private practice (retired) and clinical associate professor of medicine emerita at the Cornell University medical school in New York City, where she was interviewed on November 4, 1999.

WILBERT "BILL" LOCKLIN, B.S.'57, was assistant to Johns Hopkins president Milton Eisenhower before becoming president of Springfield College in 1965. He now heads Locklin Management Services in Longmeadow, Massachusetts. He was interviewed in Reston, Virginia, on December 23, 1999.

PROFESSOR RICHARD MACKSEY, M.A.'53, PH.D.'57, holds joint appointments in the Humanities Center, the Writing Seminars, and the Department of History of Science, Medicine, and Technology. He was interviewed on June 24, 1999.

PRISCILLA MASON served as administrative assistant to three deans at the School of Advanced International Studies before she retired in 1967 and took a seat on the school's Advisory Council. She was interviewed at her home in Washington, D.C., on December 1, 1999.

VICTOR MCKUSICK, M.D.'46, is University Professor of Medical Genetics and the former William Osler Professor and director of the Department of Medicine. He also holds appointments in epidemiology at the School of Public Health and in biology at the School of Arts and Sciences. In 1997 he received the Albert Lasker Medical Research Award for his pioneering work in medical genetics. He was interviewed on December 20, 1999.

KISHIN MOORJANI is editor-in-chief and chair of the editorial board of the *Johns Hopkins APL Technical Digest* and chair of the G.W.C. Whiting School of Engineering's programs at the Applied Physics Laboratory. He was interviewed on April 4, 2000.

STEVEN MULLER served as president of The Johns Hopkins University from 1972 to 1990 and of The Johns Hopkins Hospital from 1972 to 1983. He is on the faculty of the School of Advanced International Studies in Washington, D.C., where he was interviewed on September 28, 1999.

DR. DANIEL NATHANS was University Professor of Molecular Biology and Genetics and a senior investigator at the Howard Hughes Medical Institute. He shared the Nobel Prize for Medicine or Physiology in 1978 and received the U.S. Medal of Science in 1993. Dr. Nathans served as interim president of The Johns Hopkins University from 1995 to1996. The quotation on page 165 is excerpted from a commencement address he gave on May 20, 1998. Daniel Nathans died on November 16, 1999.

NANEEN HUNTER NEUBOHN, M.A.'64, is managing director of Morgan Stanley in London and serves on the Advisory Council of the School of Advanced International Studies' Bologna Center. She was interviewed on February 13, 2000.

CHRISTOPHER NIEDT, B.A.'99, is a graduate student at the University of California at Berkeley. He was interviewed on July 27, 1999.

ERIC NOJI, M.P.H.'87, is chief of the Emergency Health Intelligence Unit in the World Health Organization's Department of Emergency and Humanitarian Action. In the 1980s he was on the faculty of the Johns Hopkins Schools of Medicine and Public Health and an attending emergency physician at The Johns Hopkins Hospital. He was interviewed on September 16, 1999.

MORRIS W. OFFIT, B.A.'57, served as chairman of the university's board of trustees from 1990 to 1996. He is president of OFFITBANK in New York City, where he was interviewed on November 4, 1999.

SIDNEY OFFIT, B.A.'50, is a former senior editor of *Intellectual Digest*, conducts writing workshops at the New School, and is an adjunct professor at New York University. He was interviewed at his home in New York City on November 3, 1999.

E. MAGRUDER "MAC" PASSANO JR., B.S.'67, M.L.A.'69, and his family headed Waverly Press until 1998. He has been a member of the School of Professional Studies in Business and Education's Advisory Board since 1984. He was interviewed on December 13, 1999.

ROBERT POND SR. is professor emeritus of materials science at the G.W.C. Whiting School of Engineering. He was interviewed at his home in Westminster, Maryland, on December 8, 1999.

DR. RICHARD ROSS is dean emeritus of the Johns Hopkins medical faculty and professor emeritus of medicine. In 1994 he received a doctor of humane letters degree from The Johns Hopkins University. He was interviewed on April 13, 2000.

ELIZABETH SCHAAF is the archivist of the Peabody Institute and has been the curator of several exhibitions concerned with Peabody history. She was interviewed on September 14, 1999.

JEROME SCHNYDMAN, B.A.'67, is executive assistant to President William R. Brody and secretary of The Johns Hopkins University Board of Trustees. He was interviewed on June 17, 1999.

ROBERT SCOTT, B.A.'52, retired as director of athletics and head lacrosse coach at The Johns Hopkins University. He was interviewed on April 3, 2000.

PROFESSOR STELLA SHIBER is associate professor and associate dean for professional education programs and practice at the School of Nursing, where her area of expertise is community nursing and substance abuse. She was interviewed on November 22, 1999.

MARGARET SPARROW, M.A.T.'58, grew up near the Homewood campus and received her bachelor's degree from Goucher College before entering the Master of Arts in Teaching Program at McCoy College. She was interviewed on October 8, 1999.

FORREST TOBEY, M.M.'97, D.M.A.'97, is founder of the jazz/world music ensemble Off Chants and director of the 21st Century Ensemble in Alexandria, Virginia, where he was interviewed on March 21, 2000.

DR. THOMAS TURNER is dean emeritus of the Johns Hopkins medical faculty, professor emeritus of microbiology, and the author of *Heritage of Excellence, The Johns Hopkins Medical Institutions, 1914–1947*. He was interviewed on February 16, 1999.

BERT VOGELSTEIN, M.D.'74, holds joint appointments in molecular biology and genetics and is Clayton Professor of Oncology at the Johns Hopkins School of Medicine, where he has made groundbreaking discoveries in the genetic origins of colon cancer. He was interviewed on December 22, 1999.

MAME WARREN is the editor of *Johns Hopkins: Knowledge for the World*. Before coming to Hopkins, she produced a similar book for Washington and Lee University. She is also the author of six photographic books relating to Maryland history and former curator of photographs at the Maryland State Archives.

DR. LEVI WATKINS is associate dean for postdoctoral programs and a professor of cardiac surgery at the Johns Hopkins School of Medicine. He was interviewed on November 29, 1999.

CHESTER WICKWIRE came to The Johns Hopkins University in 1953 as executive secretary of the YMCA and coordinator of religious activities for university; he was later appointed university chaplain. He is retired and was interviewed on July 9, 1999.

PROFESSOR GORDON "REDS" WOLMAN, B.A.'49, is B. Howell Griswold Jr. Professor of Geography and International Affairs at the G.W.C. Whiting School of Engineering. He was interviewed on June 22, 1999.

BIBLIOGRAPHICAL ESSAY

Historical source materials at The Johns Hopkins University and the Johns Hopkins Medical Institutions are extensive and accessible. Both the Ferdinand Hamburger Jr. Archives at Homewood and the Alan M. Chesney Archives at East Baltimore include vast amounts of useful information and are staffed by very helpful, knowledgeable people.

Among the sources consulted for this book were original documents, personal and official collections, and published materials at the Ferdinand Hamburger Jr. Archives. The collection descriptions and historical summaries (which are also available online) proved a valuable resource. Thirty-two scrapbooks of newspaper clippings chronicle events and personalities from 1874 through 1928. Kept for most of those years by Registrar Thomas R. Ball, these scrapbooks, with articles culled from national (and occasionally international) papers and journals, offer a detailed portrait of the developing university. They provided much of the information on those years for captions and the chronology. Twenty-seven additional scrapbooks contain

information on specific periods, events, topics, or people. Clippings and other items collected after 1928 are filed in the Hamburger Archives vertical file and were equally helpful. Local newspapers available at the Enoch Pratt Free Library supplied additional information and dates. Meticulous and thorough biographical files maintained at the Chesney Medical Archives provided excellent background material for oral history interviews. The university website, www.jhu.edu, is a readily available source of thousands of pages of information on a myriad of topics and people and was indispensable.

The undergraduate yearbook, *Hullabaloo*, annual Circulars, and President's Reports proved invaluable for specific topics, persons, statistics, and course information. The Johns Hopkins *Alumni Magazine* and its successor, *Johns Hopkins Magazine*, include articles on a variety of subjects relating to each of the university's divisions. *Hopkins Medical News* provided fascinating reading for a nonmedical reader and offered excellent information for interview preparation. Throughout its long history, the Johns Hopkins *News-Letter* has provided insight into the concerns of the Homewood student body. Both it and the more modern *JHU Gazette*, which covers the entire university, were consulted often. *SAISphere* (published for the alumni and friends of the Paul H. Nitze School of Advanced International Studies of The Johns Hopkins University), and *Johns Hopkins APL Technical Digest* (published quarterly by the Applied Physics Laboratory) were also useful for particular topics and people.

Answers to specific questions raised by interviews or photographs were researched in other repositories as well, including the Maryland State Archives in Annapolis, the Enoch Pratt Free Library in Baltimore, and the Marylandia Room at the McKeldin Library, University of Maryland, College Park.

Each of the major divisions of the university and medical institutions has its own historical compilations. For Homewood, the following were most helpful: John C. French, *A History of the University Founded by Johns Hopkins* (Baltimore: The Johns Hopkins Press, 1946), which is a thorough, dependable, and readable account of the university's years through World War II; also John C. Schmidt, *Johns Hopkins, Portrait of a University* (Baltimore: The Johns Hopkins University, 1986); *A Brief History of the Homewood Campus, Its Buildings, Monuments, and Sculpture* (Ferdinand Hamburger Jr. Archives, Milton S. Eisenhower Library, The Johns Hopkins University, n.d.); Elise Hancock, *Benchmark, 1990–1995, A report prepared by the office of Morris W. Offit, chairman of the University Board of Trustees* (The Johns Hopkins University [1995]); Stephen E. Ambrose and Richard H. Immerman, *Milton S. Eisenhower, Educational Statesman* (Baltimore: The Johns Hopkins University Press, 1983); Abraham Flexner, *Daniel Coit Gilman, Creator of the American Type of University* (New York: Harcourt, Brace and Company, 1946); "Statements Respecting Johns Hopkins University of Baltimore," presented to the public on the twentieth anniversary, 1896; *Inaugural Address of Daniel Coit Gilman, 1876* (Baltimore: The Johns Hopkins University, n.d.); Lionel S. Lewis, *The Cold War and Academic Governance: The Lattimore Case at Johns Hopkins* (Albany: Frontiers in Education series, State University of New York, 1993); Bob Scott, *Lacrosse: Technique and Tradition* (Baltimore: The Johns Hopkins University Press, 1979), which is an exhaustive and enjoyable book, even for non-athletes; *The Organization of The Johns Hopkins University, A Statement Prepared by the Provost, June 1, 1928* (Baltimore: The Johns Hopkins Press, 1928); *The Organization of The Johns Hopkins University, A Revised Statement Prepared by the President's Office, June 1, 1933* (Baltimore: The Johns Hopkins Press, 1933); Helen Hopkins Thom, *Johns Hopkins, A Silhouette* (Baltimore: The Johns Hopkins Press, 1929); and G. Wilson Shaffer, *Recreation and Athletics at Johns Hopkins, A One-Hundred-Year History* (Baltimore: The Johns Hopkins University, 1977).

For the medical institutions: Thomas B. Turner, *Heritage of Excellence, The Johns Hopkins Medical Institutions, 1914–1947* (Baltimore: The Johns Hopkins University Press, 1974); A. McGhee Harvey, Gert H. Brieger, Susan L. Abrams, and Victor A. McKusick, *A Centennial History of Medicine at Johns Hopkins*, vol. 1 of *A Model of Its Kind* (Baltimore: The John Hopkins University Press, 1989); A. McGhee Harvey, Gert H. Brieger, Susan L. Abrams, Jonathan M.

Fishbein, and Victor A. McKusick, *A Pictorial History of Medicine at Johns Hopkins*, vol. 2 of *A Model of Its Kind* (Baltimore: The Johns Hopkins University Press, 1989); Gert H. Brieger, "The Original Plans for The Johns Hopkins Hospital and Their Historical Significance," *Bulletin of the History of Medicine* 39 (1965): 518–528; Elizabeth Fee, *Disease and Discovery, a History of the Johns Hopkins School of Hygiene and Public Health, 1916–1936* (Baltimore: The Johns Hopkins University Press, 1987); Jacqueline Baldick and Paula Einaudi, *Hopkins Nursing, 1889–1989* (The School of Nursing of The Johns Hopkins University, 1989); Ranice W. Crosby and John Cody, *Max Brödel, The Man Who Put Art Into Medicine* (New York and Berlin: Springer-Verlag, 1991); Ethel Johns and Blanch Pfefferkorn, *The Johns Hopkins Hospital School of Nursing, 1889–1949* (Baltimore: The Johns Hopkins Press, 1954); Louise Cavagnaro, "Buildings of The Johns Hopkins Medical Institutions" (1989; revised by Michael Iati, 1993; revised by L. Cavagnaro and W. R. Day Jr., 1994); and *The Johns Hopkins Hospital Seventy-Fifth Anniversary* (1964?).

For the Peabody Institute: *The Peabody, An Illustrated Guide* (Baltimore: The Peabody Institute of The Johns Hopkins University, n.d.); Elizabeth Schaaf and Anne Garside, "Peabody Timeline," (1999); Phoebe Stanton, Essay on the construction of Peabody Institute and Library, in the program *Peabody Conservatory of Music, Sunday October 9, 1983*; Elizabeth Schaaf, *The Prophetic Eye: The George Peabody Bicentenary Exhibition*, catalog of an exhibition created by The Peabody Institute of The Johns Hopkins University in collaboration with the Peabody Trust in London (1995); and Elizabeth Schaaf, *The Founding of the Colony: A View from the Nineteenth Century*, catalog for the symposium and exhibition at the Peabody Library commemorating the 350th anniversary of the Maryland colony (1984).

For the Paul F. Nitze School of Advanced International Studies: Tammi L. Gutner, *The Story of SAIS* (Washington, D.C.: School of Advanced International Studies, The Johns Hopkins University, 1987); "Center for Chinese and American Studies, Nanjing University, The Johns Hopkins University," press packet for the dedication, September 10, 1986.

For the Applied Physics Laboratory: *The First Forty Years, A Pictorial Account of the Johns Hopkins Applied Physics Laboratory Since Its Founding in 1942* (Baltimore: The Johns Hopkins University Applied Physics Laboratory, 1983); and William K. Klingaman, *APL—Fifty Years of Service to the Nation, A History of The Johns Hopkins University Applied Physics Laboratory* (Laurel, Md.: The Johns Hopkins University Applied Physics Laboratory, 1993).

For the G.W.C. Whiting School of Engineering: Stuart W. Leslie, "European Visions, American Realities: Finding a Place for Engineering at Johns Hopkins," paper presented at the Whiting School of Engineering, October 29, 1999; Robert Rosenberg, "Academic Physics and the Origins of Electrical Engineering in America," (Ph.D. diss., The Johns Hopkins University, 1990); and Mary Ruth Yoe, *Hopkins, Engineering at the University* (Baltimore: G.W.C. Whiting School of Engineering, The Johns Hopkins University, n.d.).

SOURCES & CREDITS

Roman and arabic numerals refer to page numbers.

A=above, AC=above center, AL=above left, AR=above right, B=below, BC=below center, BL=below left, BR=below right, C=center, CL=center left, CR=center right, L=left, R=right

CATALOGING DATA

The Johns Hopkins University

Johns Hopkins: Knowledge for the World

ISBN 0-8018-6614-6

1. Education—History—Pictorial Works. 2. Oral History. 3. Photographs—History.

I. Warren, Mame, 1950– , ed. II. Title.

Library of Congress Catalog Card Number 00-133973